The Special Warfare Series
from St. Martin's Paperbacks

NAKED WARRIORS by Cdr. Francis Douglas Fane, USNR (Ret.) and Don Moore

AIR COMMANDO by Philip D. Chinnery

MOBILE GUERRILLA FORCE by James C. Donahue

PROJECT ALPHA by Sedgwick Tourison

CHOPPERS by J. D. Coleman

COVERT OPS by James E. Parker, Jr.

TWILIGHT WARRIORS by Martin C. Arostegvi

FULL THROTTLE by Philip D. Chinnery

CLEARED HOT! by Col. Bob Stoffey

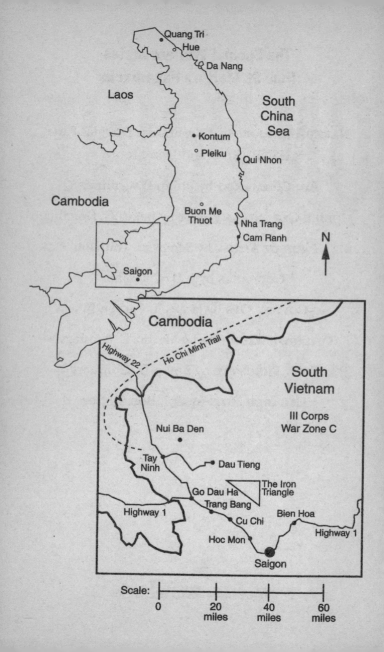

ON POINT

A Rifleman's Year in the Boonies:
Vietnam 1967–1968

ROGER HAYES

FOREWORD BY ERIC BERGERUD

St. Martin's Paperbacks

To the memory of Mary Jeanette (Marler) Hayes and to all who served in the Vietnam War, especially those of Charlie Company, First of the Fifth (Mechanized) Infantry, 25th Infantry Division. May those who did not return rest in peace; may those who did find solace.

Published by Arrangement with Presidio Press.

ON POINT

Copyright © 2000 by Roger Hayes.

All photos from the author's collection

Library of Congress Catalog Card Number: 00–022895

ISBN: 0-312-98044-2

Printed in the United States of America

Presidio Press Hardcover published 2000
St. Martin's Paperbacks edition / December 2001

St. Martin's Paperbacks are published by St. Martin's Press, 175 Fifth Avenue, New York, NY 10010.

10 9 8 7 6 5 4 3 2

CONTENTS

Foreword	viii
Introduction	xv
Acknowledgments	xx
Glossary	xxi
1. Beginnings and Forewarning	1
2. Training	4
3. In-Country	15
4. Joining the Company	26
5. Field Expediency	36
6. Learning the Ropes	55
7. Tactics	70
8. Life in the Nam	93
9. Saddle Up; We're Moving Out	112
10. The Enemy	120
11. The Year of the Monkey	124
12. In Contact	132
13. First Blood	141
14. Recuperation	147
15. Back Out	163
16. Rain and Blood	173
17. Squad Leader, Bobcat Charlie 23	186
18. Combat Operations	197
19. Last Battle	228
20. Dau Tieng	232
21. Going Home	243
Epilogue	245
Appendix	249

To truly understand any war it is important to look at both the strategic context and the view from the "bottom of the fishbowl" as seen by soldiers actually experiencing the conflict at the point of fire.

Vietnam was the quintessential infantryman's war. I think it worthwhile to analyze why this was so, because it reveals the tactical nightmare faced by tenacious soldiers like Roger Hayes and his comrades. In a conventional war both sides possess geographic areas of great value that are required for conducting military operations. In Vietnam the enemy did not have any geographic areas of importance "in-country." For political reasons that are still vigorously debated, President Johnson decided to confine ground operations to South Vietnam. No move was allowed toward Hanoi, nor were North Vietnamese sanctuaries in Cambodia and Laos allowable objectives for American attack. In addition to rice and manpower supplied by their supporters in the South, the enemy moved advanced weaponry and North Vietnamese troops down the Ho Chi Minh Trail. To make matters worse, most of the weaponry and ordnance employed by the formidable North Vietnamese Army (NVA) was shipped in from China or the USSR. In short there was no particular place or area indispensable to the enemy's war effort inside South Vietnam. Everything crucial for the enemy's struggle lay outside the grasp of United States land power.

Tactically this created terrible problems for soldiers like Roger Hayes. Because there was no point that the enemy had to defend, there was no point the Americans or the South Vietnamese could assault and bring enemy ground forces to battle. Had there been such objectives, the war would have ended victoriously in short order because of the great firepower possessed by allied forces. Instead the enemy could chose to fight for a point or not as the situation dictated. Indeed, the decision to initiate combat usually lay with the enemy. So, how were American soldiers expected to bring the enemy to battle if it could not be forced upon him? Very simply U.S. infantry had to patrol and probe as much of the countryside as possible during the day and establish ambushes at night. In practice "finding the enemy" usually meant that the Viet Cong or NVA fired first. A firefight would ensue that might be over in a minute or last several hours. With luck American soldiers, supported by artillery, helicopters, and aircraft would inflict casualties on the enemy. Often the enemy launched a quick ambush and melted away before U.S. firepower could be brought to bear. And, because no point was crucial, unlike World War II or other wars where there was a definite front line, the same battlefield might be revisited time and time again. One junior officer who saw six months of intense combat told me that the Vietnam War was like fighting a war going "around in circles."

If, on the other hand, the enemy decided to risk an assault on a U.S. fire base they had no trouble finding it. Throughout the war, Viet Cong or NVA units concentrated sizeable forces and struck American bases. Although there were some tense moments, in every case these attacks were beaten off by allied defenders, often at great loss to the enemy. Much of the war for allied combat soldiers was patrolling until fired upon, or waiting for night time enemy assaults. Vietnam was a violent war for both sides, but it was also infinitely frustrating for Americans.

Another factor made things even worse for the "grunts in the grass." American combat doctrine stressed firepower over infantry assault. As American generals liked to put it, U.S. forces would expend "bullets instead of bodies." The approach had much to recommend it. Although American and South Vietnamese losses were very painful, the enemy lost far more men. Less determined (or less brutal) governments than Hanoi might well have decided that the objective of unifying a revolutionary Vietnam by force was not worth the colossal human cost ultimately paid. The disadvantage to the American approach was that most of the Army deployed to

Vietnam was in support services. Even a combat battalion included large numbers of service personnel. When Roger Hayes was in Vietnam the American Army reached its peak strength of approximately 525,000 men. Anyone in Vietnam was in some kind of risk, but of this total less than half could be considered combat troops in any way. Many in the combat arms manned firebases or huge divisional base camps and endured relatively small risk. The number of men actually "in the grass" was rarely over 50,000. Indeed, when counting wounded, men on leave or felled by illness, it was not uncommon for an American squad to have eight men or less. I have seen all of the major reports of the 25th Infantry Division for which Hayes fought. There was not a single quarter during hostilities that the division did not match its assigned "paper strength" (usually just over 17,000). Despite this, if a unit in the boonies had 75% assigned strength present for duty it was doing very well—60% was probably more common. The enemy could never match U.S. firepower, but if one counted riflemen, Hanoi's forces very often outnumbered their American opponents by a sizeable margin. Whether one was trying to cover the countryside or survive a firefight, this fact made things difficult for those Americans on the spearpoint of combat.

Although Roger volunteered to be a combat rifleman, he entered the Army via the draft. Thus, like most of his comrades, he had no say in the time or place he would serve in Vietnam. As luck would have it, Roger and the men around him, found themselves in one of the most hazardous places and most dangerous periods of the entire war. Generally, American soldiers faced two types of enemy forces in the field. One was the revolutionary militia, the classic "barefoot guerrilla" glorified by Hanoi's propaganda machine. Lightly armed and simply trained, the militia could still make life beastly for U.S. soldiers. Until decimated during the fighting of 1968, almost all militia were local residents. Some of the peasants in the field might set a trip-wire at night. Other small units hid during the day within a very short distance of a hamlet and entered it at night, reestablishing Viet Cong control or influence over many villages across the country. It was they who laid many of the dreaded mines and booby traps that made movement across country so dangerous for the infantry. The better armed and trained among the militia launched thousands of small ambushes aimed at causing allied casualties and lowering allied morale. In addition, guerrillas established secret supply points containing rice and ammunition, allowing more heavily armed enemy units to move with great speed through allied territory. Although the guerrillas paid a heavy price, they often achieved all objectives and were a constant plague on the American infantryman.

Behind the local militia stood the "main force" Viet Cong and NVA infantry units. Although North Vietnamese units were somewhat better equipped, the difference was only of degree. Although extremely resourceful and economical in their employment of firepower, main force VC and NVA units made up a very good light infantry army. Far from the barefoot guerrillas in the rice paddies, main force units were well trained and equipped with some very powerful weapons including mortars, rocket launchers, antitank weapons, machine guns, heavy mines and fully automatic rifles. Although they lacked air support or mechanization, these units compensated by moving quietly and picking the point of attack.

To one degree or another every U.S. division faced both enemy guerrillas and heavy units from the Viet Cong or NVA. Normally, one or the other of the heavy units was the dominant problem facing the American unit in question. However, the 25th Division faced a heavy challenge from both sides of this deadly equation. The southern portion of the division's area of operation was heavily populated. Unfortunately for the Americans, this area was a long time Viet Cong stronghold. Cu Chi, the village next door to the divisional base camp that shared the same name, was one of the oldest revolutionary bastions in South Vietnam. The Viet Cong strongholds in the area were very close to the Cambodian border. A Cambodian salient which American soldiers called the "Parrot's Beak," was less than forty miles from Saigon. Naturally it included several enemy sanctuaries. Several infiltration routes existed running from the Parrot's Beak into VC strongholds in Hau Nghia and Long An provinces. Many, perhaps most, of the peasantry had no love for the Viet Cong. VC followers, however, were numerous and deeply committed. The men of the 25th Division, particularly when operating near or south of Cu Chi, had to contend with a fierce and discouraging guerrilla war.

The northern part of the 25's operational area, consisting of Tay Ninh and a part of Binh Duong provinces, was more rugged and much less densely populated. This did not mean fewer problems, however. Just inside the Cambodian border with northern Tay Ninh province was the southern terminus of the Ho Chi Minh Trail. This same point was served as the head of several infiltration routes for NVA and VC main force units toward the Saigon area or the large enemy strongpoint in Tay Ninh we called War Zone C. Because Roger was in a mechanized unit best suited for heavy combat he and his friends spent much of their time in Tay Ninh frequently confronting the best armed and best trained enemy forces available to Hanoi.

One last piece completed the ugly jigsaw puzzle. Between the heavily populated areas of Hau Nghia and the "boonies" of Tay Ninh lay a heavily fortified zone made up of the Ho Bo Woods, the Boi Loi Woods and the Iron Triangle. Alarmingly close to Saigon, and the jumping off point for units that attacked the capital during the Tet Offensive, this area was filled with mines and crisscrossed with an astounding maze of tunnels. This area, like most of the 25th Division's "turf" was not jungle but woods similar to those found in the American South. (Heavily bombed, ultimately this zone looked like the surface of the moon. It was never, however, cleared of the enemy.) A sweep into the Ho Bo or Boi Loi Woods was guaranteed to send a shiver down a soldier's spine. Studded with mines and booby traps this area might also have been the temporary home of powerful enemy main force units. Guerrilla forces were always there in strength. It did not sweeten the pill knowing that this fortified zone began a stone's throw to the north of the 25th Division's main base camp at Cu Chi.

In short, enemy existed of all types in large numbers throughout the 25th Division's area of operation. No place was genuinely safe. The base camps at Tay Ninh, Dau Tieng, and Cu Chi often suffered mortar or sapper attacks. Fire bases received night assaults large and small. The road network, necessary to keep American positions supplied, had to be kept clear daily and was a tempting target for enemy ambush. Any village, whether considered friendly or not, could be the scene of an ambush. I can think of very few areas in Vietnam that would have been more hazardous than that inhabited by the 25th Division.

Lastly, Roger Hayes might well have reconsidered his decision to volunteer as a rifleman had he known he was going to serve during the most violent year of the American phase of the Vietnam War. Beginning in October 1967 (the month Roger arrived in Vietnam) the enemy began what Hanoi termed the great General Offensive. The first stage, from October 1967 through January 1968, consisted of a series of NVA initiated battles along the Cambodian border for the purpose, some historians feel, of drawing American forces toward the border and away from Vietnam's cities. The second phase was what American journalists dubbed the Tet Offensive. Beginning at the end of January 1968 Viet Cong units of all types attacked targets of value across the entire country. The fiercest fighting, along with the siege of Khe Sanh, was in the Saigon area. It was soon obvious that the enemy had made two tremendous blunders. First, American intelligence picked up signs of the impending attack two weeks before it was launched and pulled several battalions away from Cambodia and closer to the cities. Some of these saved the South Vietnamese and American command from some serious defeats near Saigon. Second, the Viet Cong believed that the South Vietnamese Army and South Vietnamese people were weary of war and supported the revolution. Despite being weakened by soldiers home on leave for the Tet holiday, South Vietnamese units fought stoutly and the Vietnamese population failed to rise up as Hanoi anticipated. The initial wave of the General Offensive was a stunning military defeat for the Viet Cong and Hanoi.

Despite the American press' fixation on the dramatic events of Tet, the communist offensive was only beginning. After a lull in April 1968, another attack was launched against the Saigon area, nearly as large as the first. It too failed. During the rainy season local fighting remained at a much higher level than in earlier years. In August the NVA made a large attack into Tay Ninh province, causing some of the most dangerous moments for the 25th Division of the war. After another lull, the enemy launched another attack during Tet 1969 and continued a high level of activity until June of that year. By mid-1969 it was obvious to the communist leadership that further attacks could only reinforce military defeat. Shredded by losses incomprehensible to an American commander, Viet Cong forces either scattered or retreated into Cambodia.

I will let others argue whether the General Offensive was worth the price paid. The period between October 1967-October 1968, a time coinciding with Roger Hayes's tour of duty, was the most violent twelve months of the Vietnam War for American forces. Because the 25th Division was so deeply involved from start to finish, they suffered badly. Throughout the war the 25th lost 4,500 men killed, the second highest total suffered by any division in the army.

I will let Roger Hayes describe how all of the factors I have mentioned played out at the point of fire. Roger has written a splendid combat memoir. He learned the hard way that young men, despite their initial beliefs, are not immortal. Although he dedicated himself to honing his combat skills, Roger also discovered that training and prowess could not overcome deadly fortune on the battlefield. Some of the battle descriptions leave the palms sweaty. Roger gives vivid descriptions of the horrid climate and many other hardships that made Vietnam such a gruelling war. He justly criticizes the army's foolish policy of rapid officer rotation. His views of the Vietnamese people are sensitive and intelligent.

There are many extras to be found in *On Point*. Roger writes with some of the dark GI humor that was so much a part of their conversation. He also shows the reader how things worked on the battlefield. He looks at weapons, tactics, and the strengths and weaknesses of the armored personnel carriers that he served on in Vietnam. Roger also finds an affirmative side of this harsh war. He describes the confidence built by teamwork and survival in combat. Roger also discusses the importance and depth of the bonds made between the men that faced death together.

Anyone interested in men at war will learn much from Roger Hayes's moving and very well told story.

Eric Bergerud

INTRODUCTION

Possibly the most succinct war story that captured the essence of the art form emerged from the American Civil War. It went something like this. "We went up the hill to engage the enemy and not all of us made it down the hill. That's all there is except for the details." Here's my version. In 1967, when I was twenty years old, I was drafted by the U.S. Army. I was sent to Vietnam, where I served as a combat infantryman. The experience reshaped many of my values. Although war is the most difficult and horrible of human endeavors, it affected my life mostly in positive ways. Included herein are the details.

During my tour in Vietnam, I wrote more than eighty letters to my mother, Mary Jeanette (Marler) Hayes. At the time, she was separated from my father, Stanley, and was about a year away from a divorce. In the mid-1980s, my mother surprised me with every letter that I had written to her from overseas. She had kept them in neat, chronological stacks held in place by rubber bands. Many of the events described here—especially our whereabouts, some of our activities, and the dates on which they occurred—were resurrected from my memory by the letters I had written to my mom. Without them, much of this story would have been irretrievable. A few of the letters are contained in the text and coincide with the story line.

Many aspects of the Vietnam War differed from the American military engagements that preceded it. The war occurred during a time of social upheaval, the 1960s, during which America reexamined many of its values. The movement was spearheaded by our country's younger generation, the baby boomers, but no faction of society would be unaffected by the changes that were stimulated during those tempestuous years. Some of us of that generation, like those before us, went to war.

The average age of an infantryman in Vietnam was nineteen, six years younger than our World War II counterparts. There were no front lines. For the most part, the war was fought by the sons of America's blue-collar workers and minorities. Draft dodging became an art form for which people won admiration. With only one exception, no congressman's son served in Vietnam. The war became the cornerstone of the most divisive American period of the twentieth century, surpassed only by the Civil War in the history of our country.

The Vietnam War obscured the sense of reality for those of us who served in the infantry. After being in-country, as we called it, for a few months, home became something that was only dreamed of. We told one another of our lives before the war and of the aspirations and dreams we hoped to fulfill if we returned home. We used the word "if" deliberately. Those of us who were fortunate to return did so forever changed.

A Brief History of the Vietnam War

Ten years after returning home from Vietnam, I was lying in bed one evening thinking that I didn't know why I was there in 1967 and 1968, and that the intervening years hadn't done anything to shed light on the mystery. I made a resolution to find out. Over the next few years, I read almost everything I could get my hands on about Vietnam. Each book was like a piece of a jigsaw puzzle, and over time several of them became linked together. As I took a step backward and looked at the big picture, I was at first a little uncomfortable with what I found.

When I was growing up, we had never heard of Vietnam. It was known then, and described in our high school history classes, as French Indochina. Vietnam and portions of the countries of Laos and Cambodia were colonized by the French in the latter portion of the nineteenth century. Like a lot of countries during that time,

France was in search of natural resources. For the next ninety years or so, the French utilized the populations of these countries as labor to produce rice and rubber, the profits of which went not to the workers who were responsible for the products but to France. The indigenous peasants working the rubber plantations or rice paddies were allowed to keep enough of the fruits of their labor to enable them to feed their families, but hardly more.

As one would expect, the peasant workers didn't like this lifestyle and rose up against the French on several occasions in attempts to free themselves of foreign oppression. These uprisings were brutally squelched by the French, who were better trained, better equipped, and better armed. They rounded up and executed many who were suspected of organizing or taking part in the revolts. But after a few decades, the lessons of the uprisings faded and others were attempted.

This cycle was broken in 1940 during World War II when Japan invaded French Indochina and within approximately two weeks conquered the French, killing a large portion of them and imprisoning the remainder. For the first time, the Vietnamese people realized that European soldiers were defeatable in battle by Asians. It was a lesson they would not forget.

When World War II ended, Japan surrendered in place. Allied leaders sent Chinese Nationalists to the portion of Vietnam north of the seventeenth parallel—what later became a separate country named North Vietnam—to disarm the Japanese. British troops were sent to perform the same function in the southern half of the country.

The United Kingdom, because it was so far away, sent only a small force, but one with a plan. The objective was to free French prisoners who had been conquered and imprisoned by the Japanese to assist in disarming the Japanese. Meanwhile, the French economy was beginning to suffer because rice and rubber profits had stopped flowing to France during World War II, and France seized the opportunity to regain its colony.

At about the same time, Ho Chi Minh delivered the Vietnamese Declaration of Independence in a square in Hanoi. It began, "We hold the truth that all men are created equal, that they are endowed by their Creator with certain unalienable rights, among them life, liberty, and the pursuit of happiness." From there it deviated from that of our country, but it is clear that what the Vietnamese were trying to do was rid themselves of foreign domination, just as America had done when we broke away from England.

Our government didn't trust Ho Chi Minh and was not terribly concerned with what was happening to this small land on the opposite side of the globe. We didn't trust him because he was a Communist. Ho had joined the Communist Party in 1920 after his attempts to seek assistance for his homeland from elsewhere in the world, including our own country, failed to evoke a positive response. Several letters that he wrote to the president of the United States were never answered. The Communists offered him what at that time was the best opportunity to rid Vietnam of the French.

In addition, France emerged from World War II as one of our country's most important allies, and we worked out a deal with the French. We would help them in their attempt to regain their colony in Southeast Asia, a move that they billed as a means to stop the spread of communism, and in return they would give us land for three military bases in France to respond to what we were beginning to perceive as the Communist threat from the Soviet Union. As a result, we financed the majority of France's war with Vietnam, beginning in 1946 and ending in 1954 after the classic battle of Dien Bien Phu. The cost of the war to our country exceeded $2 billion during some of the intervening years.

When France lost the war in Vietnam, a short time elapsed before we picked up the sword that they dropped, doing so in the name of the domino theory. This doctrine, which history has proven false, stated that if South Vietnam fell to communism, it would soon be followed by Cambodia, Laos, Thailand, South Korea, the Philippine Islands, and Hawaii. It wouldn't be long before the Communists were landing on the shores of California. For better or worse, our country resolved to stop communism in the mountains, rice paddies, and rain forests of Vietnam.

So, when I and millions of other young Americans received the telegram that began, "Greetings," calling us to military service, we knew little about what was going on in Southeast Asia. We, including those who were against the war, certainly knew much less than the Pentagon, Congress, the Central Intelligence Agency (CIA), the United Nations, and the administration about a place called Vietnam. Simply put, our country called and we showed up as requested.

This is one story among many. It is not unusual or unique. Perhaps it is significant only because it is representative of so many of the 2.8 million Americans who served in our country's longest war.

ACKNOWLEDGMENTS

I wish to express appreciation to my wife, Velonne (Lonnie) for her unconditional love and support, and to my sons, Casey and Chad, for the close bonds that we share. They gave me the confidence and courage to tell my tale.

Dennis Hackin provided support and guidance to me while we were in Vietnam and again during the development of this book. His advice, based on his considerable knowledge of the entertainment industry, has been unselfish and sound. Ted Chadwick, who stood nearest me in combat, has helped refresh my memory and enthusiastically lent his support. Other members of Charlie Company have also shared their experiences and, in doing so, have plugged some of the holes in my story and added valuable insight regarding some of the complicated events we experienced. Among them are Jimmy Sutton, Philip Strittmatter, Andy Gimma, Bob Ordy, Steve Solomon, James Slagle, James Marschewski, and John Theologos. These men, great soldiers all, have my everlasting admiration and affection.

I wish to thank Dr. Eric Bergerud, one of our country's foremost authorities on the 25th Infantry Division, for developing the foreword and encouraging and helping me along the way.

Last, but not least, I wish to thank my publisher, Presidio Press, for believing in me and my work. Without the efforts of Richard Kane, Bob Kane, E. J. McCarthy, and the rest of their talented staff, including Barbara Feller-Roth, a proficient copy editor, this story would not have come to life.

GLOSSARY

AIT: advanced individual training
AK: Kalashnokov assault rifle, as in AK-47
APC: armored personnel carrier
ARVN: Army of the Republic of Vietnam
C-4: plastic explosive
CIB: combat infantryman's badge
CO: commanding officer
COSVN: Central Office, South Vietnam (national VC headquarters)
CQ: charge of quarters
E-3: enlisted man, third grade, a rank meaning private first class
E&E: escape and evasion
FNG: new guy; F means graphic, illustrative nomenclature
GI: government issue, refers to soldiers
H&I: harassment and interdiction
klick: kilometer
LAW: light antitank weapon
LP: listening post
MOS: military occupational specialty; job
MP: military police
NCO: noncommissioned officer
NCOIC: noncommissioned officer in charge
NVA: North Vietnamese Army
OP: observation post
PT: physical training

PX: post exchange
RPG: rocket-propelled grenade, armor piercing
RTO: radiotelephone operator
TC: machine-gun turret, from tank command or turret control
VC: Viet Cong, also Victor Charlie or Charlie

BEGINNINGS AND FOREWARNING

Drafted

My first military experience occurred long before I was inducted into the U.S. Army. When I turned eighteen in February 1965, I was summoned to Chicago from my home in Freeport, Illinois, for a draft board physical. About thirty of us from my high school class traveled to Chicago on a bus. Upon boarding early in the morning, I noticed that most of the young men with whom I would be traveling carried an envelope. Afraid that I was missing important documentation, I asked several of them about the contents. Each of them replied that it was something that pertained only to them. It turned out that the papers they were carrying were letters or documents from family physicians providing evidence of existing medical conditions that rendered each of them unfit for military service, thereby causing them to flunk the draft board physical examination. Several active members of our high school football and basketball teams who were there that day had bad backs or knees. Despite the resulting pain and discomfort, these individuals continued to compete on the school teams, thereby establishing evidence that the most athletically gifted and strongest of my high school counterparts were not physically eligible to be soldiers. Only three of us on the bus were considered fit enough to pass the physical.

In October 1966, at the age of nineteen, while in my third semester at a community college, I received a letter from my local draft board advising me that I had been reclassified 1-A, which signaled that I was ready to be drafted. I had previously been assigned a 2-S rating, which meant student deferment.

I visited the local draft board. "I am enrolled in college," I explained. "Here are my grades from last semester and my enrollment papers. Why am I now 1-A?"

"You didn't fill out our questionnaire," came the response.

"What questionnaire?"

"There was a notice on the bulletin board at your college."

"I didn't see it," I responded. "Can I fill it out now?"

"Nope, it's too late."

I thought for a moment. "Enrollment for next semester is next month," I said. "Would I be wasting my money by signing up?"

"Yes, you'll probably be drafted in May," I was told.

They had my number and probably had a quota to fill. If I had asked, they probably could have told me the date of my induction. Seven months later, in late April 1967, I received a telegram, the one that began with the word "Greetings," advising me that I had indeed been drafted and would enter military service on May 8, 1967. A letter to my congressman probably could have altered this situation, but my family was not like that. If the government needed you and called, it was time to go.

Because I knew well in advance that I would be a soldier, I had plenty of time, seven months, to become mentally prepared for leaving home and entering the army. The more usual way of getting drafted was to receive a telegram mandating induction within about two weeks. Most draftees had only fourteen days to get their affairs in order. With seven months to prepare, I was ready by the time May rolled around.

I found that the waiting period was similar to learning that you are to become a parent. In the nine months before the baby is born, the mother and father go through a period of mental and physical preparation, and by the time the baby arrives, they're ready.

The difference in being drafted was that rather than taking on the responsibility of caring for a dependent little one, I and other draftees were plucked out of the comfortable lives we knew and placed in a new and totally different environment. All ties with our previous world were cut off, except for those that came through the U.S. mail.

The experience was probably more traumatic because of our tender ages. We had only begun to explore the adult world we had not yet fully entered. Our family ties were still strong; most of us still lived under our parents' roofs.

I have concluded that people as young as we were, between the ages of nineteen and twenty-five, make the best soldiers for the same reason that they make the worst drivers: They have not yet realized their own mortality. People of that age do not know how easily death can occur. As a result, they take chances and willingly perform numerous dangerous tasks. I was no different.

During the months I had to prepare for being drafted, I had time to think about what was going on in the world. Of course, I was aware that my country was involved in a war in a land I had heard of on the news but could not locate on a map. I decided that if I was going to be a soldier, I wanted to be where the action was. I was certain that nothing would happen to me. *All I have to do is be careful,* I thought. One of the first lessons each of us learned in Vietnam, one that struck home quickly, was that this concept was about as wrong as it could be.

I would soon learn two things: First, there are certain things that soldiers in combat can do to reduce their chances of becoming a casualty; second, there are more ways to increase those chances. Both lessons had to be learned quickly, and most of the details were not taught during our training. Unfortunately, these skills and knowledge increased but did not guarantee a soldier's chance of surviving. In the end, those who died or were wounded terribly were not the poorest soldiers. They were not the least prepared or the least careful. Too many of them were simply in the wrong place at the wrong time. It could have easily been someone else. It was, to a certain extent, the luck of the draw.

TRAINING

Fort Leonard Wood

After being inducted into the U.S. Army in Chicago on May 8, 1967, I was sent to Fort Leonard Wood, in Missouri, for basic training. Several new inductees, including me, from northern Illinois were put on a train late in the evening of my first day in the military.

We rode throughout the night, and the next morning I awoke to excited chatter. My companions were gesturing and pointing to something outside the window. I joined them and received my first glimpse of the St. Louis arch across the Mississippi River. We crossed the river into St. Louis, Missouri, within half a mile of the famous landmark, then pulled into Union Station, where we would change trains. A few hours later I stood on the platform of the last train car as we traveled through the rural countryside of Missouri. As I watched the tracks disappear behind us, it occurred to me that these tracks were carrying me from the life I knew into a whole new world. But I had yet to realize that it would be a world filled with adventure, rich new relationships, and where danger would always lurk nearby.

My traveling companions and I spent the first day at Fort Leonard Wood in the civilian clothes we'd had on when we arrived. It felt strange standing in formation while wearing blue jeans. Most of us felt out of place because everyone else wore army fatigues. Later that day, we lined up for our first army haircut. Some of the guys joked, "Just a little off the sides," but everyone received the closest cut the barber could provide. For the first time since infancy, my scalp was exposed. Trying to place some of the guys I had come to know a little proved challenging with our new haircuts, and we laughed at one another's appearance.

The next day we were issued fatigues. Wearing them made us feel a lot more like soldiers, whether we wanted to or not. All of us had a long way to go, however, before the army would think of us as soldiers.

I was assigned to a basic training company that had been established in World War II–style Quonset huts in a previously unused field. All of the newer brick barracks were already in use, because so many troops were being pushed through training during the years when our country was engaged in war. Most training battalions are made up of three or four companies. The battalion to which I was assigned had six companies. I was in F Company, 1st Battalion, 3d Training Brigade.

Each of the eight Quonset huts that made up our company area consisted of a long, arched structure with the roof curving from one side to the other, forming a semicircle over our heads. The floor was concrete. Each hut housed a platoon of between thirty and forty men. Army bunks were arranged perpendicularly to the two walls, one after another, with an aisle down the middle. At the end of each bunk was a foot locker. Near the head of each bunk against the wall was an upright locker for storing our uniforms.

There was no plumbing in the platoon huts. A separate building held those facilities, and there we congregated each morning to shave, shower, and use the bathroom.

If we awoke in the night and had to go to the bathroom, we put on our pants and trudged to the latrine across the open area between the two rows of huts. I was grateful that my training was in May; this would not be fun in January.

Over the next few weeks we were taught to march, stand at attention, and recognize the rank insignia and other uniform characteristics that identified officers and noncommissioned officers (NCOs). We learned how to execute a proper salute, which we would use each time we encountered anyone at or above the rank of lieutenant.

One evening, a few of us were returning from the post exchange (PX), the store where we could purchase snacks, stationery, shoe polish, books, transistor radios, and other items. A military sedan carrying a major passed us on the street. The car circled around the block and pulled to a stop along the curb near us. The major emerged and chewed us out for not saluting him. We had not yet learned to recognize the flags on the front of the olive-drab vehicles that displayed the rank of the officer riding inside.

On another occasion, about halfway through the training cycle, I was the last of our company to leave the mess hall. In my right hand I was carrying a cookie, which I intended to enjoy later at my bunk. The last person I expected to see coming through the door as I exited was a lieutenant. In an instant I considered my alternatives. Do I transfer the cookie to my left hand so I can salute with my right? No, by the time I do that, the lieutenant will be past me. Almost instinctively, I threw up my left hand and performed a perfect salute, albeit with the wrong hand.

"Good evening, sir."

"Good evening," he responded, returning my salute.

I made it about half a dozen steps.

"Wait a minute. Get back here."

"Yes, sir?"

"Didn't they teach you the proper way to salute an officer? You never salute with your left hand. Now, drop and give me twenty-five push-ups."

My cookie waited for me on the sidewalk as I executed the prescribed exercises. To make sure the proper method of saluting was ingrained in my brain, the lieutenant had me salute him with my right hand before he excused me.

Basic Training Objectives and a Personal Victory

While in basic training—which is, in part, the indoctrination into military life—I snapped out of what I considered one of the world's biggest inferiority complexes. I realize, though, that to those who have them, they all seem large. Throughout my high school years, I suffered from an acute lack of self-confidence. In addition, my family was poor, and I and my brother and sister seldom had nice clothes to wear to school. My graduating class numbered more than four hundred, distributed among about four levels of social strata. I hovered comfortably near the bottom. I felt that I didn't know enough to hold up my end of a conversation on a wide variety of topics. In basic training, however, things changed for me.

The military has three main objectives in basic training, called boot camp by the U.S. Navy and the U.S. Marines. One objective, of course, is to familiarize recruits—called trainees by the sergeants who composed the cadre—with military life. Through a series of lectures, lessons, and experiences, new soldiers learn how things work in the military and where they, as soldiers, fit in.

A second objective is to condition new soldiers to follow orders without question. A sergeant on a battlefield, for example, does not have the time, inclination, or opportunity to explain to the members of his platoon his decisions concerning the placement of weapons or people. To indoctrinate recruits with this concept, trainees are assigned a multitude of tasks that have no apparent purpose. The intention is that by the time the trainees get to a battlefield, they will be used to doing what they are told unquestioningly and not debate the sergeant on the placement of a machine gun or anything else.

The third objective of basic training, and the one that eliminated my inferiority complex, is the development of teamwork. For military effectiveness, it is important that soldiers learn that a group of individuals can accomplish feats that individual soldiers cannot. To be effective, one must become part of a team.

The first step in the progression toward teamwork is the elimination of those factors that make individuals unique. To accomplish this, the military sees to it that all trainees have the same haircut, wear the same clothes, and eat the same food, together as a group. They get up at the same time each morning and go to bed at the same time each night. They have the same schedule for polishing their boots and writing letters to mothers and wives or girlfriends. They clean the barracks as a team. Daily training activities are performed as a platoon, squad, or company. If it were possible, the army would probably have us all go to the bathroom at the same time, too, although that would place undue presure on the plumbing infrastructure.

Sometime during this process, I discovered that I was like everyone else, that no one was better or worse than the others. There were no football stars and no members of the most popular group of kids; none of us was considered smarter or dumber than anyone else. We were simply the same, which is exactly what the military expected. With this realization, my sense of inferiority that had kept me company for years went away, never to return. Basic training accomplished that. The war would soon begin to build a high degree of self-confidence.

The process of self-discipline is the next step in developing what the military calls unit cohesiveness, or teamwork. This involves the success or failure of the platoon, not of each individual therein. It also involves group punishment.

When individual soldiers break the rules or otherwise mess up, as they inevitably do, the platoon as a whole is punished for the acts of its individual members. If the shine on a soldier's boots does not meet the drill sergeant's approval, the entire platoon performs push-ups, goes into chow last, or is dealt some other form of punishment.

At first, members of the platoon feel sorry for the individuals who are the cause of the group's punishment and offer to help them. Eventually, however, the group resents being punished for the acts of those who never seem to get it. Some of the group will begin avoiding the troublemaker, although some will still attempt to help.

If this procedure is successful, the individual will fit in with the group and all will be forgiven, which results in unit cohesion. But if the individual fails to learn or try, the platoon builds up the pressure, which can lead to intimidation at the least and possibly violence, including acts sometimes referred to as blanket parties—a form of anonymous group punishment.

In this manner, people who fail to become integrated members of the platoon are weeded out or corrected. The army does not care which. The platoon takes care of its own problems. Although this process appears cruel, it is necessary in order to create a group of soldiers who can act as a single unit, as an effective military force.

After going through this process, soldiers are more easily assimilated into whatever units they are assigned at the completion of training.

Training Routines

Because we were restricted to our company area during much of our training, we provided our own entertainment. In the evening after chow, we gathered on the low hillside outside the back door of our Quonset huts and told stories, talked about our girlfriends, and bragged of sexual exploits. Some of the guys brought out coffee cans and played them like conga drums, and we sang the songs of the day. I joined a few men who could sing harmony, and we sometimes performed for the others.

My favorite part of training was the rifle range. We marched, drilled, and learned to shoot M14 rifles, which were produced after World War II. We had heard of the newer M16 rifle, but none of us saw this weapon until we reached advanced individual training (AIT) for infantry. In my youth, I had shot my dad's .22 rifle a few times, but the M14 was the first serious rifle I had held. Our weapons training began with classroom blocks of instruction. It would be three weeks before any of our rifles were loaded with live rounds.

Once on the range, I learned that I was a natural marksman and qualified expert with the weapon, the highest rating possible. Qualifying involved identifying and firing at olive-drab pop-up targets that appeared at distances ranging from twenty-five to four hundred meters. Each target stayed up for only a few seconds, so it was advantageous to find the target as soon as possible, then aim and fire. For the farthest targets, I aimed at the head and was pleased to see the target drop when my round struck home.

Each morning we ran a mile before breakfast. After eating, we performed physical training (PT) led by one of our drill instructors from a raised wooden platform. Other sergeants circulated among the trainees to provide further guidance for specific exercises or, more commonly, to harass those who failed to complete the prescribed number of repetitions.

Because we did not have regular barracks and had been set up in a small, previously empty area, we didn't have a good spot to do our exercises. We performed them in a gravel parking lot. Dents formed in our hands during push-ups. Gravel dug into our backs during the ground exercises. A beginning routine developed that consisted of kicking some of the larger stones out of the way to make our immediate area more comfortable.

The live-fire exercise was one of the highlights of basic training. For the first time, we experienced machine-gun rounds fired over our heads as we negotiated a course. Two M60 machine guns were positioned on one end of the range and we began on the opposite end. The machine gun fired continuously as we crawled the distance. We were told that in a previous cycle, someone had stood up and was shot and killed. We were to utilize what was called the low crawl, which is performed with one's chest never leaving the ground. If we doubted that live rounds were being fired, all we had to do was glance up to see the red tracers zipping over our heads.

Multiple rows of barbed wire stretched throughout the course, and paths had been formed where trainees from other companies had crawled, then clawed their way under the rows of wire. It was easiest to follow these trails and low spots under the wire. Unfortunately, it had rained recently and the indentations were filled with water.

As we concluded the course, we were allowed to stand behind the machine guns and watch as our fellow trainees followed us. I was surprised to see that steel bars had been placed parallel to the ground under the barrel of each gun. This was to prevent the machine gunner from accidentally shooting any of us. In a way, it was a disappointment. We had believed that this was a life-threatening exercise. In actuality, we could have stood up and not been endangered.

Toward the end of our training, as we began performing as a unit and demonstrating the qualifications of someone who could make it in the army, the drill sergeants hinted that we were something more than "trainees," a term used in a derogatory way to describe civilians who had not yet made the successful transition to military life. We were proud to hear the word "soldier" enter our sergeants' vocabulary. They slowly began to treat us with less disdain. By the end of training, some of these sergeants became almost likable, something we would not have believed a few weeks previously.

I did not excel in every aspect of training, but I performed well enough to finish in the top third of the company. The scores came from written exams, physical training, weapon qualification, and completion of the various classes, ranges, and lectures. As a result, I—along with the others in the upper third of the company—was promoted to private E-2 upon graduation. Because there was no stripe for this grade in those days, the higher rank meant nothing more than a few more dollars on payday.

Fort Polk

Upon graduation from basic training, I was ready for the next step. I was sent to Fort Polk, in Louisiana, for advanced individual training along with others who had the military occupational specialty (MOS), or job, of infantryman. Our training brigade area was nicknamed Tiger Land. There was an arch over the entrance to the brigade area with a tiger painted on it. Every time we passed under the arch on the way in or out, we were to growl ferociously.

While in basic training, I volunteered for the infantry, not a difficult achievement during time of war. At Fort Polk, I was assigned to the mortar platoon of my infantry training company. I didn't want to be a mortar man, and I approached our first sergeant and asked if I could be transferred to a rifle platoon. He advised me that once I was in Vietnam, I'd probably be a rifleman anyway and, once I was, I might be glad that I had received mortar training. It would teach me to discern whether an unexploded round was ours or the enemy's, and what type of round it was. I'm pretty sure he was just politely putting me off to avoid hassling with the paperwork, but it actually turned out the way he described, although probably based more on coincidence than anything else.

So I was trained as a mortar man. We operated in teams of three, learning how to set up the mortar tubes, then peering through the side-mounted sights and aligning crosshairs on red and white aiming stakes a short distance away. The stakes were one of the few things in the army that were not olive drab or black.

The platoon fired the mortars only once, and I was sick that day. To qualify with mortars, however, all we had to do was set them up properly within a specified time period. The team I was with had learned well; all of us were able to perform each role. We aced the qualification and were assigned the rating of expert with the 81mm mortar. Firing the mortars consisted only of attaching the appropriate number of charges on the fins, which determined how far the round would fly, then dropping the round in the tube once the gun was set up. The more critical act was aiming the tube, and we excelled at that.

One of the most memorable events of advanced individual training (AIT) was the escape and evasion (E&E) course. For this exercise, we were trucked out to an area in the boonies and dropped off. The objective was to get back to a designated location, point A, on our own—a distance of maybe a mile, although it seemed like several. The woods were full of "aggressors," soldiers from some other permanent unit of Fort Polk, who would to try to catch us on the course. If caught, we were taken to a detention or "prisoner-of-war" camp, where we would be interrogated and "tortured."

The torture consisted of inflicting punishment and pain without causing permanent damage. We had heard stories from trainees from other companies who had gone through E&E before us. In one form of punishment, "prisoners" were placed flat on the ground with arms and legs extended as far as possible and tied to stakes in the ground. Then a wire was stretched across the upper lip of the unfortunate detainee and fastened to stakes pounded in the ground on either side of him. When the prisoner failed to respond to questions to which the correct response was more than name, rank, and serial number, the aggressors would kick his feet. Some of our peers came back from the detainee camp with cuts on their upper lips. This infuriated us; our peers were being brutally mistreated, and the physical scars were against the rules of engagement.

Others were forced to do push-ups until they could do no more. Some were placed naked in a fifty-five-gallon drum and a large block of ice was dropped in their laps, then the lid was put in place and the drum was beaten with clubs.

There was no way I was going to end up in the prisoner-of-war camp. But then, I've always been good at sneaking around in the woods. The most dangerous part of the course came when the group I was with approached a road that had to be crossed to reach point A, our objective. There were plenty of secluded locations offering a good view of the road where we supposed the lazy or more unimaginative aggressors would be hiding.

A few of us gathered in the darkness where we could see the road, whispering to one another and wondering where to cross. Someone volunteered to try it, and he was chased. The rest of us made a mass run for it while the aggressors were busy. I was pursued briefly, but I melted easily into the woods. For the remainder of the course, I stuck to the swamps, where I figured that no aggressors would be lurking. I saw or heard a few, but they were easy to evade.

Afterward, a few of us who were upset about the treatment that our fellow trainees had received in the detention camp began making plans to return to the camp over the weekend and burn it to the ground. On Friday morning, however, our sergeants handed out three-day passes, the first we had received since we arrived at Fort Polk. We were being given a holiday off base. Our priorities quickly changed, and we forgot all about revenge. Perhaps the timing of the three-day passes was more than coincidental.

In AIT, we qualified with M16s. Those of us in the mortar platoon also trained and qualified with the .45-caliber pistol. Once again I excelled in shooting and qualified expert with each weapon, as well as the mortars.

The .45 was the most difficult. This weapon was designed and produced with interchangeable parts, and the action was loose enough so that it could be fired after being dropped in mud, dirt, or sand. It was reliable only at short range. To qualify expert required hitting a human silhouette placed twenty-five meters away at least twenty-five out of thirty times. I was lucky and made the minimum number of hits to qualify expert. I'm not sure I could have done it twice.

As in basic training, I graduated from AIT in the upper third of my class and was promoted to private first class, E-3 (enlistment grade 3). Receiving my first stripe was a short-lived glory, though, because of a regulation mandating that no one under the rank of E-3 could be sent to Vietnam. That hurdle, if the rumors were true, was overcome by promoting to private first class everyone who arrived in Vietnam who had not yet attained the coveted grade.

I didn't have long to swagger around with my one stripe. I had been in the army for six months, and within days I would begin a month's leave prior to being shipped to Vietnam.

Arrival and First Impressions

After thirty days' leave, most of which I spent in my hometown with my girlfriend and family, I took a late-night train to Chicago. It was difficult saying good-bye to my girlfriend. We promised to wait for each other and resume our relationship when I returned.

In Chicago, I boarded a plane for Oakland, California. It was from there, at Travis Air Force Base, that most of the soldiers who served in Vietnam departed. I arrived in Oakland a day early with a friend from Chicago named Kirk from my AIT unit who was also heading to Vietnam, and we spent the time touring San Francisco. When we reported to the Oakland center, we found bunks next to each other. During the last evening we would spend in the USA for a year, we stood on a fire escape landing with a few others headed for Vietnam and watched the lights of a residential area as darkness descended. It occurred to us that the people who lived in the homes we could see would go on with their normal lives as we went overseas to fight for our country. The thought produced both excitement and a feeling of isolation.

Loudspeakers placed throughout the huge hangars, which were filled with bunk beds, announced flights and the names of the soldiers who were to be passengers. My name was called in the middle of the night. I said good-bye to Kirk and, as instructed, lined up to board a bus that would take us to the plane.

The flight took twenty-two hours. The plane stopped in Seattle for fuel, then headed across the Pacific Ocean. We chatted, ate, played cards, watched the waves below us, and slept in our seats.

My first view of Vietnam was of the coastline as the plane approached, then glided over the beautiful green land. A hush fell over the entire plane. Training had been, in a way, playing games. Sure, we knew that preparing for war was serious business, but we also knew that the real war was on the opposite side of the world. Now, suddenly, this beautiful and mysterious land below us was the real thing. I watched out the window as we flew over huge expanses of forest. I expected to see battles in progress, but I saw nothing indicating that this was a land torn by war.

My arrival in-country was typical. The plane glided to a stop at an airport near the city of Bien Hoa, sixteen miles northeast of Saigon. As I moved down the aisle of the air-conditioned plane, working my way toward the door, I became immersed in the oppressive heat and humidity of Southeast Asia, which I would not escape for a year.

We were lined up with our duffel bags and loaded onto buses that would transport us to the 90th Replacement Battalion, where we would await orders sending us to our units. We were told that the chicken wire mesh on the buses was to prevent hand grenades from being tossed into the vehicles. Some of us infantrymen knew, however, that we were in the safest environment we would encounter in the coming year. As FNGs (F stands for graphic, illustrative nomenclature; NG means new guys), we did not yet constitute a serious threat to the enemy. We didn't even have rifles. We were just a bus full of green kids who, except for the training we had received, could just as well have been on a school outing.

The next day we received orders assigning us to our new homes. As directed, I gathered with the others who were heading to the same division. About a dozen of us were loaded on the back of a two-and-a-half-ton dump truck, nicknamed deuce and a half, that was part of a convoy of military vehicles. There were sandbags in the bed of the truck and in the driver's compartment as protection against shrapnel if the truck hit a mine. We settled into a semicomfortable position on the wooden side benches, and soon the engine roared to life. The convoy moved out on its way to Cu Chi, a base camp thirty kilometers (nineteen miles) due northwest of Saigon. Cu Chi, headquarters of the 25th Infantry Division, was located right outside a town of the same name.

Our trip took more than an hour due to the poor condition of the road. En route, we received our first glimpse of the Asian world we had entered. For much of the journey, I stood leaning on the back of the cab watching the sights and scenery ahead of us. There were no telephone poles, streetlights, stoplights, curbs, or sidewalks. Most of the streets were hard-packed dirt. Other than U.S. military vehicles, there were few automobiles. The few *lambrettas*, or rickety-looking buses, that served as mass transportation were packed with people. Cages containing chickens or other fowl were tied to the tops of the vehicles. Small motorcycles and pedicabs, a reverse-style tricycle with a seat for a passenger on the front, were common. The whine of their motors blended with the sounds of Vietnamese chatter when the convoy slowed down.

Small shops were set up on the street. Numerous old men and women wearing the conical straw hats that are ubiquitous in Asia passed on bicycles or carried some type of cargo. A common sight was women balancing five- or six-foot-long poles across their shoulders with bundles or pottery containers swinging a foot or so below each end. Judging by how much the poles bounced while they walked, I guessed that some of these burdens were heavy, but the women never seemed to slow down or break stride. These women were slight but strong, a description that probably fits most Vietnamese people.

Children were abundant and the most outgoing. When the truck slowed down, they approached and asked for food by holding out a hand with their palm up and yelling, "Gimme chop chop." We new guys didn't yet have any "chop chop." A can of C rations would have done the trick.

Some of the young women wore a tight-fitting, ankle-length dress split to the hips over black or white slacks. The dress, which appeared in many different pastel colors, was referred to by the Vietnamese phrase for dress, *mot cai ao dai.* We thought that the garment was beautiful and feminine looking.

Outside of town, we passed through a land of giant rice paddies, some of which seemed to stretch to the horizon. They were lovely pools of water reflecting the sky and surrounded or crisscrossed with low earthen dikes. Small boys riding on the backs of water buffalo seemed to direct the animals by kicking gently with a heel on the side indicating the desired direction of travel. The villages were smaller here in the rural areas, and the hootches (buildings) had roofs and sides made of thatch.

We passed through the town of Cu Chi, which looked like a less populated version of the outskirts of Saigon, then entered the heavily fortified base camp through the main gate. The Cu Chi base possessed complete military facilities, including an airstrip, a helicopter pad, artillery units, a PX, division headquarters, medical facilities, and even a prisoner detention center. Each unit had assigned areas that included a motor pool, hootches for the troops, a mess hall, and battalion, brigade, or company headquarters or orderly rooms. Bunkers made of sandbags were everywhere and were used as refuge during mortar or rocket attacks, which we were told were common.

We spent a week in the relative safety of the base camp attending orientation sessions, which we called a school. To hasten our acclimatization to the hot, humid tropics, we were seated during the lectures in sets of bleachers placed in the sun. Although it was hot, I eventually learned that it would take much more than sitting in the sun for a week to become accustomed to this climate.

20 Oct 67

Dear Mrs. Hayes,

Recently your son Roger was assigned to my unit, the 1st Battalion (Mechanized), 5th Infantry, known as the Bobcats. The 5th Infantry is the third oldest regiment in the United States Army and over the years has distinguished itself in service to our country.

The Bobcats are proud to have your son join our outfit. Initially Roger will be assigned to Company C, where he will perform as a rifleman. Every man in an infantry battalion is essential and contributes to the success of the unit. I am sure Roger will perform his duties in an outstanding manner and that he will always be proud of his service with the 5th Infantry.

The primary mission of this unit is to conduct military operations against the Viet Cong/NVA. Naturally my time and efforts, as well as your son's, must be directed towards successful completion of that assignment. However, I fully appreciate your concern and interest in the activities of Roger and I will encourage him to write you often. Nevertheless, if you feel that I could be of assistance to you, please do not hesitate to write me.

Sincerely,
Chandler Goodnow
LTC Infantry Commanding

My mother, Mary Jeanette (Marler) Hayes, was my lifeline to "the world," as we called everyplace outside of Vietnam, especially the USA. My mother wrote to me often and filled me in on what was happening back home. Letters from home, like good food, constituted one of the most significant, positive morale boosters for troops in Vietnam. For the few minutes that it took to read a letter, a soldier was mentally transported back home, to the opposite side of the globe, a momentary escape from Vietnam and the war. Everyone loved to get letters.

I was aware that Mom checked her mailbox every day for a letter from me. If four or five days went by without one, she worried that I had been killed. Because of this, I wrote to her as often as I could. Over the course of the year, I averaged a letter every four days, describing for her our location and activities. My mom, who knew that I was in the infantry, wanted to experience the war through my letters, and I obliged her curiosity, withholding only a few of the details that would cause undue worry.

During my first evening in Cu Chi, I and several other new arrivals watched and listened to a battle that was occurring several kilometers outside our base camp. Red tracers from a minigun, capable of firing thousands of rounds per minute, came from a plane flying over the battle. We assumed that the tracers were spaced every four or five rounds or more, although from our perspective they appeared as a solid red line that waved back and forth slowly and gracefully as the gunner adjusted his aim. We'd been told that it appeared to the Vietnamese as the flaming tongue of a dragon.

20 Oct 67

Mom,

I've been here 3 days. We landed at Bien Hoa then took a truck to a reception station. We had to stay there til they confirmed our orders. I left the next day and came here. It's the headquarters camp for the 25th Inf. Div.

The fighting is pretty close. All night we could hear mortars shooting and the rounds going off about a mile or two away. The only thing we have to worry about here is mortar attacks. They have sandbag bunkers beside each hootch (barracks) that we have to jump in. They usually have 1 attack each month and they haven't had one this month yet.

On the way here we went through a part of Saigon. I was riding on the back of a truck and could see good. It was right after a rain storm and we were standing in formation then, so we were all soaked. In some places the water was half a foot deep in the streets cause they don't have sewers.

There were people everywhere. Hondas all over but none very big cause the roads are so bad. The stores were all open and they don't have any doors on them, just 3 walls. Some are pretty nice.

Outside of Saigon, we saw carts pulled by water buffalo, people working in rice paddies, a few temples.

Everywhere you go you see guys in the Army and there are installations, camps, motor pools, air strips, all over. We came through a training camp for the South Vietnamese Army. We saw the troops marching along the road and some of them weren't older than 13 or 14. The oldest not older than 18 or 19.

We're waiting to be shipped to our units. The weather isn't as bad as they say. The first day it was 100 degrees. But the monsoon isn't over yet and the skies are cloudy and it's about 70 or 75 when the sun's not shining.

I'll write when I get another chance. Love, Roger

I was assigned to Charlie Company, one of three companies that composed the 1st of the 5th Mechanized Infantry Battalion, usually shortened to 1/5 (Mech). The other new arrivals and I slept in one of the hootches that housed our company. They had been empty because the company was operating out in the field. For the first few days, we attended classes during the day and were sometimes assigned additional duties at night.

My first assignments consisted of guard duty. On my first evening in Vietnam, I guarded the ammo dump and motor pool in the middle of the night. This was our company's storage point for ammunition. For the remainder of my tour, I never noticed a guard posted at this location, but in the event of sapper infiltration, a guard could have prevented the loss of these supplies, equipment, and vehicles. On the other hand, it's possible and more probable that we new arrivals were put in these locations to keep us busy and out of trouble.

The division base camp at Cu Chi was as large as a small town, with sandbagged two-story bunkers lining its rectangular perimeter. Outside the bunker line were several rows of concertina wire, like barbed wire but with razorlike blades every few inches, along with trip flares, numerous Claymore mines, and other surprises to slow down enemy infiltration. Each bunker was equipped with a .50-caliber machine gun, perhaps a grenade launcher, detonating devices for Claymore mines, red and green star clusters for alerting others of attack, and the small-arms weapons carried by soldiers performing bunker guard.

On the morning of October 21, I performed my first shift of bunker guard duty with another soldier from my company. I explored the place, familiarized myself with the weapons and equipment within, and closely examined the area to our front. These bunkers guarding the huge base camp were staffed constantly, and we would remain here until we were relieved by the next shift late in the afternoon or early evening.

During the afternoon, we received a call on the field phone in the bunker from someone in one of the observation towers spaced along the perimeter. The call alerted us that a colonel was making the rounds of some of the bunkers so we shouldn't go to sleep. Not to worry. I was as close as I had yet come to enemy territory, and my adrenaline level made sleep impossible.

During the afternoon, we watched smoke drift from the Hobo Woods, several miles to the north. My experienced bunker mate explained to me that the Hobo Woods was a stronghold for the Viet Cong dating back to the Viet Minh in the 1940s and had tunnels throughout its entire area. Had we known that some of them extended underneath our Cu Chi base camp, we would have felt a bit less comfortable.

Just before suppertime we were relieved by the soldiers who would continue guard duty at our bunker throughout the night.

During my first few weeks at Cu Chi, I remained a young, wide-eyed, innocent soldier. I was taking in everything around me and enjoying learning about my new surroundings and how things were supposed to work. Of course I knew that my company was actively engaged in combat, but the war's terrible toll hadn't yet hit me. The bullet with my name on it was still probably working its way down the Ho Chi Minh trail.

Strategic Area

For military purposes, Vietnam had been divided into four separate areas called corps, which were designated with roman numerals. I Corps was up north, adjacent to the demilitarized zone (DMZ); IV Corps was at the southern end of the country.

Our division's area of operations, War Zone C of III Corps, was a strategic area for the Communist forces. Although we did not know it at the time, the Central Office of South Vietnam (COSVN)—the national headquarters for the National Liberation Front, which the administration of South Vietnam's past president Ngo Dinh Diem had nicknamed the Viet Cong (VC)—was located along the Cambodian border, forty-six kilometers (twenty-nine miles) due north of Tay Ninh in the area known as the Fishhook because of the geographical configuration of that portion of the Cambodian border.

Tay Ninh, eighty-three kilometers, or klicks (fifty miles), north-west of Saigon and near the Cambodian border, was the center of the powerful Cao Dai, Vietnam's only indigenous religion. It evolved into political activism opposing the Diem regime. The Cao Dai religion had a militia, as did several if not most of Vietnam's numerous sects, and its forces became allies of the Communist movement. Later, they became original members of the National Liberation Front, the Viet Cong.

Tay Ninh, for reasons possibly linked to the aforementioned, was also an exit point of the Ho Chi Minh trail. A series of paths, which later became roads, the Ho Chi Minh trail was used to transport troops, weapons, and military equipment from North Vietnam into Laos and from there points farther south. Some of the trail passed through Cambodia. These circuitous routes bypassed the American and ARVN military presence and led into South Vietnam in numerous places, the southernmost in Tay Ninh.

Soldiers of the North Vietnamese Army (NVA) entering South Vietnam in our division's area of operations were within a day's march of Saigon, the capital of South Vietnam's "puppet regime." The area was sparsely populated and had good vegetative cover where a buildup of forces could be concealed. Our division had been placed here in 1966 because of the threat that such a gathering of hostile forces in this area would pose to Saigon. Our mission was to plug the hole.

I spent the next few days going through the division's orientation school learning about the proper conduct of soldiers in Vietnam, how to treat the Vietnamese people, and numerous combat topics including booby traps, tactics, and patrolling the boonies.

We began hearing the first of numerous rumors that would continue throughout my tour concerning the location and mission of our company. Word was passed around that the company, currently out on an operation, would return to Cu Chi on October 29 and remain for six days. When the company returned to the field, I would go along. At least that was the plan. As it turned out, the plan changed.

Infantrymen were at the bottom of the chain of command and were the last to learn the news, even if it directly affected them, such as a unit's missions, assignments, and changes to the company's plans. As a result, rumors were an important means of learning our fate. Sometimes the rumors were accurate; other times, the plans simply changed. In the end, we seldom learned of upcoming events until we were involved in them.

As with other military organizations in other wars, we often heard rumors while visiting another unit's latrine while passing through its area and striking up a conversation with one of the soldiers.

"Hi. Which unit are you with?"

"First of the Fifth Mech, Charlie Company."

"Really? I heard that you guys will be heading to Tay Ninh day after tomorrow."

"No kidding. News to me, but thanks for the info."

These were called latrine rumors, but we usually used more colorful slang in place of "latrine." Upon returning to our units, we passed around the information, whereupon someone would ask where we heard it.

"It's a latrine rumor" was the usual reply.

In my experience, a lot of these rumors, although certainly not all, were highly accurate.

The next day, October 25, our company began wearing the new soft hat that we called a bush hat. It was made of olive-drab canvas and had a brim all the way around to keep the sun off our faces and shed rain. We wore the hats in the rear and during combat missions at night.

During our week of school, we heard reports of a company near our perimeter that had been on an ambush patrol and was hit by a VC unit that dropped three rifle grenades on its position as the men were setting up. During the subsequent firefight, which lasted an hour, seven Americans and almost all of the VC were killed. At the time, I and the other new soldiers were on a night firing range, and we watched as red and green tracers from the battle caromed high into the dark sky. I was told that the red tracers were ours and the green ones belonged to the VC. I was within sight of the enemy.

During our last evening of the school, we held a make-believe ambush outside the base camp's perimeter. It was pretty spooky just after the recent battle, but the evening passed uneventfully. The sergeant who led our small patrol was pleased that we moved quietly, which was difficult to do with all of our equipment on.

My last day of school was Friday, October 27. I was told that I might join the company in the field that night or the next day, because the company wasn't coming back to the base camp anymore.

JOINING THE COMPANY

MOS Change

When I was first told that I would be assigned to a mechanized infantry unit, I didn't know what that meant. Although I had received
six months of training, I had never heard the term *mechanized infantry*. I found out that these units were equipped with M113 armored personnel carriers (APCs). I had not heard of them or seen
any, not even in a photograph, before arriving in Vietnam.

I joined Charlie Company, 1st of the 5th (Mechanized) Infantry,
on October 28, 1967, the day after completing the orientation
school. I arrived via a huge Chinook helicopter, the army's largest,
with two rotors. In flight, the eight-foot-square cargo hatch in the
floor of the chopper was open, and we stood near it and watched as
the countryside glided surrealistically below us. In addition to carrying a few of us new arrivals, the helicopter was also transporting
bags of mail for the troops and the unit's evening chow in insulated
Mermite containers. The company's first sergeant was there to greet
us and inspect our orders as we emerged from the helicopter. We
recognized him by his rank insignia. He glanced at my paperwork
and noticed my designation as a mortar man.

"Mortar platoon, that way," he said, pointing to his left.

"Top, I'd like to go to a line platoon," I said, using the universal
nickname for first sergeants. I held my breath.

His response came immediately. "Son, you've just made the
fastest MOS [military occupational specialty] change in the history

of the U.S. Army. Second Platoon," he said as he jerked his thumb over his shoulder in the direction of my new destination.

I have never regretted not joining the mortar platoon. The first sergeant probably seized the opportunity to add one more GI to a platoon that was shorthanded. In doing so, however, he set me up to meet people with whom I would form some of the strongest bonds of my life.

Charlie Company, 2d Platoon

Charlie Company, commanded by Capt. John Theologos, who was called Captain T, was set up in a soccer field along Highway 1, the main road running through the village of Trang Bang, located between Cu Chi and Tay Ninh and fifteen klicks (nine miles) northwest of Cu Chi. Sandbag bunkers, large enough to hold a few standing men, guarded the entrance to the position off the main roadway. Concertina wire surrounded the small circular perimeter, which served as the company's temporary but heavily armored and protected base of operations. Twelve APCs, the first I had seen except for a few in Cu Chi, faced outward at evenly spaced intervals around the company's perimeter. Five or six more APCs were scattered within the interior. Four of these on the inside composed the mortar platoon. The others belonged to the company commander, the first sergeant, and a few others.

Except for the fact that the APCs on the perimeter were facing outward, it appeared from the air that these vehicles had been placed randomly. The APCs, which the GIs called tracks, were rectangular in shape and were designed to hold a full infantry squad of eleven men—although that would have been crowded—and transport them in relative safety, while protecting them at least from small-arms fire, to where they were needed.

A hydraulic ramp on the back of the APC was used as the main entrance. When we were stationary, the ramp was always down, enabling us to walk directly into the back of the track. A small door on the rear provided access when the ramp was in the up position, but we didn't use it much.

On the top of the APC was a cargo hatch about four feet square.

When we were in position, the cargo hatch was almost always open (unless it was raining) to provide fresh air and easy access to the top of the track, where a guard was posted twenty-four hours a day.

A second hatch on the top provided access from inside to the .50-caliber machine gun, which was mounted directly behind the engine wall and slightly to the right of center. Steel plating had been welded on the hatch to provide cover from small-arms fire; there were two curved pieces on either side and a third directly to the front with a slot for the machine-gun barrel. This entire structure was capable of rotating so the gun could fire in all directions.

The driver's position was in the front left-hand corner of the vehicle; a third hatch provided access to this small compartment. Usually, the driver's head protruded from the hatch, although three prisms were built in just under the driver's hatch to enable the operator to see outside and manipulate the vehicle from the inside.

A two-digit number was painted on both sides of the rear flank of each vehicle. The first digit designated the platoon; the second designated the squad. The numbering system was similar to that of our radio call signs.

Tracks were operated like bulldozers; two upright handles called laterals were used to maneuver the vehicles. To go forward, the driver pushed both laterals forward, which engaged the tracks on each side. To negotiate a turn, one handle was pulled back, slowing down the track on the corresponding side and turning the vehicle. From a stopped position, pushing one handle forward and the other back created a spin in place. Pulling both laterals backward moved the vehicle to the rear. It was pretty simple once one got the hang of it, and the tracks were fun to drive.

After we began regularly hitting land mines, our mechanics back in Cu Chi made lateral extensions composed of steel tubing that fit over the accelerator handles and protruded upward through the driver's hatch. They enabled the driver to operate the vehicle without having to sit inside. It was much safer on top if a mine was hit or if we were attacked with rocket-propelled grenades (RPGs). In such instances, most of those on top would be thrown or blown off. Anyone riding inside was likely to be killed or severely wounded. We found by experience that this hypothesis was true, and it became standard operating procedure for everyone to ride on top. Although this exposed us to small-arms fire, that was less of a threat than a land mine or an RPG, which could kill or severely wound all of us at once.

To gain access to the top of the vehicle, we stood on one of the bulldozer-like treads that propelled the vehicle, grabbed something on the top, and pulled ourselves up. There was no ladder or stair-like device.

The original APCs came with fender skirts over the upper portion of the treads. We removed the skirts, probably because mud or dirt became clogged inside them. With the skirts removed, debris was thrown out along the top by the centrifugal force of the rotating tread.

I eventually realized that being assigned to a mechanized infantry company had disadvantages as well as advantages. Because we moved around in motorized vehicles—the only ones in the neighborhood—the enemy had no trouble locating us. They probably knew where we were at all times. Their scouts had only to follow our easily discerned trail, a feat that was possible even during darkness, to learn the exact location of our company. The advantage was that because the enemy knew our location anyway, our company could afford to helicopter in hot chow for morning and evening meals. We were usually on the move or otherwise engaged during the noon hour and ate C rations for that meal. Helicopters also delivered mail almost every day and ice when it was available, plus additional ammunition and other necessary equipment and supplies. These conveniences were unheard of in most other infantry assignments, regardless of the war or theater of operations.

Often we heard the helicopters flying to our perimeter before they became visible. They flew in and hovered over a cleared landing zone, then slowly settled to the ground. Their rotors kicked up dust and debris, which moved in waves as the strong wind blew outward from the chopper. We closed our eyes to keep out the dust and dirt and hung onto our hats or held down items we didn't want to blow away. The wind cooled us, but when the chopper left, the dust settled and it got hot and still once again.

On one of my first nights in the field, I was assigned guard duty on the top of my assigned squad's APC. When darkness fell, some of the men went to bed, if you want to call it that, on the ground with perhaps a few sandbags outlining their sleeping positions. Some of the men had a light blanket, but others simply lay down on the bare ground. Still others milled about in small, quiet groups.

I was seated in the armored rotating turret behind the .50-caliber machine gun. My mission was to watch for enemy activity to our front, along with other guards on the other APCs forming our circular perimeter. The machine gun I was sitting behind was the largest made and had a mounted starlight scope, a device that magnified existing light from stars or other low-intensity sources and provided a view of the landscape illuminated in green and white.

The moon provided some light and the starlight scope was working well. The terrain to my front consisted of open rice paddies, so I could see everything within a mile or so. After a while, even though this was my first combat mission and I should have been at least nervous or uneasy, I concluded that there was nothing to fear to our front. I turned the starlight scope inward to see what my new fellow company members were up to. As I scanned the perimeter, I noticed activity near the wire surrounding our position. A few guys were sneaking a prostitute, called a boom-boom girl, into the perimeter. They disappeared from my view when they led her inside a bunker.

Later in the evening, we watched as tracers flew high into the sky from a battle a mile or two away. It was odd that something so beautiful could portend something so ominous. Somewhere in the distance beneath the tracers, people were dying. The lion was out there, and the lion was hungry.

Within a few days of joining the company, I went on my first patrol. We trudged along the top of a rice paddy dike with ten meters separating each member of the patrol so that one booby trap or mortar round wouldn't kill us all. To reduce the chances of hitting a booby trap, each man followed the footsteps of the soldier to his front.

With the sun beating down on my olive-drab fatigues, I soon became so exhausted that all I could concentrate on was proceeding in an upright position. I stopped caring where I placed each foot; I was just happy that I could keep them moving. Sniper fire would have been a welcome excuse to lie down and rest. This period of adjusting to the climate would gradually pass, but I would remember it when I saw more recent arrivals suffer from the same heat exhaustion.

On some days, we stayed inside the perimeter and had a bit of free time. The soccer field in which we were set up was on the edge of the village of Trang Bang, and civilians were numerous. A group of kids hung around the main gate, and we joked with them and gave them C-ration cans or tropical chocolate bars. Two of them saw me eyeing a cute girl one day and taught me a Vietnamese phrase to say to her. After they were satisfied with my pronunciation, they urged me to go to her and repeat it. When I delivered the message to the girl, they clutched their sides and laughed so hard that they could barely stand up. I realized that I'd been had. I concluded that the phrase was something sexually suggestive and the boys were having fun at my expense. I had just been introduced to Vietnamese humor, which is similar to humor everywhere.

The girl must have figured out what happened, because she waved and smiled to me every time we saw each other after that day. She made a few trips over to our front gate to chat with me, but the relationship didn't progress further than that.

For months afterward, however, when our unit went through Trang Bang, I saw her looking for me. When she spotted me, her face lit up and she smiled and gave me a big wave. I often wondered how she knew when our unit was passing through her town. I think that Americans never understood the extent of the Vietnamese communications network.

On November 1, our company was moved to a new location away from the large villages. We performed day and night security for a road that was being built by engineers. In the mornings, we operated minesweepers to check for explosives placed by VC forces, then guarded the road while the engineers worked. At the end of the day, they packed up and headed back to wherever they came from. We remained and guarded the site overnight.

On the first night out, I was placed on listening post (LP) with two other guys from our platoon. We spent the night about two hundred meters outside the perimeter to provide early warning of attacks. The next night, we were warned that a VC force, a thousand soldiers strong, was in the area. We prepared for a mass attack, but it never came.

The Language Barrier

Communication between GIs and the Vietnamese relied on pidgin English, a combination of words and phrases from both languages, with a little French tossed in for good measure. Some of the highlights included:

> *beaucoup:* big (from the French, pronounced "boocoo")
> *ti ti:* small (also from the French, petite)
> **number one:** good
> **number ten:** bad
> **number ten thou:** very bad (*thou* is short for thousand)
> **chop chop:** goodies or handouts, usually food
> *di di mau:* go away (literally, "go, go quickly")
> *dien khe dau:* crazy (pronounced "dinky dow")
> **same same:** the same as, or alike
> *xin loi:* sorry about that, or excuse me

An unfortunate aspect of relations between Americans and Vietnamese, and I suspect those involved in other conflicts as well, was the language barrier. In Vietnam, it was probably a little worse than in other wars because of the sound of the language. Vietnamese, like Chinese, Thai, Cambodian, Laotian, and several other Asian languages, utilizes tones. In Vietnamese, the word *ma*, for example, has six different meanings, depending on the inflection with which it is spoken.

My cohorts and I had no idea of the tonal nature of the language. When we heard Vietnamese people talking among themselves, we didn't think their speech sounded like a language. It sounded to us like sing-songy gibberish because it lacked the inflections we were accustomed to. This, among other things, led us to think of ourselves as superior to the Vietnamese people, which of course wasn't true at all. In some ways we dehumanized our enemy and, in association, the Vietnamese people as well. This is a common trait in warfare, with the exception of wars between people who speak the same language, such as civil wars.

A few days after I joined the company in the field, the LP for the 1st Platoon came in contact with the enemy. A small VC force crawled slowly and stealthily to the front of the three-man position and turned around one of their Claymore mines. These directional mines are not buried but are positioned aboveground and held in place by wire legs inserted into the soil. The mine can be aimed, but it produces a back blast. The fortunate thing about Claymores is that they are removed upon departure, not left in place to harm civilians.

One of the LP's mines was later detonated, either by the enemy—who must have had a detonator—or by the Americans after contact was initiated. In any event, the mine was misdirected and no damage was inflicted. The enemy fired machine guns into the LP position but missed everyone.

Earlier that night, VC forces shot six RPGs at one of our tracks; only one hit. It didn't cause much damage to the tracks, but it wounded one man in the throat.

The next night, I was on LP in front of our platoon's position and once again the 1st Platoon was hit by the VC. Soldiers along their platoon's sector of the perimeter observed thirty VC and opened up on them. Before their LP withdrew inside the perimeter, having fulfilled their mission of delivering early warnings of attack, they reported that the VC soldiers were moving around the perimeter toward my platoon's sector.

We were outside of our perimeter in our LP position, and our pucker factor rose in geometric proportions. We had a starlight scope with us, and we watched and listened anxiously for any sign of the enemy, but we didn't see or hear anyone. The enemy force must have withdrawn.

On November 11, during a daytime patrol, Sgt. Anderson Turner of my platoon was killed, the first casualty since my arrival. He found a live mortar round and was in the process of blowing it in place with a Chinese Communist (Chi-Com) grenade he had been carrying. His plan was to pull the pin on the grenade, place the grenade next to the mortar round, and run. That process works; I employed it myself on several occasions later in my tour. This time, though, things went wrong.

We were taking a break while he worked when the grenade explosion ripped through the air. When the initial confusion died down, I stood over him and watched while our medics worked on him, trying to keep him alive until the dust-off chopper arrived. He looked normal except for numerous small puncture wounds on his face and chest. We heard that he died in the helicopter before reaching the rear, where further medical attention awaited.

Some of our guys speculated that the Chi-Com grenade had a faulty fuse and may have been planted by the VC in hopes that one of us would find it and use it. Sergeant Turner had been a nice guy. The war was becoming real.

I fell into the routine of being out in the field with the company. We slept on the ground around our tracks. Depending on the number of men in the squad, each of us pulled guard for an hour or so in the middle of the night—on top of the track behind the .50-caliber machine gun. During the day, we went out on patrols, and each night our platoons sent out three guys on listening post and several more on ambush patrols. We were near the end of the monsoon season, but it still rained a little every day and night.

My mom was curious about my life in Vietnam. One of her letters asked if I was eating okay. I answered as best I could.

"When I got over here I had a little trouble getting used to Army food again, but since I came out to the field, I've been eating pretty good. We get 2 hot meals a day flown in by helicopter. Yesterday for breakfast I had 3 cups of coffee and 4 eggs. For lunch, C-rations as always. Last night we had pork chops, potatoes, gravy, salad, beans, bread, ice cream and pop or beer, which we have to pay for ourselves. They feed us on paper plates so there are no dishes to wash. You should see my suntan."

My mom was attempting to follow our unit's progress on a map of Vietnam that she had obtained from the National Geographic Society. She had questions concerning where we were, but I wasn't too sure, which is normal at the lowest levels of the infantry. I told her that I had landed at Bien Hoa, spent the night there, then passed through the outskirts of Saigon on the way to Cu Chi. Our company remained for a week at the old base camp at Trang Bang, where I had joined the company, before we were moved closer to the road we were guarding for the engineers. After the road was finished, we were told that we'd move about sixty miles north, but I had no idea what towns, if any, we would be near.

Mom also asked about the Vietnamese economy. My response was that the Vietnamese people were so poor that a box of C rations was a luxury for them. I was interested in the way they lived. During operations that necessitated searching hootches, I wandered around looking at their possessions and attempted to get a glimpse of their lifestyle.

Most homes that I observed consisted of three thatched structures. The main one, the living quarters, held the beds: low tables of coffee table height with bamboo sleeping mats, which were often rolled up during the day. I presume that the beds were off the ground to avoid rodents, snakes, and other pests. This arrangement also provided more fresh air and, during the rainy season, drier accommodations than sleeping on the ground.

The Vietnamese lit their homes with kerosene lamps, but few of them had glass chimneys; perhaps they had all been broken. I sometimes used the lamps when checking out a home's bomb shelter. Each hootch had one to provide shelter for the family if a battle occurred nearby. One day a woman showed me a hole in her roof where a mortar round had dropped in. Upon closer inspection, I could see evidence of the explosion in the form of damage to the thatched walls.

Another building, often adjoining the main one, was used for cooking, which was performed over an open fire using one or two crude pots hung from a tripod or placed on a grating. Food, usually rice and chicken, was stored in bags, which were hung above the ground to prevent pilfering by animals.

The third structure served as an animal pen. Almost every hootch outside a village had pigs, chickens, and water buffalo.

Transportation was limited to bicycles, small minibikes or motorcycles, or carts pulled by water buffalo or oxen.

These were common reminders that we were in one of the world's poorest countries.

FIELD EXPEDIENCY

Sleeping

We did not get a lot of sleep in Vietnam. There were few nights when we did not pull some type of guard duty, usually lasting about an hour and a half. Throughout our tour, it seemed as if we spent more nights outside our perimeter than we did inside, either on an LP or an ambush patrol. As a result, we seldom were well rested.

Early in my tour, when it was time to get some rest, most of us bedded down on the open ground. Later, as the frequency of our contact with enemy forces and the likelihood of mortar attacks increased, we were told to sleep inside a ring of sandbags, which provided at least some protection against shrapnel. Later still, we progressed to digging a hole deep enough to enable us to sleep entirely belowground. We used the soil from the hole to fill sandbags, which we placed around the edge of the hole. Next, our orders called for two layers of sandbags around our sleeping positions, which began to double as fighting positions. We were no longer permitted to sleep in random locations but were to construct our positions along the outer edge of the circular perimeter, where we could, if necessary, return enemy fire without having to move from another position farther inside the perimeter. Eventually, we built full bunkers with overhead protection, door openings in the back, firing ports to the front, and a raised earthen shelf for a machine gun.

While on operations away from our perimeter, we slept wherever we happened to be. On ambush patrol or listening post, we slept on the open ground wherever we fought or pulled watch.

Within the perimeter, the squad leader and the driver of each squad slept inside the tracks, on narrow benches along the sides. When we had enough squad members to man the bunkers, a few guys hung hammocks inside the track, and one of our squad members slept on a litter or stretcher, which was a little shorter than the width of the track. The litter was suspended between two equipment racks, sort of like shelves, and made a fine bed.

Each soldier was issued a poncho and poncho liner. The latter was a lightweight, but surprisingly warm, quilted cover the same size as the poncho. Ties sewed on the outer edge of the liner aligned with the eyelets on the poncho. The two items could be joined to make a waterproof, warm sleeping bag.

The official army description of the poncho liner was "Liner, wet weather poncho." A tag on a corner provided operating instructions:

1. Spread the poncho flat on the ground, making sure that the hood opening is tightly closed and on the underside.

2. Place liner on poncho, matching the tie-tapes on liner with the grommets on the poncho and tie together.

3. If the poncho and liner combination is to be used as a sleeping bag, snap the sides of the poncho together along their entire length and tuck the foot end under to keep the feet from sticking out.

CAUTION: Do not fasten the snap fasteners together when used as a sleeping bag in combat areas; it cannot be opened quickly.

4. Poncho and liner combination can be used as a wrap-around sleeping bag or as a blanket.

5. The liner, without the poncho, can be used as a blanket when sleeping under cover or in a jungle hammock.

6. Keep liner away from open fire and sparks. *DO NOT SMOKE* in bed when using liner as a blanket or sleeping bag.

7. When necessary, liner can be hand laundered. Use a mild soap and *lukewarm* water. Do not boil.

8. Do not dry clean.

We had no trouble complying with item 8.

The outer shell of the poncho liner was nylon and had a property that made it invaluable in the humid tropics: Sticky flesh did not adhere to it. This meant more comfortable sleeping.

Unfortunately, the liner I was issued disappeared on about the third day of my tour. It was probably scrounged, the army's word for stolen, by someone who had lost his own. I never got a replacement, and I wasn't mean enough to scrounge somebody else's.

I slept on a poncho, which I carried in my butt pack at all times. I spread it out entirely and lay on half of it, with my M16 next to my body. In the middle of the night, if I awoke with a slight chill or if it began to rain, I flipped the other half over me. To prevent my usually moist flesh from sticking to the fabric of the poncho, I slept with my clothes on. Most of the guys slept fully dressed except for their boots. This prevented delays in getting dressed, which we could ill afford if combat situations arose in the night. Instant reaction was a necessity, and we were always prepared to engage in combat immediately.

The poncho liner was one of only two items of standard issue that were made of camouflage fabric. The other was the cloth helmet cover, which we assumed was intended to reduce the shine of our World War II–style steel pots. Buttonholes were sewn at regular intervals on the helmet cover. At first, we poked grass or leafy twigs into the buttonholes, but instead of making us more difficult to see, they made it harder for us to get out of sight. We discovered that the best use of the buttonholes was to hold vegetation that pointed downward, not upward, which served to break up the easily discernible silhouette created by our heads and shoulders.

Our jungle fatigues and almost every other piece of military hardware, equipment, or apparel were olive drab—a color that most GIs grew to dislike—or black. Olive drab is generally the color of shadows in a forest. Guys seemed to disappear once inside a closed canopy. Sweat and mud added some mottling to our uniforms and helped us blend in.

Vietnamese Weather

I arrived in Vietnam in October, near the end of the monsoon season. The Vietnamese climate has two parts: the rainy season and the dry season. The dry season is subdivided into what we called the cold dry season and the hot dry season. Year-round highs in South Vietnam near Saigon averaged between the upper eighties and low nineties, and it was always humid. Lows ranged from the mid- to upper seventies. The record low for Saigon is slightly below sixty degrees. Not much chance for a white Christmas.

During the rainy season, it rains hard several times per day, every day. In a six-month period, more than eighty inches of rain falls. The earth turns to mud and rice paddies fill with water. During this season in this beautiful tropical place, there are two parts of the landscape—water and green.

In November, the rain stops and usually doesn't resume until May. The rice paddies slowly dry up. The areas that had been saturated become dry and as hard as concrete. The dirt roads turn from sticky mud to fine dust, the consistency of flour, several inches deep. When we would jump down from the top of the track, our feet kicked up clouds of dust. Once, I jumped down, raising a cloud of dust, then I remained motionless. When the dust settled, I could not see the tops of my boots.

It took me a month or more to become fully adjusted to the tropical climate. For my entire tour I dreaded the sight of the rising sun because of the unbearable heat it would produce, heat that beat on our shoulders and scorched and faded the olive-drab shirts and trousers that were our uniforms.

Because our company was a mechanized infantry unit, we set up in the open. Each squad had an armored personnel carrier, which transported us quickly to trouble spots or assigned areas and served as a storehouse for our supplies, ammunition, and gear. Unlike our cousins, the ground-pounding infantry, who sneaked through the jungle in an attempt to locate the enemy before the enemy found them, we were constantly prepared for attack. Because of the engine noise of our APCs, the enemy always knew where we were. Our philosophy was, we're ready to fight whenever you are. Setting up our defensive perimeters in the open created an exposed area that the enemy attack had to cross. This provided us with a forewarning and discouraged enemy forces from getting too close. Unfortunately, this also meant that we baked in the sun each day.

Driven by the desire to escape the sun's heat, if only for a short time, we devised ingenious methods of producing shade. Even small amounts of it were welcome. We strung ponchos and poncho liners between makeshift poles and our tracks, or between radio antennas on top of the tracks. Ponchos and their liners were valued as much for their shade-providing capabilities as they were for their intended purpose.

During the monsoon season, this same ingenuity—called field expediency by the military—was applied to the prospect of staying dry. When it rained during the daytime, we got wet. We didn't have the luxury of a shelter or even an umbrella. When the first drop of moisture soaked through to the skin, we felt uncomfortable. Being thoroughly soaked, however, didn't bother us. I found that if I kept my head reasonably dry, I felt as comfortable as possible under the circumstances. My helmet or, preferably, my bush hat served this purpose well.

At night, or while inside a base camp or perimeter, it was easier to stay dry. My companions and I spent hours, when the opportunity presented itself, creating shelters. Ponchos or shelter halves (pieces of canvas, two of which formed a pup tent) were fastened or tied together, then suspended a few feet above the ground from poles or whatever was available.

One afternoon inside the perimeter, a few friends and I gathered several ponchos and shelter halves and spent the afternoon constructing an elaborate fourteen-foot-square canopy that we suspended about two feet above the ground on sticks inserted into the soil. That evening, as we were luxuriating inside our structure during a gentle rain, our perimeter was hit by an enemy force of undetermined size. We left the relative comfort of our carefully constructed shelter to get up on line with the tracks, bunkers, and other infantrymen to return fire. With green tracers zipping over our heads, we grabbed our weapons and dove for a firing position. A few of us landed in a puddle and became thoroughly drenched. After the firing was over, there was no reason to reenter our shelter, because we were already soaked. We slept the remainder of the night in the puddle with water up to our waists. At least it was warm.

6 Nov 67

Mom,

How's everything back home?

Tonight I go on my first ambush. I have to take the sling off my rifle and fix everything else that makes noise.

Later . . . Hi again. That ambush last night wasn't exactly an ambush. We sat in the middle of a road. We were security for a radar station to see if anybody was coming down the road or planting mines on it.

I have to burn all the letters I get. I don't have room to store them all and if I throw them away & the VC find them, they'd write to you saying I was dead & all that stuff.

I loaf around all day cause I was on the ambush last night. Tonight I'll probably be on LP.

I've made a few friends but not very good ones.

The ARVNs are here. That's Army of the Republic of Vietnam. They're just passing through. They got 4 VC today.

It's around noon & the sun is real hot so I put up a little shelter with my poncho to get out of the sun. Last night I wore a mosquito net over my head. This morning my hands are full of mosquito bites. You can hear them all over. Millions of them. They aren't so bad in the daytime but terrible at night when you're near a rice paddy & we're surrounded by them.

There isn't much jungle up here. Banana trees and fruit like I've never seen before.

We should be eating chow pretty soon. I'll write more next time I have a chance. Roger

Out on patrol, we spent time in the woods, out of the sun, but the combination of the higher humidity in the forested areas, the additional weight we carried, and the exertion of the march made us just as hot, if not hotter, than when we baked in the sun. We drank a lot of water. Sometimes, while crossing streams, we filled our steel pots and poured water over ourselves. We didn't mind getting wet on hot afternoons. The water evaporating from our shirts and trousers felt good. Our boots stayed wet and cool for a long time. Southeast Asia is known for having the heaviest rainfall in the world. During some of the downpours a few of us ventured out naked with a bar of soap to bathe. Once, while standing in a tent in our company area at Cu Chi, I was amazed that I could not see the tent across the company street, only thirty feet away, because it was raining so hard.

At Cu Chi, our company constructed a shower from an old airplane wing suspended above a wooden floor. The sun warmed the water in the wing during the day. When the company returned from operations in the field, there were warm showers for the first twenty-five or so soldiers. Upon our unit's arrival in the company area, men stripped off their clothes and raced for the showers in hopes of enjoying warm water to wash away the sweat and filth that were inherent in field operations.

At times, we went three weeks or longer without a shower or bath. We often worked shirtless and were proud of the tans we developed—that is, until we took a shower. Then the soap washed away the "tan."

Once while in the rear, I witnessed several of our permanent base camp staff (company clerks, supply gofers, mail handlers, and so on) drop what they were doing during the late afternoon and take showers before the company returned. These individuals prevented some of our infantrymen from enjoying a warm shower. In doing so, they demonstrated the reason for the infantryman's inherent mistrust and dislike of rear-echelon troops, the guys who worked in the larger bases and never went outside the perimeter.

One day after returning to Cu Chi from an extended time in the field, I was on my way to the PX. While in the field I had lost my bush hat, which every soldier in Cu Chi was supposed to wear, and headed into the PX hatless. A military policeman (MP) refused to allow me to enter because I was out of uniform without a hat. While I was trying to explain that I could not wear a hat because at the moment I did not have one, several others from my platoon came by and overheard the conversation during their approach.

Without stopping, they grabbed me and pulled me along with them, saying, "He's with us." The MP was outnumbered, and I made it inside the PX.

The PX story illustrates some of the close bonds that form between men at war. The guys from my platoon who dragged me past the MP were not my best friends, but simply being in the same unit was enough to make me feel as though I was one of them and made them want to help me. Members of the same unit were treated like family, especially when mixed with other troops in the larger base camps. It was in the field that we became close. We depended on one another for safety, security, and our very survival. In a sense, we stood back to back against the rest of the world, ready to take on any group that had the guts to challenge us. We also depended on one another for entertainment. We had radios but no televisions and saw only an occasional movie. As a result, we engaged in extensive conversations and learned little things about one another that were usually reserved for family members. Each of us found others with whom we shared values and felt comfortable.

The longest lasting and closest relationships that I am aware of were between men who lived together in the field and shared the good times and comforted one another during the bad. We looked out for, and cared for, one another. When we went to sleep, we literally placed our lives in the hands of those who were awake and on guard.

Nicknames

Soldiers in the Vietnam War had a propensity for nicknames. We referred to one another by our last names, which were sewn on our uniforms and therefore the easiest to learn. If someone's name was forgotten, a glance at the name tag refreshed our memory. As we got to know one another, we assigned nicknames, possibly as a socially acceptable form of showing affection. It was also a means of remembering something about a new person that helped in getting to know him, which is important in a group of fighting men. Some nicknames were shortened last names. Hackin became Hack. Chadwick became Chad. Solomon became Solly.

Hack was a dark-complected guy with dark, curly hair and an infectious laugh. He remembers when I joined the company at Trang Bang, but my first memory of him was later, when our platoon was

lying in a deep ditch waiting for an operation to resume. He spent
the time making funny remarks about something, causing everyone
to giggle. Because he was witty and funny, most of the guys were
drawn to him.

Bob Ordy, from Pennsylvania, and I had a lot in common and became close. Leroy Thomas, a black guy with a quick, friendly grin,
was good with an M79 grenade launcher. Sam Stewart, another
black soldier, was liked by everyone for his sense of humor. Darrell
Guffey looked younger than the rest of us and was considered a little brother. Goode, another likable black soldier, was also proficient
with the M79.

James Bell joined the company a month after I did. He was
known at first for taking the war too seriously. After breaking
through hedgerows while on a sweep, he would dive into a prone
position with his M16 up and ready to fire. The rest of us, who had
developed a sense for when the enemy wasn't around, rolled our
eyes at one another. Bell caught on eventually to the same clues that
we had learned and became one of us. He was known for never using profanity, which was almost unheard of in an infantryman. Instead he used the term "mother fletch" several times daily. Bell
became a good soldier and one of our best track drivers. He performed some of the bravest acts I witnessed in combat.

In addition to nicknames for one another, we assigned them to
other divisions or units. The 4th Infantry Division became known as
the 4-H Division because of the design of their patch. The 9th Infantry Division was called Flower Power or Cookie Division, for the
resemblance of its unit patch to these two objects. The 1st Infantry
Division's self-assigned nickname was the Big Red One, with em-
phasis on the last word. We switched it, emphasizing the middle
word, which gave the phrase a new meaning. The 101st Airborne,
known as the Screaming Eagles because of its patch, was called the
Pukin' Buzzards.

Our unit patch, worn on the left shoulder of our uniform, was a
red leaf from a taro tree, a tropical species, with a gold lightning
bolt superimposed in the middle of the leaf. The outer edge of the
patch was also gold. For the most part, the patches we wore overseas
had subdued colors, consisting of olive drab and black, rather than

bright red and gold. The subdued patches allowed us to blend in better with the environment.

The design of our unit patch symbolized Tropic Lightning, the division's nickname. We were told that the name was assigned by the division commander when the new unit's first mission—capturing an enemy-held area—was accomplished ahead of schedule. To other units, we became the Electric Strawberry. The Beatles's song "Strawberry Fields Forever" took on special meaning.

I carried an official Boy Scout compass in my shirt pocket, and it came in handy on several occasions. On November 13, I was assigned to an LP with two fellow platoon members. Our lieutenant wanted us near a cemetery that we could see from our perimeter, and during the afternoon I shot an azimuth (compass reading) and rotated the north arrow so that the directional arrow pointed to the cemetery. After dark, while we were en route to our position, the cemetery wasn't visible and we weren't sure which way to go. I held up my compass to the stars and looked at it from underneath—the only way I could see the directional arrow in the dark. I pointed to where I thought we should go. One of my companions looked in that direction with a starlight scope and found the cemetery.

Until now, my squad didn't have a squad leader. The previous one had a wounded foot, the result of a booby trap, and was in the rear recovering. On November 17, we were assigned a new squad leader named Jones.

One of the tropical diseases we were exposed to was malaria, which is carried by female mosquitoes. These insects were more numerous than bullets in Vietnam. To ward off this life-threatening disease, we took pills. Each Monday one of our medics stood at the end of the chow line with a container of large orange pills and gave one to each of us. This event was the only indication we had of what day of the week it was. Otherwise, one day was no different than any other; our daily routines were the same.

In addition to the weekly orange pills, we took small white ones each day. Either this medication or our diet affected our stools, resulting in semidiarrhea. I suspected that the orange malaria pills caused the problem. Some guys stopped taking the pills because of the side effects.

During an evening inside our company perimeter, I noticed Solly off by himself, lying down. This was unusual for Solly, who had been a successful amateur boxer before becoming a soldier. He was well liked and usually socialized with the guys. When I noticed him away from the others, I went over to check on him and found him under a blanket shivering with a high fever and slightly disoriented.

I notified our platoon sergeant, who checked him too. Solly was medevacked (medical evacuation) to the rear for treatment. The next day we received word that he had malaria. He was back with us a few days later but would continue to suffer periodically from the tropical disease.

Road Security

The terrain in our area of operations can be described in one word: flat. A notable exception was Nui Ba Den, the Black Lady Mountain, eight klicks (five miles) north-northeast of Tay Ninh and 800 meters (approximately 2,600 feet) in height. All soldiers in our area of operations called it the Black Virgin Mountain, but the literal translation includes the word "lady." Legend has it that a young woman was abducted and taken to the top of the mountain by a group of thugs who intended to rape her. While they were resting after the climb, she threw herself off one of the cliffs and died.

Because the surrounding terrain was flat, this mountain could be seen for miles. I once flew from the Saigon area into Cu Chi, and as we approached the base camp we could see this mountain although it was fifty-three klicks (thirty-three miles) to the north. The mountain was formed by a volcano, which accounts for its dark color, and is honeycombed with caves. It was reportedly occupied by a battalion of NVA and/or VC who came down from the mountain during the night, attacked American or South Vietnamese positions or placed land mines in nearby roads, then returned to the mountain. Because the mountain was a religious symbol, we were not allowed to place any ordnance on it larger than a mortar. Inside the many crevices and caves, the enemy was safe.

The company's favorite duty was what we called road security, which was performed within easy viewing and walking distance of the mountain. It involved guarding the twenty-five-kilometer (sixteen-mile) road running between the bases of Tay Ninh and Dau Tieng against attack, ambush, or the placement of mines or booby traps.

While on road security detail, the company often spent the night at an engineering compound at the base of the mountain where rock was crushed to produce gravel. During the day, we guarded the road; at night we set up on the perimeter of the rock crusher compound and provided security for the engineers and other personnel who were stationed there.

We left the rock crusher each morning shortly after dawn. One platoon cleared the road, with one squad walking down the middle—operating a mine detector or two—and checking for other signs of enemy activity. Two other squads provided flank security, one on either side of the road, slightly ahead of the team on the roadway. The remainder of the company followed behind on the tracks. The APC in the rear peeled off and set up facing into the woods and rubber plantations, with the road at its rear. The next APC did the same a little farther along on the opposite side of the road, and so on. From the air, I imagined that the placement of our tracks along the road appeared like a long zipper.

Once we were in place, we could not see the tracks on either side of us but could hear them on the radio. We posted one man on guard, then spent the remainder of the day resting in the shade, writing letters, cleaning our weapons, sleeping, or socializing with the numerous Vietnamese civilians who came out in hopes of selling us their wares.

They carried just about anything they thought we might purchase. Over the course of the year, I bought a wristwatch; a souvenir photo album; a whetstone, which I and other members of my squad used to sharpen knives; tasty sandwiches; and numerous soft drinks. Some of the vendors sold cigarette lighters that read, "Yea, though I walk through the valley of shadow I shall fear no evil, for I am the evilest son of a bitch in the valley." Armed to the teeth as we were, and constantly on the lookout and prepared for action, we could empathize with this sentiment.

In most areas, civilians approached us if the enemy was not nearby, so we used the friendliness of the locals as an indication of our relative security. Two of the children who sold Coca-Cola were special to me. We called one of them Susie. Most GIs had trouble learning and pronouncing Vietnamese names, so the kids took on American nicknames. Susie was a beautiful twelve-year-old girl with a friendly personality. All of the guys in our company liked her and looked out for her. I became the best of friends with an eleven-year-old boy we called Jerry. Both of them were from Tay Ninh.

These two kids rode bicycles with front-mounted baskets lined with plastic and filled with ice and twelve-ounce bottles of Coca-Cola. They purchased the bottles from the Saigon Coca-Cola Bottling Company for twenty-five cents each and sold them to us for fifty cents. Because of the long distances they had to pedal their bikes to reach us, and because we liked them, we didn't mind the markup. They used their profits to help support their families.

After Jerry sold his Cokes, he would find our squad and spend some time with us before making another run. I told him stories of America and he taught me Vietnamese words. He showed me how to throw a knife, and we often competed in best-out-of-ten contests throwing bayonets at the rubber trees that lined the road. He usually won.

The men and I often wondered about Jerry's family and which side his father was on—that is, if Jerry had a father. He did not speak much about his dad. In any case, his father's political persuasion would not have changed the way we felt about this bright, friendly boy.

The fathers of these two kids were most likely fighting on one of the two sides of the conflict, as were most men of military age. That had to have a negative impact on the country's economy. To add to that, the American military machine turned the economy of Vietnam, and I suspect other countries in which it operated, upside down. A typical Vietnamese family subsisted on an annual budget of well under the equivalent of a hundred dollars U.S. currency. Because of the war, most professional pursuits by male heads of household were interrupted, at best.

Into this mixture came GIs with half a year's Vietnamese income in their pockets as discretionary funds. Suddenly, children such as Susie and Jerry could earn their father's equivalent annual salary in a few weeks. A boom-boom girl could earn that much in an afternoon. This temptation was too great for many attractive girls. It was an ugly side effect of the war. I once saw a mother trying to interest us in her two teenaged daughters. She was pulling up their skirts and saying *ti ti*, meaning small or tight.

One night in the third week of November, my platoon was on its way to an ambush site. We paused in place to allow our three point men to check out a hedgerow to our front. Back in the column, we crouched in the darkness, with every other GI facing to the right while the remainder of the patrol faced left. The last man in the column faced to the rear. Our lieutenant, in the center of the column, monitored the radio.

Several bursts of automatic fire broke the silence to our front. The firing lasted only a few seconds, then it became quiet again.

Our point men returned to the column and reported that while they were checking the hedgerow, they spotted three VC walking down a trail that ran along the opposite side of the hedgerow. The two forces saw each other at the same time and opened fire, then the VC fled.

The next week, our company moved farther north and was operating near the large town of Tay Ninh, not far from the Black Virgin Mountain, Nui Ba Den.

During a daytime operation shortly after we arrived, I was with a few others who were searching a hootch. I decided to check out the bomb shelter to see if it held any weapons or other military equipment. I found a kerosene lamp and lit it, then lowered myself into the opening and held out the lamp to light the way. Instead of finding a small earthen room, typical of most bomb shelters, I saw a tunnel leading off to the right. I borrowed a .45 from someone and entered the tunnel.

The floor was flat; the walls rose vertically for about a foot and a half, then arched over my head. I passed a discarded thong sandal, which most likely had floated to its present position from the recent rain. The walls and floor of the tunnel were hardened and appeared porous. Once water drained away, there was no evidence of it having been there, except for the sandal.

I saw light ahead and continued crawling for a distance of twenty-five feet or so, holding the lamp and resting the .45 on the floor in my other hand as I moved. As I approached the light, I noticed that it was coming from above. A shaft led straight up. On the other side of the shaft was the shelter. I checked it out but found nothing unusual, so I blew out the lamp and cautiously raised myself into the shaft. I found myself in an area near a tree line between several hootches. It appeared that this shelter was used by several families.

I reentered the hootch, where several of my companions were waiting for me to emerge from the tunnel entrance. They were surprised to find me behind them.

On November 28, we joined up with two other companies, one of them a tank outfit. It was reported that two battalions of VC were in the vicinity, and we were on a search and destroy mission.

We knew we had found them when firing erupted to our front where some of our other platoons had made contact. My platoon wasn't directly involved in this battle. We provided rear security while the rest of our company, and the others with whom we were attached, engaged the enemy.

While monitoring the radio as the battle progressed, we learned that two soldiers in one of the other companies had been killed and five were wounded. That was the extent of our casualties; no one in my company had been injured. After an hour or so, the enemy broke contact and disappeared, as they had a knack of doing. We regrouped and headed back to our perimeters.

Mistrust of New Arrivals

Because the Vietnam War was different than any war the United States had previously experienced, and because our training consisted of World War II tactics that were not used here, new replacements were fully trusted only after they proved their competency and effectiveness in battle. After even the best training, it was difficult if not impossible for an individual to know how he would react when bullets zip in his direction for the first time. This is not to say that our training was poor, but it is hard to duplicate life-threatening circumstances in a classroom or at a range.

In any event, we learned how we would react to incoming mortars, rockets, sniper fire, firefights, booby traps, and battle only when they occurred. Fellow soldiers judged our reactions and either developed confidence in us or kept their distance. We did not discuss this, possibly because some of it was subconscious, but each of us went through such a test and later applied the same test to those who arrived after us and upon whom our lives would depend.

Another reason for the testing process was the 365-day rotation. With the exception of the initial insertion of our unit, each of us who served with the company during the six years it was stationed in Vietnam joined an established and experienced company in the field. We replaced someone who either became a casualty or had rotated home. As such, each person in the company had more time in-country than did new arrivals and would rotate home before they did. Men in the company had already proved themselves; new arrivals were unknown quantities.

New replacement troops also had to prove their willingness to pull their share of the many tasks that were necessary to keep a company operating. We had no room for slackers.

Rotation of Officers

Another factor that made life in the company uncertain, and resulted in decreased safety for us infantrymen, was the rotation of officers in combat assignments. Vietnam was the first war the United States engaged in since 1953, and the majority of career officers did not have combat experience, upon which the army—and I suspect the other branches of our military—places high value. In order to remedy that for as many officers as possible, it was decided that each officer would serve a maximum of six months in a field assignment as a platoon leader or company commander. After that, each would be reassigned to a staff position at the battalion or brigade level and be replaced by an inexperienced, new officer, usually one fresh in-country. Even battalion commanders rotated.

For example, the Bobcats, 1/5 (Mech) Infantry, had six battalion commanders during the year I served with them. Lieutenant Colonel Chandler Goodnow commanded from May to October 1967, which was considered a full tour for a command position. Lieutenant Colonel Fremont Hodson commanded the battalion from October to December. Major Ralph Hook held the reins from December to January 1968. He was followed by Lt. Col. Henry Murphy, who served as commander from January to February. Lieutenant Colonel Thomas Lodge was in command from February to June. Finally, Lt. Col. Andy Anderson took the lead in June and remained in command for the remainder of my tour. He was medically evacuated after his command track was struck by an RPG in October, the month I left Vietnam.

My platoon had seven platoon leaders, a lieutenant position, during my tour. This isn't a good example of the rotation of officers, however, because most of them became casualties. Three captains commanded our company during my tour.

In the long run, perhaps this action plan of rotating officers to optimize the number of them with combat experience resulted in improvements to the military. In the short run, however, life in the platoons and companies was more complex and dangerous. Often, by the time an officer learned the nuances of combat in Vietnam, which differed significantly from those of previous engagements, he was rotated out and was replaced by someone who, regardless of rank or time in the military, knew less than many of our privates about the war and our enemy. These officers were placed in command positions and made daily decisions affecting the lives of those they led. The smallest mistakes could lead to the death of an infantryman. Some of these poor decisions resulted in the deaths of some of my fellow soldiers.

Some of the new officers, but certainly not all, seized the opportunity to make a name for themselves. These men took aggressive action that led to increased danger for those under their command. The platoon watched new officers for signs of trustworthiness. Officers, as with all new arrivals, were tested before they were accepted.

Once the officers were accepted and learned the ropes, the platoon's trust was earned, and the combat troops would follow them almost anywhere and preferred to keep them rather than lose them to a staff position. Most infantrymen felt that the trusted officers' knowledge and experience would have been better spent keeping Americans alive. Their green replacements had to learn from the beginning. The policy of rotating officers contributed to the amount of black granite that was used during the construction of the Vietnam Veterans Memorial in our nation's capital.

One of the changes between the stateside army and the one to which I now belonged had to do with saluting and identifying officers. Because we always assumed that the enemy was watching, we were not required to salute officers. If we did, a sniper or scout could tell who the officers were. They would then become the priority targets. However, there were other ways to determine who the officers were. During operations, the enemy learned that officers were usually the ones walking just ahead of the guy carrying the radio.

Our officers had radio contact with the rear and could quickly pour huge amounts of armament down on top of the enemy. They were the individuals who gave orders and the men whom the other men followed. As such, they were the most desirable targets. If the platoon leader or platoon sergeant was killed, the rest of the platoon was less effective and therefore less of a threat. The Asian's way of expressing this notion was, "To slay a dragon, cut off its head."

To be less conspicuous and increase their chances, our officers wore the same uniforms that we did, with only black rank insignia worn on the lapel, not visible for more than a few yards. Now, I could carry a cookie in my right hand without having to worry if I would encounter an officer.

Early in my tour, I was not able to contribute much to my platoon. During patrols when we walked for miles in the hot sun and high temperatures, I was too exhausted to think of much more than placing one foot in front of the other. I was a new guy and not accepted by the others until I proved my usefulness. My first friends were other new arrivals, the guys who came about the same time I did. They were the ones with whom I shared the duties that were assigned to the new replacements, such as constructing bunkers, performing guard duty, going out on observation and listening posts, and, when in the rear, burning the human waste that was produced by our company.

I do not remember when I became something more than a FNG to the others in my platoon. The first sign that I recognized as acceptance was during a hot afternoon I spent working on a bunker. I was filling sandbags by myself in an attempt to improve our bunker and my sleeping position but also to kill time. Several of my platoon members nearby noticed my efforts in the hot sun, and one of them remarked, "That guy's a worker."

Although I was working to relieve boredom because there was not much else to do, I was pleased with the remark. At that moment I began to feel as though I belonged to my platoon.

LEARNING THE ROPES

Back at Fort Polk, a sergeant on one of the numerous ranges where we received training had explained to us how the Vietnam War differed from anything the army had experienced previously. He advised us that if we wanted to learn quickly what was going on, we should find someone who knew his stuff and follow him around.

As I became familiar with the members of my unit, I thought of the old sergeant's advice. It made sense to me and I decided to try it. The guy I picked to learn from was Jimmy Sutton, a specialist fourth class, the same rank as corporal, from Georgia. He had been in Vietnam for about six months by the time I arrived. He wasn't an infantryman; he was a tanker. I'm not sure how he ended up in our unit, but a replacement was probably needed, and tanks are sort of like tracks, right?

Sutton and I were in the same squad for a while, but he eventually became the leader of one of our sister units. He seemed to know his stuff pretty well. He was also somewhat eccentric and a legend in our unit. He didn't seem to have many close friends. Yet, our officers and senior NCOs valued and sought out his opinions. He was only nineteen when he arrived in Vietnam, but because of his experience, he seemed a lot older to us new guys.

We used the term "older" to denote soldiers who had more time in-country. The "younger" ones where those who had arrived in Vietnam later than we had. Experience in Vietnam was everything; those who had been there longer were more exposed to combat and proved that they were survivors. Age was only a number. I'm sure that soldiers in other wars felt the same.

Probably the strangest thing about Sutton was that after overrunning an enemy position or when operating in or near an area recently occupied by the VC or NVA, he went off by himself and explored the enemy's bunkers and tunnels. He had good powers of observation and logic and could discern significant bits of information about how the enemy lived and operated. By exploring bunkers and base camps, he was exposed to a lot of information, most of which he added to his knowledge base. Because he so willingly explored enemy positions on his own, he was used by our company commander as the unit's tunnel rat.

I began following Sutton when he went on his excursions. At first he would see me coming and try to get me to go away, usually by growling with his Georgian drawl, "What are you doing here? Get away from me."

I wouldn't leave, though, and he eventually but grudgingly tolerated my presence, provided I didn't come too close. After a while he let me ask questions. After a couple of weeks, he accepted me. Eventually, when he found bunkers or something else to explore, he came to get me and we went off together.

We were both interested in enemy soldiers. They took on an almost spiritual dimension because we seldom saw them. We did, however, have plenty of opportunities to explore their camps, and we carefully examined everything we found to learn how they lived and, if possible, how they fought.

One day Sutton took me into an enemy bunker that had been constructed, like many of them, by digging a rectangular hole, placing logs over it to form a roof, and covering the logs with the soil that had been removed from the hole. To camouflage the bunker, vegetation was transplanted to the top and sides.

Inside the bunker, Sutton pointed up at the ceiling. "See that? What do you think that is?" he asked.

I looked up and noticed a few sheets of paper tied to one of the logs that formed the roof of the bunker. Cords had been tied around the log, probably during construction, and the paper had been inserted into the cords so that it hugged the log. I couldn't figure it out.

"I don't know," I said.

"It's writing paper," Sutton explained. "The wood draws moisture out of the paper and the paper stays dry."

Of course. I had not been thinking of it in the right way. In the tropical humidity, documents or paper left in the open became too soggy to write on. We all carried plastic bags to hold our letters, pictures, wallets, and other important documents. Otherwise, they would disintegrate.

Sutton's observation amazed me. No one had told him this; he had noticed it and figured it out on his own. He knew more about how the enemy lived and operated than anyone I've met, before or since. That's why he was a legend in our unit.

The company commander used me as a tunnel rat, too. I explored a few tunnels for the company. Fortunately, I never ran into anyone in them. I would take a .45 and a flashlight, check for booby traps, and go down. If I suspected that someone was waiting for me, I would toss in a grenade first. A lot of the tunnels began with a four- to five-foot drop, then became horizontal. I always suspected booby traps, especially in the tunnel entrances that were easy to find, and stayed away from the hard-packed soil in the center of the entrance-way as I lowered myself into the tunnel. Once inside the opening, I waited for a few minutes, listening and allowing my eyes to adjust to the reduced light, then flicked on my flashlight and began moving.

Several times, while the company waited at the entrance, I crawled through a tunnel and popped up someplace else. I probably missed some trapdoors leading to lower levels, and maybe it's a good thing. The tunnels in and near our area of operations were a lot more sophisticated than any of us expected. Anyone in them would probably have been in the lower levels, hoping that intruders would miss the trapdoors.

Once I followed a tunnel that opened into a bunker with a firing port that offered a good view of the surrounding terrain. There was a ledge for a machine gun near the firing port, and lying on the ledge was a starlight scope. It was disconcerting to think that our enemy had somehow acquired this expensive, U.S.-made night vision device. It meant that the enemy could see our every movement during hours of darkness. I checked the scope for booby traps and took it topside.

When I handed it to our lieutenant, I told him, "I'm not going out after dark anymore for a while."

Unfortunately, that humorous tactic didn't work. All of us were out after dark regularly throughout our tour.

On December 1 we became involved in a large operation of which we had little if any forewarning. We left Tay Ninh and drove down Highway 1 to Cu Chi, our division base camp. We assumed that we would receive a short stand-down, but we didn't stop. We moved on to a road that led to a forested area about two miles to the west. Tracks from other units were lined up, waiting for us, along the entire length of the road. The 2d Platoon was down to two tracks because our other two had broken down. Our platoon was crowded onto the tops of the two remaining tracks, and we went to the head of the line. It took about forty-five minutes to negotiate the crowded road while avoiding the inevitable artillery and bomb craters.

Ahead of us, jet fighters and artillery were pounding a tree line. We watched the air show as we drew continuously closer. When we arrived at the assailed tree line, we dismounted and lined up our platoon to sweep the woods. We waited until the bombing stopped, then moved in. The vegetative growth was so thick that it took five minutes to go ten to fifteen feet. Once inside the wood line, we couldn't see one another and had to call to those on either side in order to stay on line. We swept like that from around noon until half past four. We found a VC body but no live soldiers.

We established a perimeter in a clearing to spend the night. That evening I went out on an ambush patrol, sharing duties as the point man with our new squad leader, a specialist fourth class named Maldonado. Jones, our previous squad leader, had been transferred to a different squad.

While we were out, our company perimeter was mortared. One man from another company who was attached to ours was killed, and several others were wounded. At the ambush site all was quiet, but we could hear small-arms fire as another company's night defensive perimeter was being visited by Charlie (from Victor Charlie, the phonetic alphabet slang for the VC). For about half an hour, tracers from the battle passed over our heads. Several of us were lying in a crater made by an artillery round, so we weren't in immediate danger from the tracers—which were coming from enemy fire—but we were scared nevertheless. We would have been outnumbered had the enemy force moved in our direction and made contact with us.

A little while later, after leaving the protection of the crater, a few of us were lying on the side of a large mound of soil waiting for the call to move out. Throughout the battle we could hear the whine of artillery and mortar shells as they passed overhead on their way to their intended targets. Suddenly an artillery round sounded different than the rest; it was heading right toward us. The telltale whistle grew steadily louder until the round hit and exploded on the opposite side of the mound of soil we were lying against. We were shaken but unhurt. We didn't want to be on the receiving end of American artillery anymore.

The next day we packed up and continued our sweep. Pilots overhead reported seeing bunkers two hundred meters ahead of us, a sure sign of an enemy stronghold. Once again the air force and artillery were called in. We fired our .50-caliber machine guns in the general direction of the bunkers, to make withdrawal difficult.

That afternoon we found several foxholes with positions dug in on the inside, most likely to help evade shrapnel from artillery and bombs from fighters. As we searched the enemy area, our lieutenant found one of the bunkers and thought that the side extension was a tunnel entrance. He called for a tunnel rat but nobody answered. So I went over, took off my equipment, got a .45 pistol and a flashlight, and stuck my head inside the bunker. I came back up.

"Sir, that's just a hole."

I spent an hour checking out what guys thought were tunnels but were only foxholes, similar to the one the lieutenant had found with dug-in positions.

That night we set up another night defensive perimeter and passed an uneventful evening. We were too deep in enemy territory to send out LPs, so we fired harassment and interdiction (H&I)

rounds with our M79 grenade launchers all night just in case Charlie got any ideas. It might make him think twice.

Each of us was handed an M79 when we took over on guard duty. Our regular grenadiers carried their rounds in a medic's bag because it was larger and held more rounds more comfortably than the ammo pouches designed for holding M79 rounds. When it was time for my watch, someone handed me one of the medic's bags filled with grenades. During my watch I probably fired several dozen rounds, aiming over the trees to our front so that the rounds would land where enemy troops might be gathering. I wondered what would happen if the enemy was closer than my rounds were falling, and I concluded that it would be a good idea to have a few land closer. I didn't know how far up to aim, though, to have the rounds land just outside our perimeter. I tried one, aiming a little less than straight up.

It seemed to take forever for the round to land. While it was in the air, I was afraid that I may have aimed wrong and the round might land inside our perimeter, perhaps near me. Just when I was beginning to wonder if it would land at all, I heard the *crump* of an explosion to my front, not too far outside our perimeter. I decided that maybe it would be best to interdict possible enemy movement before they had a chance to come that close to us.

The next day we moved into the area where the planes had reported the bunkers. When the first bunker was found, the lieutenant called for me to check it out. I entered, being cautious about booby traps. The bunker was clear and empty. I checked out five or six others. After a while, Sutton, who had taught me what I know about enemy bunkers but was now a leader for one of the other squads in our platoon, helped me check them out. After exploring enemy bunkers on our own, we felt confident in our abilities.

I found two mines, some web gear, and some morphine. I didn't know what the latter was until Sutton told me. Later, a lieutenant found some and didn't know what it was, so I told him. Sutton was making me look good. We also found rice, ponchos, hats, a little ammunition, some web gear and ammo pouches, pistol belts, and flashlight batteries, which were used to detonate mines. The enemy had departed hastily, probably when it became obvious that we were moving in their direction. When the bombing began, they most likely decided that it was best to withdraw and fight again another day when the odds were more in their favor. They had their own military goals, and if engaging us in combat wasn't in the best interest of completing their present mission, they avoided us.

I found only one tunnel, this one emanating from a bunker. I entered with the customary .45-caliber pistol and a flashlight. After going about twenty feet, I emerged without incident into another bunker. We spent most of the day in the recently occupied enemy base camp.

The next day we conducted sweeps through more of the enemy area. I found a few tunnels, but they didn't go anywhere. Or if they did, I missed the trapdoors leading to the lower, more dangerous levels. At the end of the day, we returned to our battalion base camp. By December 5, five days after the operation began, the enemy base camp was adequately cleared, and we headed back to Tay Ninh.

After the operation was over, we were told that the area we'd been exploring was a battalion-sized VC base camp. The VC had hastily withdrawn when we began moving toward their camp, as we suspected. We heard that another company had been approaching the same base camp from a different direction and was hit by the enemy, suffering one killed and one wounded by sniper fire. Our company suffered no casualties.

I have always looked younger than my age. One of our platoon's sergeants often teased me about this, especially in the presence of Vietnamese women. They giggled when he called me "baby-san GI."

One day while on an operation, this sergeant called me over. "You're the tunnel rat, aren't you? I found a tunnel and I want you to check it out."

I glanced where he indicated. "That's not a tunnel, Sergeant. It's a latrine."

Our enemy had devised a clever way of building a latrine that prevented odors, which might otherwise lead to discovery of their position. A square hole was dug a foot or so deep. Straight twigs of

bamboo were placed side by side along the top of the hole, extending about a third of the way across from each side. More twigs were
placed at a 90-degree angle, leaving a small square hole in the center. A little soil was used to fill any spaces, and a few large leaves were
used as a lid to cover the hole when the latrine was not in use. Sutton and I had seen dozens of these latrines while exploring enemy
positions, but this was the first this sergeant had seen.

"I want you to check it out anyway. It might have a false bottom."

Although I wondered how an enemy soldier would enter such a
tunnel entrance while avoiding the excrement, I did as I was told. I
found a long tree branch and, while the sergeant watched, I inserted it into the latrine and stirred it around. I then held it up for
his inspection. "Here, smell this."

He took a whiff and doubled over with dry heaves. I maintained
my composure, but on the inside I was gleeful.

Later in my tour, this same sergeant, who had a tendency to be
cocky, performed one of the few acts of cowardice I witnessed in
combat. We were on our way into battle, moving through a lightly
wooded area with low wooden structures—possibly for use by livestock—scattered here and there. We could hear the sounds of the
firefight to our front and became involved in the battle as soon as
we arrived. Because we were busy, we didn't notice that the sergeant
wasn't with us. When the enemy broke contact and the firing
stopped, we headed back the way we had come. As I passed one of
the low wooden structures, on impulse I glanced inside. There was
the sergeant, huddled in a corner and shivering. I shook my head
and walked away. He never spoke to me again, which was fine with
me. He had hidden in one of the huts rather than help us in combat. By doing so, he showed that he was not to be counted upon.

We were operating fifteen to twenty miles from the Cambodian
border, and the word was that we would be in Tay Ninh that night.
In this part of the country, I noticed a population of folks who had
darker skin but features more like those of Caucasions. I was told
that they were Mongolians.

Some of the local kids, who were entrepreneurial in spirit, ped-
aled their bikes out to where we were operating and sold us goods.
One of them was selling a frozen concoction that was cut into

squares with a piece of wood inserted as a handle. The orange ones tasted just like orange sherbet. The lime-flavored ones were good but tasted odd.

During our stay in Tay Ninh, preventive maintenance was performed on our APCs. My squad's APC received new tracks on both sides, and the motor was worked on all day by the mechanic assigned to our platoon. Our mechanics accompanied us to the field, at least in the early part of my tour, but remained with the APCs when we went out on operations.

Some of the guys with small transistor radios had them tuned to the only American programming in-country, an armed forces network, this one emanating from Saigon. The programming was music most of the day, with *Gunsmoke*, starring William Conrad, on Wednesday nights. I liked to listen to that when I could.

On the radio news, we heard that 159 North Vietnamese soldiers had been killed during two days of fighting with a mechanized infantry unit such as ours. American casualties were said to be light. The location wasn't given, so we had no idea which unit it was.

Sutton, like a lot of the guys, had a bout with immersion foot. This condition was usually caused when a GI went several weeks or more without removing his boots. During the day, and sometimes at night, our feet became drenched, either from sweat, monsoon rains, or wading through rice paddies or streams. Tropical fungi liked these conditions. The soles of the feet became soft and either absorbed or grew through the fabric of our socks. In severe cases, the sole of the boot became incorporated into the sole of the foot. Affected GIs could not remove their footwear without tearing off parts of their skin. Sometimes the boots had to be cut off by our medics, a painful procedure.

In some respects, our medics were like our moms. They were not in our chain of command, but they cajoled us into performing preventive measures that would avoid such things as immersion foot. Their incentive was partly not wanting to treat someone with the condition and partly wanting to ensure that we remained healthy and available for duty. They accomplished this by practicing preventive medicine.

If any of us had questions concerning anything medical, we went to one of our medics. Although they were not doctors, these men were knowledgeable. Of course, their most important responsibility was to keep the wounded alive until they could be transported to the rear for further medical attention.

Sutton, and most of us, learned the lesson of removing our boots whenever possible, which was the only way to dry our feet thoroughly. Our medics told us that the sun would kill some of the damaging fungi. They also said that fresh air was the best thing for our feet. Because of that, many of us removed our boots whenever possible, even if only for an hour or two.

Sutton often went without his boots for days and occasionally went barefooted on an overnight ambush. Although this was unusual for an American, our enemy, especially the Viet Cong, often wore nothing more than inexpensive thong sandals.

I developed the habit of always sleeping with my boots off. Overnight my feet would dry completely and could withstand another full day of being moist or wet. On patrol, I would sit down near a stream when possible, remove my boots, rinse out my socks, wring them out as best I could, and put them back on. Although they were a little wet, they felt much more comfortable.

One day in early December, I received the piece of mail that every GI dreaded, a Dear John letter. My girlfriend, who had promised to wait for me, decided that she couldn't. She wrote to break up with me. I was crushed; it was one of the most helpless feelings I had ever known. We had been very close, and I was sure that if I could talk to her, I could fix whatever was wrong and convince her to change her mind. But there was no way I could reach her. There was no phone where I was on the opposite side of the world. A letter would take five to seven days to reach her, and I didn't know if she would open it or respond. I was devastated, although it would have been worse had we been married. Some of my married friends went through much more traumatic times.

I knew it was difficult for the girlfriends we left behind. The person they depended on for entertainment, emotional support, and friendship had suddenly been plucked away to a far corner of the earth. The closest visual connection between the two worlds was the orbiting moon. In the meantime, there were other young men close by, and as our girlfriends' dependency and emotional attachment for us faded, it was only natural for them to be attracted to someone nearby. We even had a name for the guy back home who was trying to steal our girls. We called him Jody.

But I was young and not thinking logically about my predicament. I still loved my girlfriend and was sure that if I were still home, she would be at my side. Unfortunately, that served only to make the pain worse.

I wrote to her, but when it became obvious that she wasn't going to answer, I decided I had to put her out of my mind. To achieve that objective, I threw myself into my duties. I wanted to keep my mind occupied with anything except her. Our relationship had become a casualty of war, the first that affected me personally.

I was on guard on top of the track one day and decided to clean the .50-caliber machine gun. Taking it apart would keep my mind busy. I placed my M16 within reach and went to work.

Although the .50 caliber was a huge weapon, there wasn't much to it. The bolt came out, and the chamber could be cleaned. There were few other moving parts. To make it a little more complicated, I decided to take apart the bolt. After working on it for what seemed like hours, I had it apart in fifty-two pieces. It was like a heavy, complicated puzzle. As I studied the different components, I concentrated on how they came apart.

Putting them back together was more difficult, and it continued to keep my mind busy. I eventually got the gun back together with no pieces left over, then stripped it again and reassembled it once more. I repeated the entire process a few more times until I committed it to memory. Because my girlfriend had left me, I became a whiz at disassembling and reassembling the bolt of the .50-caliber machine gun.

Word got around about my expertise, and a few weeks later someone from another platoon on the opposite side of our company perimeter came to get me. They had taken apart the bolt of their

.50 and were having trouble getting it back together without left-over pieces. I quickly took it apart and then reassembled it correctly, showing them what they had done wrong.

11 Dec 67

Dear Mom,

We're sitting in a perimeter about a mile from that big mountain (Nui Ba Den). They told us to get ready to move at 1:00. Now it's almost 5:00 and they're still trying to decide if & where we'll move to. We moved in here yesterday & they said we'd stay 2 weeks. Oh well . . .

I've got girl problems. You probably know about it. Every time I think of Milly it hurts so I try not to think of her. Today I cleaned two .50 caliber machine guns & 2 rifles, about an hour apiece. There's nothing else to do so I decided to write to you.

Today one of our guys went on R&R. I think he's going to Hong Kong. He's been here 8 months. He's a Spec 4 [specialist fourth class].

By the way, my squad leader put me in for Spec 4 this month. But I doubt that I'll get it cause we have a new lieutenant & I haven't been here long enough. Now we have a new squad leader. He used to be squad leader of this track but stepped on a booby trap & messed up his foot. That was about 2 or 3 weeks before I got here. He came back yesterday. He's a sergeant.

We've had 3 new men in our squad since I've been here. One has been here 6 months but transferred over here to be with our machine gunner. They tried to put me on that thing but I wouldn't take it. I don't want anything except my M-16.

Every night when we stop & set up a perimeter, we have to first unload the track, [then] take out everybody's duffel bags, water cans, ammunition, and supplies. Then concertina wire, on a roll, has to go out. It goes all the way around the perimeter every night. Then, dig positions for a ground mounted .50 caliber machine gun & the M-60 machine gun. It's a hole behind the gun big enough for 1 or 2 men to crouch in. Sandbags are placed around it leaving a place for the gun to shoot. Every man has to sleep below the surface of the ground in case of mortar attack. Then comes trip flares, a flare tied to a stake with a trip wire. They're put outside the wire in case Charlie decides to come close. And Claymores have to be put out at each position. A man has to be behind the .50 cal. machine gun on top of the track at all times. So, I have guard duty every night.

It's impossible for us to set up before dark tonight. We probably won't stop anywhere before dark, if we do move, that is.

For the last 2 weeks, we've moved to a different place almost every night. We had to set up a perimeter every night except when we were at Tay Ninh. There, we just park the tracks, clean weapons, & move out to chow, shower, and the E.M. [enlisted men's] club for beer and pop. That's why everybody likes to go to Tay Ninh or Cu Chi. We haven't seen Cu Chi since Thanksgiving but I'm pretty sure we'll be there for Christmas, but we might be out in the sticks someplace, too. I haven't heard for sure.

They're going to get our mail now. I hope I get one from Milly but I doubt it. I'll write again soon. Bye for now, Roger

---

Equipment and Web Gear

Because we conducted almost all of our operations on foot, we carried the items we needed and a lot more that might come in handy. My usual gear consisted of a web belt holding a canteen or two, with two ammo pouches mounted on the front, each carrying four magazines. A bayonet was placed on the web belt over my right hip. On the back of the belt, we placed small, low-riding packs called butt packs. The weight was supported by heavy webbed suspenders that connected to the top of the butt pack on the backside and crossed over our shoulders to attach to the front of the web belt. Additional gear, such as field dressings, a compass, and several grenades, was hung on or attached to the front of the suspenders.

Most of us also carried a cloth bandolier that held seven more M16 magazines and was draped over a shoulder, crossing the chest. Added to this was surplus ammunition for the M60 machine gunner, who could not carry the amount that would be expended in an average firefight. Ammo for the M60 came in boxes of a hundred linked rounds each. When the two ends were connected, they formed loops just the right size to be worn comfortably over our shoulders, crisscrossing our chests, Poncho Villa style.

Additional equipment might include, depending on the operation, a Claymore mine, also worn over a shoulder, and a light anti-tank weapon (LAW), slung over our backs. At times we added to all of this a gas mask, which was worn on a hip.

In my butt pack I carried a poncho and enough C rations to last for the operation. If an operation lasted several days, there wouldn't be room in the pack to store all the rations we needed. In that case, we placed C-ration cans inside an extra sock and tied it somewhere on our gear.

All of this gear was heavy, and the weight increased our fatigue. Our gear wasn't nearly as heavy as that of the infantry units, though, which weren't mechanized. Other infantrymen carried rucksacks, which added even more weight. We didn't know how they did it, but their operations were usually of shorter duration than ours. They went back to the main base camps more than we did. The fact that we could be resupplied in the field meant that we could be out much longer.

Our helmets, which we called steel pots, were worn during daytime operations. They weighed about two pounds, and wearing one for just a single day developed good neck muscles. We usually wore our soft jungle hats at night unless we had been out all day, in which case we still had our steel pots with us.

Unnecessary noise was dangerous during night operations, and we did all we could to eliminate it. We jumped up and down before leaving the perimeter to make sure that none of our equipment banged together. Anything that clanked was taped, tied down, or repositioned.

We carried our weapons everywhere we went. My rifle was seldom outside arm's reach. In the field, it was always in contact with my body so I wouldn't have to grope for it. I removed the sling and discarded it. In a war with no front lines, the enemy could appear anytime, anywhere. It was tempting to sling the heavy rifle over a shoulder, but I preferred to have it in my hands, where it was always ready.

Our standard rule was to be prepared to pack up everything we owned and move out with one minute's notice. On several occasions, we were called upon to do just that. We could not afford to have many personal possessions that did not fit in our pockets. An exception for us in the mechanized infantry was the personal box that each of us kept in our APCs. These were empty .50-caliber machine-gun ammo boxes measuring eleven inches long, five and a half inches wide, and a little more than six and a half inches deep. A rubber seal along the opening made the container watertight when it was snapped shut. We used the boxes to store letters, stationery, pens, photos, and an assortment of personal effects. We wrote our names on the boxes with a marking pen and stored them beneath the seats in the track. Our total individual equipment, then, consisted of the personal box, a duffel bag containing uniforms, a laundry bag containing our dirty clothes, our web gear, and whatever fit in our pockets.

I spent my youth tramping through the woods of northern Illinois with my brother and friends. When I was ten our family moved outside of town, where our summers took on a lifestyle similar to camping—with evenings spent sitting around a fire and sleeping under the stars, and days spent exploring the rural countryside. Through this lifestyle, as well as my experiences as a Boy Scout and many things I picked up from my dad, who served as our scoutmaster, I learned the skills that made outdoor life enjoyable. Walking point in Vietnam was, in some respects, similar to sneaking through the woods with my brother and the other members of my scout troop, except for knowing that others in the jungle with equal or better skills would kill us on sight. And, of course, Boy Scouts do not carry weapons, at least they didn't in my troop.

We were operating near the Cambodian border not far from Tay Ninh and were escorting tanks and huge, self-propelled artillery pieces. Because of the heavy infiltration into South Vietnam via the Ho Chi Minh trail, there were enemy positions all over the area we were moving through.

One day as we were traveling on a road leading across the border into Cambodia, we were hit with RPGs. These lethal weapons with shaped charges could drill through the armored walls of a track or tank and explode on the inside. One round hit one of our men in the chest, killing him. He lost both hands and was cut almost in half. We also had five wounded.

Five of the trucks that were with the artillery unit hit land mines on the road we were following, blowing tires off but not killing or wounding anyone. Our tracked vehicles passed harmlessly over them, but the trucks seemed to hit more mines. I theorized that each of the four truck tires exerted enough pressure on the surface of the road to detonate the mines. The treads of our armored personnel carriers distributed weight over a larger surface, so that although an APC weighed more than a truck, the pressure on the ground at any given point was less than that exerted by a truck tire.

That night I was selected to walk point for an ambush patrol that would set up at the scene of the RPG attack. Our officers felt that the enemy might show up there. We watched the location from our concealed ambush position but didn't see a thing all night, which was fine with us.

On one of the days of this operation, I found a VC mine. My squad was on foot, serving as the point element. We came to a bridge, the type with concrete slabs on the sides and two huge culverts under the road. It seemed like a reasonable spot for the enemy to place a command-detonated mine, one that could be blown by someone watching when we passed over the explosives and into the kill zone. I left the road and checked out the area. In the second culvert I found two cans and some wire. I told my squad leader, and he radioed our lieutenant.

"Two-six, this is Two-two. Over."

"This is Two-six. Go ahead, Two-two."

"Two-six, we've located what looks like a mine under the bridge up here. Over."

"Roger that, Two-two. See if you can get it out of there, but watch for booby traps."

"Roger. Wilco. Two-two. Out."

"Two-six. Out."

Radio call signs indicated the platoon and squad or position in the squad. The first number identifies the platoon; the second, the squad or position. Two-one designated 2d Platoon, 1st Squad. Two-two was 2d Platoon, 2d Squad, and so on. There were only four squads. Two-five was the platoon sergeant. Two-six was the lieutenant who was the platoon leader or his radio telephone operator (RTO). The company commander was Charlie 6, which identified him as the commander of C Company. Our battalion radio call sign was Bobcat, our nickname. So, the 1st Squad of 2d Platoon's full radio call sign was Bobcat Charlie Two-one, but we usually shortened it to just Two-one. The squad leader was referred to as Two-one actual. The driver was Two-two delta. Anyone else in the squad was Two-one x-ray. Wilco was the radio abbreviation for "will comply."

I entered the culvert and checked the cans and wire for booby traps. The wires weren't hooked up to anything, and I couldn't see anything under them, either. Just in case, I carefully dragged one of the wires outside the culvert and gave it a tug. Nothing happened. I concluded that it was harmless and dragged it into the open. The cans were filled with TNT, and one of them appeared to be half blown. We surmised that the enemy had tried to blow the mine but it failed, possibly due to moisture.

Later in the day, I relaxed before a smokeless fire waiting for a bed of coals to form, over which I intended to heat my C rations. If I had been in a hurry, I could have had my meal already heated up, but watching the fire was relaxing. Sitting near a campfire always brought back memories of camping trips and outings into the woods of home. It was a peaceful time of reflection.

On Point

In Vietnam, I was selected to walk point often and did not mind. I felt safest there and volunteered for it from time to time. I felt confident in my ability to navigate and learned to detect trip wires, booby traps, or the presence of enemy forces. Back in the column, with someone else up front, I felt less in control and more vulnerable.

I liked the responsibility of going first, up ahead and out of sight of the platoon, company, or patrol, checking out the safest route, then leading the rest of the unit. In our company, the point man was the pacesetter. When on point, we were empowered to go as quickly or as slowly as we thought prudent. If I heard noises to the front, I crouched down, listened, and waited. I quickly learned that all of my senses were important on point. Like my comrades, I never stopped scanning the terrain before me, looking for anything that was not natural. Nothing was unimportant. My eyes constantly moved from the ground I was about to step on to as far to the front as I could see. Because I was alone, it was important to keep an eye on my flanks, too, so that I wouldn't be cut off from the rest of the unit. I even watched the tops of the trees, where snipers were sometimes positioned, some of them tied in place. Freshly dug soil, any man-made object, a footprint, a broken branch, or a slight indentation in the turf where someone may have walked could indicate the presence of our enemy. I listened for the slightest hint of human activity, such as a cough, a twig breaking, or the sound of fabric rubbing together or on vegetation. I watched bird activity, which can indicate the presence of others. Birds rise or flush suddenly when they are startled or disturbed. Normal bird activity usually meant that we were alone in the woods.

Others in my platoon claimed that they could smell the enemy because of a fish sauce called *nuoc mam*. *Sauce de poisson,* as the French called it, was made by wrapping alternating layers of fish and salt in banana leaves and letting it ferment in the sun. A liquid resulted that was further refined and bottled after being mixed with spices such as garlic and hot peppers. It had a pungent smell that turned the stomach of some American GIs, while others came to enjoy it immensely. During a Vietnamese meal, a small bowl of *nuoc mam* was placed in the center of the table for dipping bits of food held with chopsticks. Some local peasants would offer us tastes of the fish sauce, knowing full well our prejudice against the smell. They laughed hilariously at polite refusals or the faces we made. Sometimes, the Vietnamese cooked with the sauce, and the smell permeated entire villages. It was this odor that some soldiers claimed they could detect at considerable distances. On the other hand, some Vietnamese claimed that they could detect American troops by their smell because of our meat-oriented diet. I didn't doubt that a bit.

Early in my tour, walking point and exploring bunkers and tunnels made me feel as though I was contributing something to the platoon. It enhanced my feeling of belonging.

Walking point at night, however, could be spooky. If I heard suspicious noises to the front, I crouched to wait and listen. There were few other alternatives. After a reasonable delay, however, I had to do something. Should I stand up and proceed? Is there someone up ahead who has seen my shadowy movement in the night or heard my pant leg brush against a branch? Is someone waiting and listening the way I am? Eventually, I would stand up and move forward, bracing for the impact of bullets in my chest. After finding no one, I would heave a sigh of relief, go back and signal the others, then lead them forward; I would then do it all over again until we reached our objective.

While in the Boy Scouts, I learned map reading and navigation skills. I knew how to locate the North Star and used it to find my way to an objective during darkness. Often, while on point, I was given a compass reading or an azimuth to follow that would take us to our destination. Of course, I couldn't risk using a flashlight to read my compass; besides, it would destroy my night vision. I could use my compass if I read it from the bottom, but I could see only the directional arrow, not the numbers indicating degrees. So I found the North Star and used it as a reference, adding or subtracting the appropriate number of degrees to determine the correct direction of travel. As we moved, I kept an eye on the North Star—or on the Big Dipper, which is used as a reference to locate the North Star—and adjusted our direction of travel accordingly. Of course, I had to make adjustments for terrain features that we went around for stealth and safety reasons.

Navigation was trickier with a cloud cover. On overcast nights, there was less light coming from the sky unless a bright moon pushed through the clouds. Generally, however, overcast evenings were incredibly dark. There were no streetlights in Vietnam except in the largest cities. There were no lighted billboards, no neon signs, and no porch lights. Although this hampered our vision, it also created an advantage. Our bodies were not silhouetted against a lit background.

Navigating on pitch dark nights was done by what little we could see and by the glow-in-the-dark compass direction arrows on our military compasses. If our direction of travel was known while some daylight existed, we set the azimuth on our compasses. Then, while on the move after dark, we lined up the north arrow between the two indicator dots on the compass, all of which was luminous, then followed the direction arrow to our objective.

At night, especially in a combat situation, darkness and silence can be the infantryman's best defensive tactic. Sitting quietly in the darkness while concentrating ⌐n detecting sounds or movement that can give away the presence of enemy forces can produce a feeling of security. After a short time sitting quietly, it would become evident whether anyone is near. We could hear their movements or see them as they approached. It would be possible that someone would be doing the same as us, but if so they would not constitute an immediate threat.

All of us took pains to observe what the army calls noise and light discipline. While on listening post, ambush patrol, or walking point, I felt relatively safe as long as I was still and quiet. I even opened my mouth and throat wider than normal to silence my breathing so I'd be able to hear any soft rustling noises, which could mean that someone was near.

It was when I had to move that I felt vulnerable. The slightest noise, or my silhouette against the night sky, would betray my presence to enemy soldiers who would also be quietly listening to the sounds of the night.

Although operations in Cambodia were forbidden, because the war was an undeclared one, we moved across the border a few days after I found the mine under the bridge. There were no border markings, however, and none of us knew our exact location. We moved through the jungle, with our platoon performing security on the left flank, walking along a trail that paralleled the road. The road was used by tracks and tanks that had been attached to us from an armor company.

This was a dangerous mission that infiltrated what had been an enemy safe zone. The enemy knew that we weren't supposed to be operating outside of Vietnam, so they set up large base camps and assembly points for sizable concentrations of NVA troops who had come down the Ho Chi Minh trail. They wouldn't consider our intrusion a neighborly act and would hurt us badly if the opportunity presented itself.

We had not been resupplied in about two weeks, and our cooks had been feeding us powdered eggs for breakfast. The stuff was green when served, which I presumed meant the mixture was past its prime. To say the least, it didn't agree with me. I became nauseated about an hour after eating, then vomited as I lay in the undergrowth at the edge of the trail. My strength was sapped, and all I could do was lie there. Several guys from our platoon tossed me onto the back of one of the tanks on the road. I rested there for about a half hour and regained some of my strength, then returned to the trail. I ate the green eggs the next day, and the same thing happened. After figuring out what had made me ill, I lost my taste for eggs and didn't eat them again for three years.

On December 16, when we reached our destination for the day, we set up a circular, temporary perimeter in a small clearing. A short time later, a small VC or NVA force sneaked in close to a clump of shrubbery right in front of my squad's track. They fired automatic weapons into our perimeter and aimed an RPG at the track two down to our left. I assumed that they didn't fire the RPG at us because they could aim at the other vehicle without exposing themselves, or perhaps they thought our lieutenant was on that track. The other track also offered a wider side aspect, which made it an easier target than the narrower front of our track. Or they might have chosen the other track to have a better chance of blowing the gas tank as a secondary explosion. Sure enough, whether by design or luck, the gas tank exploded when the RPG round hit.

Our APCs were gasoline powered at that time, and the exploding tank sprayed burning gasoline on two GIs who were in the track or nearby. One of the victims burned where he had been lying just inside the track at the top of the hydraulic rear ramp. The other crawled screaming for fifteen feet or so with flames shooting about ten feet off his body. Soon, he stopped moving and dropped dead. There was nothing anyone could have done for him.

Our platoon leader organized a quick reactive force, which included me, to chase after the VC, who had fled the scene. We ran into the lightly forested cover a distance of a hundred meters or so but couldn't find any sign of the enemy. They may have disappeared into a nearby tunnel, or they had too much of a head start. After a short but frantic search for any sign of the enemy, we gave up the chase and headed back to our perimeter. Several soldiers walked backward with weapons aimed at the enemy terrain. Upon arriving at the perimeter, we checked out the shrubbery where the VC had launched their short attack, and we found brass casings from their AK-47 assault rifles. Our enemy excelled at hit-and-run attacks, inflicting maximum damage to us while minimizing the risk to their personnel. This was the best tactic for our enemy, who excelled at guerilla warfare, to use against a superior armed force.

It was events such as this that demoralized us. We were losing someone every few weeks with little to show for it. We were America's best-equipped, best-trained, and most highly educated army, but we were having difficulty even finding our enemy, not to mention kicking his butt.

During the short attack, a lieutenant who had just joined our unit dove under a deuce-and-a-half truck. Our company commander dove under the truck with him and, while the battle ensued, pinned a combat infantryman's badge (CIB) on his chest.

The CIB is one of the infantryman's most treasured medals. It is awarded only to people with an infantry military occupational specialty who were assigned to an army infantry unit during its participation in a major combat operation. The rule of thumb during the Vietnam War, at least in my division, was that the CIB went to infantry soldiers who had spent at least thirty days out in the field with the company.

The CIB is one of the few medals that is worn on all classes of uniforms, including fatigues; it appears above the U.S. Army designation on the left side of the chest. It consists of a blue rectangle with a rifle, superimposed over an oval wreath. One glance at a recipient's uniform indicates that the wearer has had combat experience.

When the excitement of the burning track died down and the vehicle cooled sufficiently to allow approach, a few of us wandered over to see what was left. The soldier who had been lying at the top of the ramp was still where he had died. He was reduced to a pile of black ash several inches high between a helmet at one end and a pair of partially burned boots at the other. The only discernible part of his body was a short section of unburned intestine.

Three days later, we were in the Boi Loi Woods, north of Cu Chi, back in more familiar territory. I had been out on ambush the night before, so I and a few other guys remained in the perimeter to rest and man our bunkers while the remainder of the company escorted a convoy to Tay Ninh. The rumor was that they would remain overnight in the Tay Ninh base camp, which was smaller than Cu Chi. We were set up with another company from our battalion and would secure our company's sector until they returned. There were only six of us in each of our platoons, but on the opposite side of the perimeter was a full infantry company, so we didn't feel too vulnerable.

During the afternoon, another guy and I were sent out on an observation post (OP). It was like an LP except that our mission was to look for the enemy rather than listen for them. We were sitting in dense vegetation but could hear anyone who approached. Although we preferred to remain inside the perimeter, these missions provided a chance to sit in the shade and watch our front while engaging in quiet conversation. It was during such discussions that we grew close.

On December 18, our company commander modified our standard operating procedures (SOPs) regarding sleeping positions. We now were to sleep in a hole sufficiently deep that our bodies would be entirely belowground with an overhead sandbag cover. Such a bunker would afford protection from all types of incoming enemy fire.

Until now, we had constructed individual sleeping positions. Rather than build an entire bunker by myself, a process that would take hours, I decided to enlist some help and asked a new guy, Jim Slagle, from Tennessee, if he wanted to join me. We began by digging a hole large enough for both of us to sleep in, making sure that the bottom was level and smooth. It was about two and a half feet deep. Around the hole we placed two layers of sandbags filled with the soil we dug to make the hole. We left open spaces in the front of the bunker, facing outside the perimeter, to be used as firing ports. In the rear, we left a space to be used as a door.

The company carried perforated steel plating (PSP) chained to the sides of our tracks for use as overhead cover for our bunkers. The steel sheets, each about eight feet long and two feet wide, were interlocking; they were designed to be quickly assembled into aircraft runways wherever one might be needed, even on bare ground.

We found that three pieces of the steel sufficed to cover the top of our bunker. We stacked the plating together, carried it over to our bunker, and lowered each piece onto the double-thick sandbag walls. Then we placed two layers of sandbags over the top of the PSP. In all, we used seventy sandbags. The bunker was strong enough to withstand direct hits by mortar or rocket rounds.

This was the beginning of an era of full bunker construction for our company. Orders were that every man had to sleep in such a bunker except for those on LP or out on an ambush patrol or any other combat mission that included spending the night in the bush. Exceptions, of course, were the squad leader and the driver, who slept in the track. Later, our company's bunker SOP was modified with the specification that each bunker hole be so deep that a D-ringed shovel, which we carried on each track, could be inserted vertically into the bunker without protruding above ground level, a depth of nearly three feet.

This was also the beginning of a close friendship with Jim Slagle. We enjoyed working with each other and found that we had a similar sense of humor. For the rest of my tour, Slagle and I, along with another guy we hung out with early in my tour, Billie Barnett, made each other laugh when we were together. Most of us decided that since we were going to be in Vietnam for an entire year whether we liked it or not, we might as well make fun of the situation. Not only did time pass more enjoyably, we were not suffering in isolation.

Observation Posts

When set up in a company perimeter, most infantry units in Vietnam employed observation posts (OPs) during the daytime to provide early warning of enemy activity or attack. One or two soldiers per platoon were sent outside the perimeter, to a location offering a good view of the surrounding terrain. This was not always an unpleasant experience. If a shady spot was located that offered a good view, the time spent on OP was enjoyable. Sometimes, while on an OP by myself, I took along a book in the cargo pocket of my jungle fatigues and kept an eye on the surroundings while reading.

Sometimes, when the enemy was not near, Vietnamese civilians visited our perimeters and bartered with GIs from outside the wire. Once, while on an observation post assignment early in my tour, my companion was showing me pictures of his wife and telling me about her. It was obvious that he was deeply in love with her. A few minutes later, a boom-boom girl came by and he took her into the bushes. I could see his white buttocks pumping up and down as they had sex. I was naive, and astounded that he could be in love with his wife yet have sex with a girl he had never seen before. It was an eye-opening experience for me.

A few weeks before receiving my Dear John letter, when I was on an OP, alone in a grove of trees about a hundred meters outside our perimeter, I was approached by a boom-boom girl. She offered me herself at a reasonable price, but I politely refused. She lowered the price, but I still said no. She finally offered herself to me free of charge. I still refrained. She sat next to me on a log, and I explained as best I could, given the language barrier, that I had a girlfriend back in the States and had promised to be true to her. We changed the subject and chatted for a while. When it was time for her to go, she kissed me on the cheek and we said good-bye. If she had come by after I received the Dear John letter and gotten over the loss of my girlfriend, I would not have been so angelic.

Listening Posts

At night, security around the perimeter was based on listening rather than observing. Teams from each platoon were positioned outside the wire, but because vision was limited, these were called listening posts rather than observation posts. The number of people involved was increased to three, in order to have sufficient people to post guard and allow each a reasonable amount of sleep. The man on guard remained awake, listening and watching for a third of the night while the others slept.

The members of the LP gathered at the edge of the perimeter about a half hour before dusk. As soft conversation and laughter drifted from groups of GIs near the perimeter's sandbag bunkers, we checked our equipment and weapons in preparation for going out. The radio equipment was checked by calling the platoon leader's RTO.

"Two-six, this is Lima Papa. Radio check. Over."

"Lima Papa, this is Two-six. I read you Lima Charlie. Over."

We used a phonetic alphabet to spell out some words so that the enemy, if listening to our radio frequency, would have trouble figuring out what we were talking about. Lima Papa is phonetic for LP. Lima Charlie is phonetic for the letters "L" and "C", which stood for loud and clear.

We used the word "niner" in place of the number nine. Supposedly this was left over from World War II when the word "nine" was confused with *nein*, the German word for no. I always thought that if the Germans, had they been listening, heard our guys say "nine" and thought it meant "no," their interpretation would be all the more difficult and confusing. So much the better. But instead we chose to make it easier for them by saying "niner," just so they'd know we meant the number nine. I've been told that sometimes I think too much.

"Roger, Two-six. Lima Papa is leaving the wire soon. Out."

"Roger, Lima Papa. Two-six. Out."

As full darkness fell, we advanced beyond the bunker line and negotiated the concertina wire by standing on the strands while trying to avoid the sharp blades that pressed inward on our legs as our weight pressed down. We avoided the Claymore mines and trip flares and stepped into enemy territory. A little way out, just inside the tree line, we crouched, paused, and listened to the sounds of the night in an attempt to detect anything indicating someone up ahead. Without speaking, but using hand signals, we advanced a short distance, then paused to listen once more.

Upon reaching our destination—which was often along the most likely avenue of approach to the perimeter now a hundred meters or so behind us, or from a vantage point offering a good view of open areas—we quietly set up our position. One or two of us crawled forward to place a Claymore mine facing to our front, screwed a blasting cap in one of the two wells on the top of the mine, and strung the detonation wire back to the LP position.

Claymores are directional land mines detonated by a handheld electrical generator. It is pumped with one hand to produce a spark, which ignites the blasting cap, thereby setting off the mine. The Claymore is a slightly curved plastic case with metal fold-down legs that are inserted into the ground to hold the mine in place and allow aiming. The back of the mine is loaded with C-4, a plastic explosive. The front consists of two hundred steel balls designed to rip into enemy forces. The aiming sight on the top made the mines resemble Polaroid cameras, at least to us.

Meanwhile, another LP member quietly and slowly spread a poncho on the ground where we would sit and sleep. The radio, which emitted a barely audible squelch noise, was placed within arm's reach. The only radio speaker was on the handset, which looked like that of a telephone but had a push-to-talk button on the side. The squelch noise, which is like a white hiss, enabled us to listen to the sounds of the night but still detect the silence caused by a broken squelch, which meant that someone was transmitting. Upon hearing the interruption of the white noise, we would bring the handset to an ear.

All site preparations were done by feel or by whatever star- or moonlight existed. When all was ready, someone depressed the push-to-talk button and whispered into the handset.

"Two-six, this is Lima Papa."

"Two-six. Over."

"We're in position. Over."

"Roger, Lima Papa. Two-six. Out."

"Lima Papa. Out."

We sat together for about an hour, listening to the sounds coming from the tropical forest. We listened for the sound of men moving through the woods and for any change in the normal night sounds of insects or amphibians that would indicate some type of disturbance.

Our position in the shadows was barely visible from a few feet away. We were secure in the knowledge that as long as we didn't make any noise, we would hear and see intruders long before our position was detected.

Later, two of us stretched out within arm's reach of the one remaining awake on watch so that everyone could be easily awakened, if necessary.

On my first LP, I sat quietly watching and listening, facing away from the perimeter, several hundred feet to our rear. The steady breathing of my comrades told me that they were asleep. I scanned the area to our front and memorized the few shapes, shadows, and landmarks that were visible. A later quick scan would indicate if anything was different that might indicate a silently moving enemy penetration.

The eyes can play tricks at night. The best way to check out an object is to look all around it rather than directly at it. This is especially true on nights without a moon or with cloud cover.

Those of us on watch whispered situation reports, known as sit-reps, every half hour to our platoon leader's RTO or whoever was on radio watch inside the perimeter. "Sit-rep normal" indicated that everything was okay.

"Two-six, this is Lima Papa. Over," I whispered into the handset.

"Lima Papa, this is Two-six. Over."

"Sit-rep normal. Over."

"Roger that, Lima Papa. Keep your eyes open out there. Two-six. Out."

When my watch was over, I nudged the man scheduled to take my place, gave him the radio handset, and lay back. With no lights within perhaps a hundred miles, the stars looked brilliant. The Milky Way was clearly discernible; it was one of the most beautiful sights I'd ever seen. Just before drifting off to sleep, I raised my head. The next guard was awake and alert. I relaxed again and was soon asleep.

Just before first light, we awakened and waited for enough light to confirm that we were alone. We retrieved our Claymore mines, hand grenades, radio, and poncho, then radioed back to the perimeter to let them know we were coming in. That word was passed to the tracks so that those on guard or awake would not mistake us for enemy soldiers when we came into view.

Once, all members of a listening post from another platoon fell asleep, the number one sin while performing guard duty. That night our perimeter was hit by an enemy force. The next morning a search patrol found all members of the LP dead. According to the reports we heard through the informal but highly developed rumor control network, the poncho they had been lying on had 140 bullet holes in it.

Early in my tour, I was assigned a listening post with two others from my platoon. The company's night defensive perimeter was in a dry rice paddy. Our lieutenant wanted us to set up on the opposite side of a small woodlot to the front of our platoon's sector. It looked fine while there was still light in the sky, but after nightfall, as we were moving outside the wire, it looked dark and ominous. We decided to set up someplace else but neglected to tell our platoon on the perimeter.

About half past twelve in the morning, we monitored radio traffic concerning reports of enemy activity in front of the platoon. We looked around but couldn't see what the perimeter was reporting. We had no idea what they were talking about. The lieutenant later called us and reported that all weapons on that sector of the perimeter, including a few tanks that had joined us for the operation, were trained on the enemy. The lieutenant was checking with us before opening fire. We were asked to verify the sighting and, if we could locate the enemy, prepare to engage them. The moon lit up the surrounding rice paddies and we could see clearly all around us, but we found no other signs of human activity.

We slowly realized that it was us that they were aiming at because we were not where the lieutenant expected us to be. We told this to the lieutenant over the radio, but he still had doubts. I suggested that he take a compass reading to our position, and I shot a back azimuth with my official Boy Scout compass, which I carried in my pocket. The moon enabled me to read the numbers. The lieutenant's reading was the same as ours, meaning that all of the weapons on our side of the perimeter were aimed at us. To be absolutely sure, however, the lieutenant had us signal with a red-filtered flashlight, which we happened to have along. The perimeter saw our red flashes and checked their weapons.

I think that whoever spotted us in the night had seen movement as I crawled a dozen feet or so away to take a leak, which—in the boonies at night—was performed while lying on our side. Standing up, of course, would have been stupid. It was shortly after I returned to our LP position that we began hearing the reports of enemy movement.

We were reprimanded when we returned inside the perimeter the next morning. The lieutenant was mad, and we learned our lesson. After that night, we made sure that we were where we were supposed to be on listening post.

Near dawn on another LP a few weeks later, when we were preparing to go back to the perimeter, I crawled forward to retrieve my Claymore mine and discovered that it had been turned around. It was facing us. If I had detonated it, all of us would have been killed or seriously wounded. We knew that sometimes the enemy did this, then made noise in hopes that we would blow the mine. The realization that an enemy soldier had silently approached close enough to find our Claymore mine, turn it around, and withdraw without us detecting him was definitely unnerving. If his intention was to make noise so we would blow the mine, it was good that we failed to hear him.

Christmas in Vietnam was, with a few exceptions, like any other day. One of the exceptions was that we spent the day inside a battalion perimeter, outside a village named Suoi Da, about a mile or so east-southeast from the Black Virgin Mountain, where we had spent the last five days. We were not assigned any missions, such as the sweeps or search and destroy operations that we had been regularly performing. It was the first day since I arrived in Vietnam that I awoke after daybreak.

I spent most of the morning completing a bunker of my own design, which incorporated 185 sandbags and a passageway with a corner for an entrance. I figured that I could turn a corner, but shrapnel couldn't.

A Christmas cease-fire went into effect at 6:00 P.M. on Christmas Eve. That night we received a ration of sodas and beer, and some of our guys bought whiskey from the villagers. A few of our tracks displayed small, poor examples of Christmas trees that had been sent from home. Decorated with Christmas cards, the trees made Charlie Brown's appear lush and festive; nevertheless, they added a touch of holiday spirit that boosted our morale. The members of our squad sat up talking until about ten o'clock in the evening.

There are few days off in the infantry, and even though this was a holiday, we still had work to do. Rocket-propelled grenades were becoming an increasing concern, and each of our squads built a bunker to hold the .50-caliber gun, which we removed from the top of our tracks. We then moved the tracks farther inside the perimeter in order to offer fewer targets for the enemy. We also dug an ammo sump, a hole with sandbags around it, to decrease the chances of a mortar round sparking secondary explosions as well as to protect our ammunition.

A community in California sent us Christmas presents of writing paper, candy, magazines, and other items to make our life a bit easier. The sentiment was genuinely appreciated.

Besides the Christmas trees mounted precariously on the top of some of our tracks, the biggest difference between this and the other days of the year was the amount of food that was available. Our cooks prepared a holiday feast for us, and most of us ate off and on all day long.

I sent my mom a Christmas message. "Here in Vietnam, there aren't very many Christmas trees or lights across the downtown district. Come to think of it, there aren't any downtown districts. Oh well, Have a very Merry Christmas and a Happy New Year."

Bob Hope and his traveling show appeared in Cu Chi, and a few people from each of our platoons were selected and taken in to see it. The rest of us conducted business as usual. I went on an overnight ambush that night

In addition to LPs, ambush patrols led us into the night. It was during hours of darkness that Charlie operated. Because there were no front lines, we Americans actually controlled only the ground we were standing on. (To some extent during daylight hours, we controlled only the ground we could see.) After dark, when the VC could move about without us detecting them, the enemy ruled. The North Vietnamese Army (NVA) and the Viet Cong (VC) lacked our superior firepower and sought to elude it. If we could fix their position during the day, we called in tons of ordnance, including helicopter gunships with rockets and machine guns, artillery, mortars, air force jet bombers with five-hundred-pound bombs and napalm canisters, and the thing that the enemy feared the most—the B-52 bomber.

During darkness, however, the enemy moved about in relative freedom. The only viable option to thwart enemy activity at night was the ambush. The only way we could slow down the enemy at night was to sneak out after dark, set up along a trail or other location where we thought they might appear, and kill them. Not surprisingly, this tactic produced only token results, because of the large area that was available to the NVA and the VC—the entire country outside American bases and company perimeters—and the relatively small number of ambush patrols we could muster.

Each company consisted of three rifle platoons and a mortar platoon. Only the rifle platoons conducted ambushes; the mortar men might be needed for fire missions if we ran into anything we couldn't handle. During my tour, our platoon and company were never full strength. A complete platoon consisted of four eleven-man squads; a platoon sergeant; a platoon leader; a radiotelephone operator (RTO), the guy who carried the leader's radio; and possibly an attached medic or two. This could total fifty people. We seldom had thirty.

Each platoon was responsible for a third of the company's perimeter. Two men always stayed with the tracks: a driver and someone behind the .50-caliber machine gun. At least two more were in bunkers built between each track. Three more platoon members were needed on LP. Either the lieutenant or the platoon sergeant remained in the perimeter. This left—during the times when we had the most men—only ten to twelve guys available for an ambush. After heavy contact with the enemy, we could be down to less than fifteen people for our entire platoon. On four occasions, our platoon was down to six men standing, which is not combat effective.

Because there were three rifle platoons per company, only three ambush patrols could be sent out. Charlie had scouts who followed us, presumably people who knew the local area and could move about quietly and remain camouflaged or hidden. Some of them might have known where our LPs and ambushes were located.

The three companies of our battalion and those of other battalions operating nearby were located far enough apart so as not to endanger one another. As a result, each company was centered in a relatively large area where they were the only American or allied force. This gave each company the flexibility to engage full fire-power all the way around their perimeter without endangering other American or allied perimeters, thus enhancing their ability to defend themselves. Unfortunately, it also meant more freedom of movement for the enemy. Into the huge void between friendly perimeters, we sent platoon ambush patrols consisting of perhaps a dozen men.

In reality, ambush patrols were a relatively insignificant means of thwarting enemy movement. Although we didn't think of it in these terms, we nevertheless understood and acknowledged that the enemy owned the night.

Members of ambush patrols carried, in addition to their own personal weapon and ammunition, extra grenades, extra ammo for the machine gunner, and a Claymore mine. Although ambush patrols were conducted after dark, if we left before dark, we switched directions once full darkness fell.

With the point man leading the way, the patrol moved slowly, quietly, and cautiously in a single-file column toward a hopefully tactical location, usually a trail suspected of heavy enemy traffic. On a few occasions, we set up ambushes along rivers and watched for sampans carrying enemy supplies.

The configuration of the ambushes we set up varied depending on the anticipated kill zone. If we were ambushing a straight section of trail, we lined up on one side a short distance away. If the kill zone was irregularly shaped, such as a trail with a curve in it, we positioned ourselves in the shape of an L or a smaller angle. A U-shaped ambush was mentioned in our training, but we didn't use this configuration because of the likelihood of shooting toward one another.

Once in position, each of us crept forward a distance of fifteen meters or so and set up our Claymore mines, as we did during listening posts. These mines, along with hand grenades, were the best method of popping an ambush, because they didn't give away our exact positions. Firing rifles initially would have provided the enemy with targets and at the same time let them know what direction to flee in or seek cover.

While operating near Tan Son Nhut, a huge air force base just north of Saigon, we sometimes conducted fourteen-klick platoon-sized ambushes. We crossed dried-up rice paddies and arrived at our destination well after midnight.

On the evening of July 4, I was on such a patrol. At midnight we crossed a huge dried-up rice paddy with a fourteen-man patrol, wondering what would happen if we contacted a battalion of NVA on their way to hit the air force base, reportedly one of the enemy's main objectives in all of South Vietnam. The jet bombers that operated from this location were a big hindrance to the VC and NVA. We figured that any enemy force that would attack the air force base would be much larger than our small patrol. We might be able to handle a mortar crew, but few larger units.

At midnight, the American bases in the vicinity decided to celebrate the Fourth of July with a fireworks demonstration of their own making. Flares, star clusters, and whatever else could be found were launched into the air from several perimeters, casting long, distinct shadows of our small patrol across the rice paddy. We hit the dirt and remained pinned down by the celebration for the better part of an hour. We laughed about it the next day, but we felt vulnerable while we were lying in the dirt wondering if we could be seen by a group of VC or NVA.

Although some of the old-timers spoke of major battles that occurred before my arrival, the company experienced a relative lull in combat action early in my tour. Although we conducted sweeps and search and destroy missions, we seldom came in contact with enemy forces. We knew that the Viet Cong were active in the area; we found evidence of their presence, and periodically one of us came across a booby trap. Occasionally a small force struck fiercely at our perimeter, then disappeared. Sometimes we received sniper fire. Generally, however, although we suffered an occasional casualty during this period, it was a relatively quiet time. The 1968 Tet Offensive was still a month or two away and the NVA was not significantly present in our area of operations, if they were there at all.

By late December, however, we had noticed a significant increase in enemy activity. We didn't know it at the time, but we were seeing the enemy buildup prior to the 1968 Tet Offensive.

It was still the holiday season, and we celebrated New Year's Eve by filling sandbags to build yet another bunker. For a change, I wasn't selected to go out on ambush or LP; I got to sleep inside the perimeter.

As I was pulling my share of guard duty, I notified the guard on the track next to ours that I'd be away from the track for a while, then I wandered over to our chow line. Our company cooks sometimes came to the field with us and had a tent on the inside of the perimeter where they slept and stored dry goods. They prepared meals there for us and served them in a series of stations spaced about ten meters apart. The spacing was designed to preclude multiple deaths in the event of a mortar attack while the men were congregated for meals. A big advantage of the cook's presence to those of us pulling guard in the middle of the night was the large pot of coffee and the sugar and cream placed where we would find it.

I got a cup of steaming coffee and carried it back to my track, where I enjoyed sipping it as I continued my watch. The night was cool and there was a breeze. The coffee hit the spot and helped keep me alert.

The next morning, our platoon's ambush patrol was en route back to our perimeter when they came in contact with two RPG teams heading for our perimeter. They opened up on them but weren't sure if they killed any. They did get the RPGs, though.

Word was passed around that a turkey dinner, complete with stuffing and pumpkin pie, was being trucked out to us from Cu Chi for our New Year's meal. When it arrived, the entire perimeter perked up in anticipation. I could see the truck working its way through our perimeter's entrance and maneuvering inside, past a garden plot that belonged to a local resident, to the vicinity of our chow line. Suddenly the truck lurched, and black dust and smoke enveloped the vehicle as the sound and concussion of an explosion spread across the perimeter. Our chow truck had hit a mine. Inspection of the damage revealed that our turkey dinner had been riddled with shrapnel and was unsafe to eat. With that explosion, the holiday became just another in a long string of days without distinction.

The word came down that we would be going to Saigon the next day, January 2. As usual, we had no idea what we would do there, but we would be stopping at Cu Chi to clean up. That had never happened before. Fashion show, maybe? Rumor had it that we'd be there for five days or maybe a week and afterward we'd receive a stand-down in Cu Chi. I went out on an ambush patrol that night.

Our track broke down again, and members of my squad, 21, were dispersed among the squads that had tracks. By this time, I had been in the company for a little more than two months and was being accepted by the platoon. I considered everyone in the unit a friend, so we didn't mind the fact that we were working with other squads.

During this week, our tracks were switched for new ones with diesel engines. I don't think the incentive was better fuel economy but rather the safety of our men. An exploding fuel tank was not an immediate danger with diesel fuel, as it was with gasoline-powered vehicles that hit a mine or were struck by an RPG. Diesel vehicles would burn for a few minutes, giving us time to evacuate the wounded or dead. Eventually, though, the ammunition, grenades, Claymore mines, and LAWs inside the track would begin cooking off, and explosions would continue for about an hour and a half, reducing the vehicle to a pile of rubble and ash several feet in height. I'm not sure why, but the insurance companies never seemed to pay when that happened.

There were seven men in my squad during this time. Two of them arrived after I did, so I wasn't the new guy anymore. Our squad leader was twenty years old and had been in the army for three years, having served previously in Germany and Korea.

On the first of the year, I received one of the most coveted infantry awards, the combat infantryman's badge. I had met the criteria for eligibility six weeks earlier, but it had taken that long to get the paperwork through—or for the company to get around to awarding it to me. I didn't mind. Everyone knew who was who in our platoon.

The fact that we were never full strength was the reason why we disliked draft dodgers. We could have used their help, especially during the firefights in which our friends were killed. More guys would have increased the chances for each of us to go home. Additional men in our platoon would have also meant that each of us could pull fewer LPs and ambush patrols and gotten more sleep.

We heard from home, usually through the new replacement troops fresh from the world, about how many young men had mastered the art of draft dodging. When we thought about the predicament that we were in, along with the fact that new soldiers did not arrive in sufficient numbers for us to approach anything near full strength, we developed resentment for draft dodgers. Because of them, it was more difficult for us to do our part to serve our country.

At the same time, some of our fellow countrymen back in the States were developing a similar resentment for us, because we were in Vietnam. Unbeknownst to us, while we fought for our country, the antiwar movement was picking up steam back home.

LIFE IN THE NAM

Insect Pests

The area of Vietnam in which we operated, between Saigon and the Cambodian border to the west and northwest, did not have a large population of tigers or snakes, which would have made life unpleasant. Or if those critters were around, we didn't encounter them regularly. There was, however, a healthy population of voracious insects.

Aggressive fire ants occupied much of the area and seemed to dislike intruders. When we came too close, dozens of them, if not hundreds, attacked and bit. Each bite felt like a bee sting, although the pain dissipated once the attack ended or the insects were brushed off. Trees often had a line of fire ants going up or down the trunk. It was common to see GIs who were taking a break examining the bark prior to sitting down and leaning back against the tree.

The ants made us miserable when we invaded their territory. The only way to get rid of them was to get out of their immediate area, then strip off clothing as quickly as possible and brush them off.

On more than one occasion when trying to escape enemy fire, we unwittingly dove into an area populated with these ants. Suddenly, priorities changed: Viet Cong or NVA rifle fire became a lower priority when compared with attacking fire ants. The unfortunate victim would stand up—exposing himself to enemy fire, drop his weapon, rip off his clothing as fast as possible, and brush away the ferocious attackers.

I knew of no soldiers enduring fire ant attacks who were shot by the NVA or VC. I always presumed that the enemy was laughing too hard at the GI's predicament to take proper aim.

Ants were not the only insect pests we encountered. While our tracks were moving through an area one day, our driver chose to pass between two trees about six inches closer together than the width of our vehicles. The trees bowed to the side as we passed between them. No one saw, until it was too late, the beehive in one of the trees. The bees had the same disposition as the fire ants. They attacked with a vengeance that I'm sure the enemy would admire and possibly emulate.

Some of the guys under attack by the bees yelled and waved their arms wildly. This attracted the attention of the bees, who were searching for tactical targets, much like a jet fighter pilot whose home base had just been bombed. With identified targets, the bees homed in. I and a few others took a different tactic. We slowly pulled our collars closed and sat still. Several bees stopped in front of my face and inspected me, then went on. I was evidently identified as a noncombatant and was not stung.

Finally the insects broke contact and withdrew. Welts covered the faces and arms of those who were attacked. Several of them required medical evacuation. One or two of them had such swollen faces that they were difficult to recognize for a while. If I had been in command, I would have made sure that these soldiers received a Purple Heart.

The insects that caused us the most misery were mosquitoes. The area where we operated seemed like the world's optimum mosquito habitat, with warm temperatures, high humidity, and plenty of standing water. They weren't too bad during daylight hours, but they were a constant menace at night.

One evening as we were en route to an ambush site, we paused along a road near a rice paddy to wait for full darkness. As the daylight faded, we heard a distant buzz, which grew steadily in volume as thousands if not millions of the blood-sucking pests descended on us. There was nothing we could do to get rid of them.

Because of the extreme heat during the day, we rolled up the sleeves of our long-sleeved jungle shirts. But at night, some of us rolled down our sleeves to reduce exposed flesh to our hands, which were usually in motion, and our faces. Although we could swat the mosquitoes when we were awake, we became free Purina mosquito chow when we dropped off to sleep each night, and we woke up with welts on our faces and exposed skin.

As it turned out, we did go to the Saigon area, as was rumored, but we didn't stop at Cu Chi on the way. So much for the bath.

7 Jan 68

Mom,

We're still by Saigon. Today is the first day we've stayed at our base camp, because of a company-sized ambush last night. There are rumors that tomorrow we're going back to the place we just came from. I sure hope we stop at Cu Chi. I haven't been to a PX since before Thanksgiving.

Now that I have some of your past letters here, I'll answer your questions.

Yes, Bob Hope was in Cu Chi but our company was way north of there as you probably know from a few letters back.

[What's a personal box?] We all have a personal box. It's a metal box used for .50 caliber ammo for the machine gun. We put stuff in them like letters & other personal stuff to keep it handy without having to dig through a duffel bag.

[Were you in Cambodia?] I don't know of any marked boundary between Vietnam and Cambodia. We were pretty close to it though & rumors are that we might be going back sometime maybe in the next month or so.

[How do you mail letters?] The first sergeant always has a mail bag tied to the back of his track. When we mail letters, we drop them in it and it goes out by chopper.

I'm anxious to get a radio. In the morning they play country & western music. All day they play all kinds of music & at night, pop music. Johnny Carson comes on at 10:30. And of course, Gunsmoke on Friday nights.

I told you we were checking out villages didn't I? The other day another guy and I were searching a hootch & the

only inhabitants were a young girl, about 23 & her baby. She
came up to me and said something in French. I about
jumped for joy. I'd been looking for someone to speak
French with ever since I've been over here. I know some of
the people [speak French] cause the French were here for
94 years & left in 1954. So anyone over 20 would be old
enough to have learned it.

It was the best conversation I've ever had with a native.
She didn't know any English and only a little French but we
could hold a regular conversation.

That guy I was with is in my squad. 26 years old from Texas
named Lindsay. He stopped to listen to me talk to her and
was real surprised that I knew French. I stopped back there
several times throughout the day to talk with her.

Better be going. Write soon. Roger

Resupply

Choppers flew out almost daily resupplies to our company perimeter when we were in the field. They brought ammunition, water,
meals, mail, beer and soft drink rations, and military supplies. Some
of the items were intended to make our existence more bearable.

Special purpose (SP) packages came from the Red Cross. They
were relatively large cardboard boxes that were periodically given to
each squad. They held an array of items that the Red Cross thought
we might like or need: soap, razors, a few toothbrushes, toothpaste,
cigarettes, a few novels, candy, gum, and other assorted goodies.

We ate C rations every day for lunch and for all meals while on an
operation or during periods when the chow supply was cut off.
There were twelve meals in each case, but only eleven different ones;
one meal appeared twice. Each meal consisted of a smaller cardboard box containing several cans or containers of various sizes.
Each meal had one of the eleven entrees, which I think were intended for supper; a B-2 unit containing crackers and cheese spread
or peanut butter, probably for lunch; and a B-3 unit with fruit, maybe
for breakfast. Theoretically, a box of C's would provide sustenance
for one GI for a full day. If that was the intent, we didn't know it; most
of us consumed the entire contents of a box during one meal.

Each box also contained a package of assorted items, including a rounded white plastic spoon, a pack of olive-drab tropical matches, a package of four cigarettes, a small bundle of toilet paper, packages of instant coffee and hot chocolate, and packets of cream, sugar, and salt.

With each case came a P-38, a tiny flip-open can opener that some of the guys wore on their dog tag chains. Each time a case was opened, the P-38 was given to someone who didn't have one.

Most of the guys had their favorite C-ration meals, and they dove for them when the case was opened. It was first come, first served.

Over the years, the type of meals differed somewhat I think, but during our tour we had:

- Spaghetti and meatballs—not bad.
- Spiced beef and gravy.
- Beans with franks in tomato sauce—everyone's favorite. We called it beanies and wienies. A preferred method of preparing this meal was to melt in the cheese from a B-2 unit. It added flavor and could be quite good.
- Scrambled eggs and ham—horrible. Most of it was thrown away. One guy could eat it. Because he liked this stuff, no one trusted him.
- Meatballs and beans in tomato sauce. I once prepared some of this for my two sons. Upon tasting it, they ran out of the house and spit it in the yard.
- Boned chicken.
- Ham loaf—not bad.
- Turkey loaf.
- Chicken and noodles.
- Beefsteak with potatoes and gravy—good if you're in the mood for it.
- Ham and lima beans—another of the least favorites, which we called ham and mothers. I could eat this meal, though, so I seldom starved.

There were dates on the bottoms of the cans, and the ones we were issued and consumed were labeled 1949. I was appalled when I first discovered that the stuff was nineteen years old.

Except for the beanies and wienies, we had to be very hungry to enjoy C rations. When the main course was opened, the first thing we noticed was congealed grease; sometimes it was so thick that the contents of the can were difficult to identify. The only way to make them palatable was to heat them, thereby melting the grease so it could be mixed in.

There were two main methods of heating C rations, neither of which consisted of burning the heat tabs that were provided for that purpose. The tabs burned long enough but produced a horrible smell and visible smoke that stung our eyes. When we had time, we built a small fire and balanced the meal on a couple of large sticks. This occupied a few minutes and was a good way to kill some time.

The much preferred method, however, and one that could be completed quickly, consisted of burning a small ball of C-4 plastic explosive. This substance came in wrapped one-pound, brick-shaped blocks about six inches in length. We always had some C-4 in the equipment rack on the inside of the track. We pulled off a small portion of the puttylike explosive and rolled it between our palms to form a perfect sphere. A ball of C-4 about three-quarters inch in diameter lit readily with a match and burned with a quiet hissing noise and a blue flame for more than a minute. One or two balls of the stuff could boil the contents of most C-ration cans. Larger balls of the explosive would burn a little longer but would shoot the flame over the sides of the can, like a gas stove turned up too high.

We were cautioned against stomping on the C-4 to put it out because it could cause detonation. And it wasn't a good idea to touch it while it was burning, because it tended to stick to flesh. All of us received minor burns before we learned the proper technique.

Methods varied for holding the can over the flame. Some soldiers held onto the lid, which they had not fully removed. Others made a usable stove from an empty B-2 can. They punched holes in the sides to let in air, set the meal on top of the stove, then placed a ball of C-4 inside the stove and lit it. Good stoves were kept for reuse later on.

During the course of the war, two-thirds of the C-4 plastic explosive sent to Vietnam was said to have been used to heat C rations.

Based on observations I made in our company, I believe that to be a low estimate. A few times when we ran out of C-4, we popped the back off a Claymore mine and used some of the C-4 from the inside, then snapped the mine back together.

The intended purpose of C-4 was for blowing up things. We didn't do that very much, though. It required placing a blasting cap in the explosive and messing around with wire or fuses. It was easier to place a hand grenade next to whatever we wanted to blow, then run. That left plenty of C-4 for heating C rations.

Beer and Soda

For most of my tour, we were issued soda and beer each day. For some reason the amount distributed rose as my tour progressed. Toward the end, we were given two-thirds of a case of each beverage per squad per day.

Although most of the beer and soda sat in the sun at a chopper pad for several hours before being helicoptered to us, large blocks of ice accompanied the beverages when it was available. The ice was purchased from local ice plants and placed inside a Huey helicopter or slung below by chains, dangling in the air with water streaming from it as it melted in the heat. Not much ice was left by the time it was delivered, but there was enough to enable us to cool a can of soda or beer.

We didn't use the ice in the drink itself, though. We assumed that the water used to make the ice was not potable. Instead, we learned that a warm can of beer or soda could be cooled to near freezing temperatures in about five minutes by rolling it on a block of ice. The most difficult part was getting started. A groove had to be melted into the ice so that the can could spin in place. This was done by holding the can in one spot and rotating it. Once this was accomplished, the can could be spun using both hands. Within a few minutes, our fingers would be too cold to continue, a not altogether unpleasant experience in the heat of the tropics.

I think we were issued beer in the field because the rear-echelon folks, the guys whose jobs enabled them to remain on the inside of the larger base camps, had access to clubs for enlisted men (EM), noncommissioned officers (NCOs), or officers during their off-duty time. In the field, we did not have off-duty time or access to clubs. To make us feel better about having to be in the field, away from creature comforts, they brought some of them to us.

An unfortunate aspect of this was that we occasionally had intoxicated people in the field. Sometimes it was okay, but we never knew when we would be in contact with the enemy, and we found that drunk soldiers didn't perform well in combat.

Because of their mobility and relatively high firepower, mechanized infantry units such as ours were used as quick response units if other outfits got into trouble and needed help. In addition to our personal weapons, our firepower included the .50-caliber machine guns mounted on our tracks. So, besides the necessity of being prepared to defend ourselves at all times in the event of attack, we were sometimes called on to serve as a reaction force to help others. Accordingly, it was preferable if our troops were sober most of the time.

The beer we were given had a low alcohol content (3.2 percent), but guys could and did get drunk on the stuff. The locals produced a beer named Ba Muoi Ba, the Vietnamese phrase for the number thirty-three. Like the American 3.2 beer, the Vietnamese beer was sufficient to produce intoxication if enough was consumed.

Our squad had a high percentage of soldiers who did not drink much or at all. As a result, we usually had extra beer. That made us popular with some of the guys from other squads, who drank their share from their squad, then came visiting and consumed our extras. These were the people who got drunk the most often.

I was on LP once with someone who was drunk. In the middle of the night, while we were supposed to be quiet and stealthy, he stood up, walked around, hummed to himself, and talked to us. I crawled back inside the perimeter and found the lieutenant.

"We've got a drunk guy out on LP, sir. He's walking around humming to himself and is going to give our position away. If he stays out there, I'm not going back."

The lieutenant went out and got the guy and gave us someone else. Although we would have prefered to remain in place, we abandoned our compromised position and moved to a new one. If the drunk soldier was punished, we didn't hear about it.

I've been in combat situations with people who were drunk and with men who were stoned on marijuana. In my experience, people who are high on marijuana can still function. When duty called, they seemed to snap out of it. People who are drunk cannot seem to do so and are generally useless in combat or any other situation in which they may be depended upon. Given a choice between someone who was drunk or stoned, I would take the latter, no question. They might have been a little loopy, but they proved, time after time, to be dependable when we were in contact with the enemy.

I think the attraction of getting stoned or drunk was that it made time go by faster. Each of us had 365 days to serve in-country. Some figured that if they passed some of the time in a blur, so much the better. When they sobered up, there were fewer days to wait to go home. I can't blame them for that. I, however, chose to do neither. That wasn't a wartime choice, it's just that I do not use drugs or drink alcohol.

While in the rear at Dau Tieng, another of our division's forward base camps, I once saw two soldiers drink beer for four hours, then decide to smoke marijuana.

They went to one of the perimeter bunkers where they knew that no high-ranking NCO or officer would show up and smoked several joints. A short time later, mortar rounds impacted within our company area. I jumped into a bunker with a doorway offering a view of an open area. The two drunk and stoned soldiers were strolling through the open area pointing and laughing hilariously as mortar rounds landed and exploded all around them, some only a few yards away. No one knows how it happened, but when the shelling stopped, these men were unhurt and still laughing.

Water

Fresh, potable water was provided as often as possible in a special trailer designed for the purpose. We called it a water pig, perhaps for its short, rounded, stubby shape. Each of us carried at least one canteen. If we were to be away from our perimeter for more than a few hours, we carried additional canteens.

When soldiers ran out of water, most bummed it from a fellow platoon member who didn't mind sharing water with someone who chose not to carry enough. Another option was to refill canteens from a stream. During operations that were conducted on foot away from our tracks for several days, there was no way that each of us could carry enough water. In those cases, we were forced to drink whatever water we found. Our rule of thumb was, if you could see the bottom of the canteen cup, only a few inches deep, the water was safe to drink. We weren't told about the toxicity or the half-life of dioxin, one of the ingredients of Agent Orange. Once in a while, someone filled a canteen from a rice paddy. This was a last resort for most of us; we knew what the Vietnamese used for fertilizer.

The army provided us with water purification tablets, but they gave the water a putrid taste. No one used them more than once, unless they added packets of presweetened Kool-Aid or lemonade sent from home.

While operating in the field, we didn't have an inexhaustible supply of water, although we received resupply almost every day. We kept two five-gallon cans on the back of the track; that was usually enough to last our squad a full day. We developed the knack of brushing our teeth, washing our face, and shaving in a steel pot (helmet) or a canteen cup filled with water. The specific order was important. We brushed our teeth first, spit the water on the ground, used a little more water from the container to rinse off our face, and used the rest to shave.

On January 10, 1968, we performed a relatively touchy operation. Our captain wanted to search a church and hospital that were operated by Buddhist monks. The buildings were in an enclosed compound near a village. We suspected that the facility supported and possibly housed the VC. In order to sustain maximum surprise, we pretended that we were going to search the village. We surrounded it with our tracks—sealing off access—and dismounted troops, who moved toward the hootches. Then, at Captain T's signal, which was a blown whistle, everyone ran for our tracks. We mounted quickly, then rushed to surround the church and hospital compound.

The 3d Platoon was pulling flank security as we raced from the village over to the mission. A booby-trapped mortar round, which had been placed between two rubber trees, went off, wounding four men, including the platoon leader, a lieutenant. The lieutenant and his RTO died from wounds received that day. Meanwhile, my squad, along with half of the company, was performing security around the compound, making sure that nobody passed in or out. The other half of the company entered the compound to conduct the search. They checked patients at the hospital to determine the extent and cause of their injuries. Bullet or shrapnel wounds made the patient a suspected VC. We heard that there were rooms constructed of steel somewhere in the compound, and we intended to break in to see what was being stored or hidden inside. The search turned up nothing of military value.

That night, we stayed in Dau Tieng, our forward base camp near the northeast corner of our division's area of operations (AO). I took my first shower since Thanksgiving, when we were in Cu Chi, a period of forty-eight days. I had cleaned up a little on most days in my steel pot, which I filled with water and splashed over myself. That helped, but it was nothing like a shower.

Vietnamese Dogs

One day on a battalion sweep, we were held in position, as we often were, while one of the companies on our flank caught up with us. I found myself in the backyard of a family hootch. A little girl was near the door, and her pet, a small dark brown dog, romped playfully nearby.

I tried calling the dog using the familiar, "Here boy, come here, fella," and whistling.

The girl watched me and figured out what I was trying to do.

She demonstrated how it is done in Vietnam by calling in a falsetto voice, "Coo coo coo coo coo." The dog scampered over to her.

She looked at me with an expression that said, That's how you do it. Wanna try?

I looked at the dog and called, "Coo coo coo coo." The dog began running to me. About halfway over, he must have realized that I was an American and he put on the brakes. Most of the animals stayed away from GIs. The girl and I smiled at each other. When we moved out a few minutes later, we exchanged good-bye waves.

I noticed that in Vietnam the dogs had curly tails. Some of their tails curled up over their backs, like the tail of a pig. Later, I read that although the Vietnamese eat dog flesh, they think that dogs with curly tails have tough meat. Consequently, they eat the ones with straight tails, and the curly-tailed dogs are left to breed. This type of unnatural selection produced dogs with a tendency toward curly tails. These types of observations reminded me of Sutton, the observant soldier who taught me how to explore enemy bunkers and tunnels.

VC Village

During daylight hours, the enemy kept a low profile because of our superior firepower. At night, however, when Americans would be held up inside perimeters, the balance of power shifted and our enemy had almost free rein.

Most villages in Vietnam probably provided support to our enemy during one time or another if not throughout the entire war. During the evenings, Viet Cong political units visited villages and held "educational" sessions heralding the merits of the liberation movement. They also enlisted new recruits and attempted to gain support from the community. The VC used several different tactics to accomplish this and sometimes committed atrocities against those who did not enthusiastically volunteer immediate assistance. Often, however, the VC's requests for help were filled willingly by sympathizers. The VC were, after all, their own countrymen. They shared the same language, culture, values, and political views. Some were neighbors, friends, or relatives.

For the most part, I felt that the average Vietnamese peasant simply wanted to be left alone to grow rice or produce a product and take care of his or her family. Most of them did not care which form of government their country had. They were, in many ways, pawns in this game between our side and the Communists.

The Viet Cong did not view friendliness between the villagers and the Americans, who were around during the day, as honorable activity, unless the friendliness was used as a means of gaining access to information that could be passed on to the VC. On the other hand, we didn't take too kindly to villagers who helped the Viet Cong, either. Those who did were considered the same as the enemy. As a result, and to stay out of trouble with either side, most villagers kept their distance from both sides. A usual response to anything spoken in English was, *"Toi khong biet,"* sometimes shortened to *"khong biet,"* meaning "don't know" and implying "I don't know what you're saying." It was a phrase that Americans heard often from those who did not speak or understand English and also by those who wanted to hide the fact that they did.

To complicate matters further, the Vietnamese believed that bad news should be delivered only by a loved one or relative. If we asked villagers if a particular trail was booby-trapped, for example, or if any VC were nearby, they invariably replied emphatically, "No VC, no VC."

The presence of the enemy was bad news; therefore, it was dishonorable for the villagers to tell us if they were around. None of us knew this, however. If evidence became available indicating that the trail we asked about was indeed booby-trapped, or if plenty of VC were in the area, the villagers' actions were interpreted as aiding the enemy, which was close to actually being the enemy.

Villages that supported the enemy were called VC villages. On January 12, Charlie Company was sent to search one. We surrounded the village and effectively blocked access in and out. The objective was to trap any VC inside the village and to prevent the arrival of reinforcements from elsewhere.

On this operation, each platoon was split in two, with half of the guys entering the village to conduct the search and the other half remaining outside on the perimeter for security. On this day, I was selected to be inside, among those searching hootches.

We often began by rounding up the civilians and herding them to a central location. This allowed us to conduct the search without worrying what the home occupants or their neighbors were doing out of our sight. My group had gone through about half a dozen hootches when we heard mortars landing somewhere near the perimeter. They weren't falling near us, so we ignored them and continued the search. Over the radio, we heard that there had been a casualty. Upon returning, we learned that Bernie Mattson, one of my friends from 2d Platoon, had been killed.

Bernie, or Matt, as we called him, was a good-looking kid from Peoria, Illinois, and we hung around together because we were from the same state and had arrived in-country at about the same time. Although I knew several of the men from our platoon who had died, Matt was the first of my friends to be killed.

Like everyone else, Matt had dived to the ground when the whine of the incoming mortars was heard, but one small piece of shrapnel entered his left side near his armpit and pierced his heart. He died quickly despite the efforts of our medics to save him.

When those we knew died, we mourned them, but because the war demanded almost all of our attention, we soon put the incidents out of our mind. There was also a psychological barrier that most GIs built around themselves to prevent being hurt too much by the death of comrades. This may be why some chose not to have many close friends. In order to avoid the depression caused by the death of fellow soldiers, some of us, myself included, developed a "better him than me" attitude. Although some of this might emerge in later life as post-traumatic stress, it was the only method we knew of dealing with the death of friends, some of whom were too young to have experienced much of what life had to offer.

Once the brief grieving process was over, it was helpful if we identified some mistake that our fallen comrade had made. It would make us feel that our chances of surviving were a little better and that death was less of a random act. We would think, all I have to do is avoid doing what he did. If I do, I'll have a better chance of making it. This was one of the ways we learned our craft.

Uniforms

Each soldier in our company was issued four sets of jungle fatigues. Designed for the tropics, they were made of lightweight, ripstop fabric, the first I had seen. They dried easily. The shirts were meant to be worn outside the trousers to facilitate airflow and cooling.

Because we didn't want a third layer of fabric, which would prevent quick drying of our clothing, we avoided underwear. This took some getting used to, but it served well in preventing fungi and bacterial infections that would have occurred had our groin area remained moist.

Once while I was in the rear for a day or two, someone who needed uniforms swiped my three extra sets of fatigues and I never got them back. We spent the next two to three months in the field, and I wore the same clothes without taking them off. They became wet every day and over the weeks turned dark with sweat and grease. They slowly rotted away to almost nothing. The pant legs became shredded, and I could feel fresh air on my crotch. Toward the end, all of me was visible to the world when I stood in some positions. I was beyond the point of caring.

I finally got out of this rut back in Cu Chi during a battalion inspection. As we stood in formation, our battalion commander passed up and down the rows, stopping to talk, question, or chat with each of us.

When he stopped in front of me, he asked, "Soldier, why aren't you in the proper uniform?"

"This is the only set of fatigues I have, sir."

"Why is that?" he asked.

"I was in the rear for a few days, sir, and when I came back my other uniforms were gone."

He turned to our commanding officer, who remained two paces behind the colonel on such inspections, and said, "See that this man gets a new uniform issue today."

I received four brand new sets of jungle fatigues that afternoon. For a while afterward, because of my clean dark olive-green uniforms, I was mistaken for a new guy by those who didn't know me. That was a bummer.

The Perimeter

Upon arriving at a new location each night in the field, we set up a complete perimeter that was capable of withstanding enemy attacks. The company commander selected a site in a strategic location that could be defended, then the first sergeant assigned sectors of the shape—usually a circle—to each of the three line platoons. Each platoon leader or platoon sergeant placed the squads of his platoon to adequately cover his sector, establish overlapping fields of fire, and tie in to those on either side. This process took only a few minutes. Once we were in place, we unloaded the unnecessary supplies out of the track and stacked them near the rear of the vehicle.

During movement, the tracks contained so much equipment, gear, and ammunition that they were difficult to enter. Gear was piled on the inside about halfway to the top. If we needed anything from within during movement, we had to jump down on top of the stuff and walk over it to get the desired item.

Each member of a squad had a duffel bag containing extra uniforms, a laundry bag, extra M16 magazines or other equipment, and a few personal effects. Duffel bags took a lot of space, and when we were in place we stacked them outside in a line near the rear of the track along with our water cans, some of the ammunition crates, the starlight scope in its case, and some other equipment. That left quite a bit of ammunition and other equipment inside the track, but most of the floor and side benches would be clear and usable.

Next, we removed concertina wire rolls from the front of the track, where we stored them while on the move, and strung them out in front of our squad, connecting with squads on either side. Once in place, this wire formed a continuous loop all the way around the perimeter. A roll of concertina wire unfolds like a giant slinky toy. It has razor-sharp shards, to make enemy infiltration more difficult.

The next step involved the construction of a machine-gun position or bunker for each squad's additional .50-caliber machine gun. Underground sleeping positions were either incorporated into the bunker or dug elsewhere so that everyone would have protection from incoming small-arms, mortar, or rocket fire while sleeping.

With one .50 on the top of the track and another for each squad in a bunker, the enemy—if he wanted to come calling—would have to contend with twenty-four machine-gun bunkers, each with a powerful .50-caliber machine gun. At times, we built a separate bunker for the M60 machine gun, and that served to increase our already high amount of available firepower.

Finally, trip flares and Claymore mines were placed outside the concertina wire. In the meantime, our mortar platoon was preparing for fire missions with ranges beginning just outside the perimeter and extending to their maximum reach of a few miles. Grid coordinates for suspected areas where enemy forces could build up were called in to artillery units. Together, these latter two items provided for quick and accurate heavy indirect fire support (trajectories that arc through the air rather than aiming directly at a target) if needed.

The entire process of setting up a perimeter took hours to complete, with each man taking part. Sometimes we moved every day and went through this process each afternoon or early evening, often finishing after full dark. We couldn't afford not to.

We were the most vulnerable immediately after establishing a perimeter. No bunkers were yet dug, no Claymores were in position, and the mortar and artillery coordinates were yet to be fully worked out. It was advantageous for the enemy to attack us during these times, except for the advantages that our side had during daylight, such as airpower. We were relatively safe as long as we were set up before dark.

We dug a latrine inside the perimeter for use by our platoon. It usually consisted of a small hole flanked on three sides by three sandbags, filled with the soil removed to make the hole. When the hole was full, we simply emptied the sandbags into it and made a new latrine.

The concertina wire made our company perimeters more difficult to penetrate than those of the regular, nonmechanized infantry units. In addition, we had a lot more firepower with our two .50-caliber machine guns per squad. These features gave us an edge that was needed because the enemy always knew where to find us. This is not intended as a slight on regular infantry units, just a comparison. Of course these same advantages meant that we could remain in the field a lot longer.

The troops in our company and others preferred to either stay in one place for a few days or go to Cu Chi, Tay Ninh, Dau Tieng, or another base camp, where there was no need to construct a company perimeter. Times in the rear or at a permanent forward base camp were like a vacation to us.

By January 17, we were still working out of Dau Tieng, east of Nui Ba Den. We began hearing rumors that we would go to Cu Chi on January 19, but we weren't sure if we believed them. We hadn't been to our division's main base camp since Thanksgiving.

On this day, while on our way to a village to pull security while another company searched the place, we received rifle and machine-gun fire from within the village. The 3d Platoon, which was closest to the firing, opened up, killing three enemy soldiers. We were still getting some fire, so we called in artillery rounds. Most of them landed within the village. We then set fire to some of the heavy vegetation near the village to flush out any VC hiding there, but we almost started a forest fire. A few of the rubber trees ignited and produced black smoke like that generated by a burning tire.

I presumed that the enemy had taken cover within the village under the assumption that we would hesitate firing back to avoid injuring civilians. But if so, they guessed wrong. We assumed, probably correctly, that when the enemy took up positions in a village, the word spread quickly and most of them took cover in bomb shelters. Small-arms fire from rifles, machine guns, and grenade launchers probably would not inflict much damage on the village. The artillery rounds, on the other hand, probably didn't win the hearts and minds of the villagers.

That night, we were back in the friendly confines of the base camp at Dau Tieng. Shortly after returning, Billie Barnett and I heard that a movie would be shown by one of the rear-echelon units. After chow, we walked over and enjoyed the show.

On January 23 we left Dau Tieng, but we didn't go to Cu Chi as was rumored. Rather, we returned to the area near the Cambodian border, about a mile northwest of Tay Ninh.

Barnett, with whom I shared duties early in my tour, and I returned from a two-day operation around half past ten at night shortly after we became established near the border. There was no room in any of our squad's bunkers for us, which meant that we would have to build a complete bunker in the dark in order to have a place to sleep. With only two of us working, we didn't finish until

3:00 A.M. I could usually make Barnett laugh, and although we were exhausted, we still managed to see the humor in our predicament. It helped keep us awake and moving. After completing the overhead cover, we collapsed inside the bunker and immediately fell to sleep.

We finished the bunker the next day. I designed it myself and was proud of it. There was a semicircular shelf for the .50; it was dug about eight inches below ground level in order to lower the silhouette of the completed bunker. The lower silhouette made a more difficult target for RPGs while allowing grazing fire from the machine gun. The remainder of the bunker, including the sleeping positions, was about three feet deep.

Life inside the company perimeter during the day was enjoyable when compared with the alternatives. Of course, guards were posted around the clock, and they usually stayed on top of the tracks so they could easily see the surrounding terrain. The rest of the guys retired to the coolness of their bunkers during the heat of the day or lounged in the back of the track. A poncho liner was spread across the open cargo hatch for shade.

Transistor radios tuned to the Saigon Armed Forces Radio Network played music throughout much of the day. Several songs of special significance to the troops were heard regularly. Bobby Vinton's "Mr. Lonely," which he wrote while stationed at Fort Dix, New Jersey, created a mood that every GI could empathize.

When Eric Burton and the Animals' "We Gotta Get Out of This Place" was played, guys in bunkers around the perimeter joined in on the chorus, singing at the top of their lungs.

Although we didn't know it, the 1968 Tet Offensive was just a few days away.

SADDLE UP; WE'RE MOVING OUT

Trouble Finding the Enemy

Before Tet, the Vietnamese lunar new year, we suffered occasional casualties, about one every two to three weeks. Though we humped through the areas where we thought we would find evidence of the enemy or come in contact with them, we managed somehow to miss them. Or, probably more accurately, they knew how to elude us.

We operated sweeps, ambush patrols, and search and destroy missions to little avail. Eventually, it began to affect our morale. We were, after all, supposedly the world's best-equipped and best-trained army, yet we had trouble locating Viet Cong soldiers, who seemed to excel in eluding us. I was in-country months before I saw a live enemy soldier.

I do not remember which battle was my first. It was probably one of those firefights during which we closed in on the enemy without us or possibly either side realizing it. When the firing started we would dive to the ground and fire in the direction of the enemy as fast and furiously as we could in an attempt to gain what the military calls fire superiority. The theory was, and still is, that if one side shoots more at the other side or shoots more accurately than the other, the recipients will have a difficult time returning accurate fire; they'll be too busy ducking, thereby providing us with the opportunity to maneuver or withdraw. The most we saw of the enemy during these contacts was fleeting glimpses of movement through dense vegetation. For some of us, the enemy began to take on spooky and surrealistic dimensions.

Weapons

M16

When I arrived in Vietnam, American forces were still using the original M16, the one with the three-pronged flash suppressor on the end. Our enemy called it the black dragon because of the peculiar angles formed by the carrying handle along the top and the front sight. The M16 was designed to inflict damage while keeping the size of the round relatively small. It replaced the M14, which fired 7.62mm rounds, the same as the M60 machine gun. Rounds from the M16 were smaller, 5.56mm, with a projectile only slightly larger in diameter than a .22-caliber rifle round. The magazines were smaller and the rounds were lighter than those of the M14. The overall weapon was shorter and lighter, weighing only about five pounds fully loaded. The hand guard and the stock were made of high-impact black plastic. The troops joked that the gun was made by Mattel, the toy company.

Compared with other weapons, the M16, so we were told, had less rifling in the barrel, so the round spun more slowly. When the round hit something, it tumbled end over end as a result of the decreased spin velocity, thereby causing considerable damage.

During firepower demonstrations back in the world, plastic milk jugs filled with water were suspended from overhead tree limbs and shot with an M14, then with an M16. The first shot made the jug jerk and caused two streams of water to pour from either side onto the ground. The second shot, the one from the M16, caused the jug to explode. We were duly impressed. We saw similar damage to the flesh of dead NVA and VC soldiers.

The original version of this weapon, with the three-pronged flash suppressor, was used as a tool in opening cases of C rations, which came in cardboard boxes wrapped with heavy-gauge wire, the way ribbon is used in gift wrapping. We didn't have wire cutters, or any other tools for that matter, but we discovered that the prongs at the end of the barrel could be fitted over the wire, which could then be snapped by standing over the case for maximum leverage and twisting the weapon. The army always finds ways to get at food.

The original M16s came with a design flaw. They jammed easily.

Dirt in or around the chamber would cause a jam, as would the expansion and contraction of the metal chamber as the weapon was fired, or so we were told. After being fired, the chamber would contract as it cooled and exert pressure on the round remaining in the chamber, resulting in that round shell not being ejected the next time the weapon was fired. To clear the jam, a cleaning rod had to be inserted into the end of the barrel to poke out the stuck shell. During contact with the enemy, it was preferable not to have that happen. A jam was difficult to clear without increasing the exposure of the unfortunate GI to enemy fire.

During firefights early in my tour or when our perimeter was attacked, all weapons in our company roared into action. After just a few seconds, only the M79 grenade launchers and the M60 and the .50-caliber machine guns were still heard. Almost every M16 jammed in the first minute of action. That didn't do much to increase our confidence in the weapon. Because of this, some of our guys carried the few M14s that were available to us.

A believer in keeping my weapon in top shape, I performed at least minimal cleaning every day. When I had the chance, I stripped the entire weapon, including the trigger assembly, which was a complicated and time-consuming job. I cleaned everything I could, then reassembled the rifle. When time didn't allow disassembly, I removed the bolt and cleaned out the chamber, bolt, and receiver as best I could.

In late November or early December, our rifles were replaced by the newer, redesigned M16s. Instead of the three-pronged flash suppressor, this version had a cylindrical one about an inch in length with slots along the sides. These weapons were much more reliable than the original M16. The only soldiers who had trouble with them were those who failed to keep them clean and lubricated. For a while, we kept a few of the original guns with the three prongs just for opening C-ration cartons.

M79 Grenade Launcher

The M79 grenade launcher was a sweet weapon. It looked, and was operated, like a sawed-off shotgun except that the barrel and rounds that it fired were 40mm (1½inches) in diameter. The rounds armed centrifugally after traveling fifteen to twenty meters; that is,

The village of Cu Chi, from the .50 caliber machine gun turret on the top of our armored personnel carrier—note machine gun barrel. With its dirt road, modest hootches, and plentiful women and children, Cu Chi was a typical village. Nearby is the main base camp for the 25th Infantry Division.

Picking their way through the mud along the road, these girls are on their way to school, each wearing an *ao dai*, the traditional Vietnamese dress. The black and white colors identify them as students. In the background are rice paddies shortly before filling with water.

Dennis (Hack) Hackin and village kids inside a family hootch. Children loved to have their pictures taken even though most would never see the results. The villages were almost always devoid of young men.

The Black Virgin Mountain, from a distance of five miles. This volcanic mountain, 800 meters in height, was reportedly the home of 1,000 VC or NVA soldiers who lived inside its many crevices and caves. Because it was a religious symbol, it wasn't bombed.

While performing road security, we provided overnight protection for a rock crusher installation at the base of Nui Ba Den, to the right of the armored personnel carrier. This mountain formed indelible impressions in the memory of GIs in our division. The APC behind us is maintaining the standard distance between our tracks while on the move.

During our stays at the rock crusher at Nui Ba Den, my squad was positioned at this location, within yards of the mountain's base. A special forces communication installation was on the mountain's crest. The enemy owned the rest. We sometimes saw NVA or VC soldiers sitting near the large white rock at the top left.

Housecleaning day during a stand-down in the Tay Ninh base camp. Hack is on the top of the track, while John (Big John) Lewis performs preventive maintenance on the left-side tread. Bob (Bo) Smith is working on equipment in the right foreground.

Our track in the Iron Triangle, an enemy stronghold dating back to the 1940s and the days of the Viet Minh. Because of heavy enemy activity, bulldozers dug trenches to lower the silhouette of our tracks on the company perimeter, making them more difficult targets for the enemy RPG gunners.

they had to spin at a fast rate in order to detonate upon impact. A locking ring moved out of the way as a result of centrifugal force. This served to protect those on our side by precluding explosions close to our forces that might occur, for example, if a round struck a tree limb.

I once was carrying an M79 on an evening when we fired harassment and interdiction (H&I) rounds in areas with known heavy enemy activity. I didn't know it but the safety button on the weapon I had was broken, and I was carrying the weapon with my finger on the trigger. To my great surprise, a round went off, embedding itself in the ground near my feet. On that occasion, I was thankful for centrifugal arming.

The grenades, once fired, flew slowly through the air. We often saw them arcing toward the enemy. The weapon made a thumping sound when it was fired. Heard from a distance, the sound had a psychological impact on the listener, who wondered where the round would land. The sound also led to the weapon's nickname: the thumper or blooper. To our enemy, it was the most feared small-arms weapon in our arsenal.

Because the round was slow and heavy, it dropped quickly. In order to hit targets beyond fifty meters or so, grenadiers had to aim above them. The farther the target, the higher the aim, up to a maximum range of about four hundred meters, approximately a quarter mile. A flip-up front sight aided in aiming at distant targets. A slide bar could be raised or lowered to marked increments on the sight that corresponded with the estimated distance to the target. The men who carried these weapons developed an admirable knack of quickly and accurately judging, without using the front sight, how high to aim to hit almost any target within range.

I always thought it would be a good idea to develop a double-barreled M79. The grenadier could fire the first round, holding the barrel in place. If the round missed, he could adjust for the second one. This would increase accuracy and firepower, which were important during initial contact. Of course, in some situations, it wasn't feasible to hold a position until the round impacted.

During the battalion inspection when I was questioned about the condition of my uniform, the colonel also spoke to the man next to me, Goode, one of our M79 grenadiers. Goode had removed the front sight from his weapon and thrown it away. When the colonel asked why he had removed the sight, Goode replied, "Well, sir, after firing several hundred rounds, I never used the front sight anymore, and it kept getting caught on branches when we moved in the woods and made noise at night."

"Very well," replied the colonel, and moved on.

Although altering a weapon was a no-no, Goode's explanation convinced the colonel that the front sight wasn't necessary if the man carrying the weapon was experienced. Soldiers in Vietnam, and other wars for that matter, developed skills beyond the norm because their life depended on it. Goode was a fine example of that.

As much as our M79 gunners were admired for their skill, the weapon itself commanded the respect of those on its receiving end. Once on our way to an ambush site, we heard Vietnamese voices off to our right in the darkness. We maneuvered on line and opened fire. Shortly thereafter, we learned that we were firing toward an ARVN compound, and they contacted us on the radio. We hadn't known that our allies were there, and their compound didn't show up on the maps we were using.

A few of the ARVN soldiers came out after the firing stopped, and we apologized to them. Although they indicated that no real harm had been done, one South Vietnamese soldier was holding a bandage to his buttocks. He approached one of our M79 gunners, patted the weapon, and said, "Number one, number one." He showed us the bloody bandage, and we surmised that he had been wounded by one of our M79 rounds. We didn't know how to react to that.

M60 Machine Gun

The workhorse of the infantry was the M60 machine gun. It provided lots of firepower and was portable enough to be carried into battle or on long operations conducted on foot. Good M60 gunners fired grazing fire, which placed rounds about a foot off the ground. The theory was that most people on the receiving end would be lying down. Anything higher than a foot would go over their heads. If they weren't lying down, they soon would be, one way or another.

There were a few guys who preferred this weapon, but not many. It was larger and much heavier than the M16. There was a noticeable difference between carrying an M16 and humping the 60. Each squad had at least one M60, and few wanted to go out on an operation without a 60 gunner. There was no way for the gunner to carry all the ammunition he might need if we ran into anything, so we all helped carry additional M60 ammunition. When the gunner ran low, he called for more ammo, and one of us would remove a belt and toss it in his direction. Other nearby soldiers passed the belt until it reached the gunner.

My friend Bob Ordy grudgingly carried an M60 during his first few months in Vietnam. In January, Phil Strittmatter, from Michigan, arrived, and Ordy was successful in having the big gun transferred to the new guy. Over the next few months, Stritt, as we called him, became one of our platoon's most trusted M60 gunners. That's not always a good thing, as Stritt found out; he was almost always requested to accompany ambush patrols. Consequently, he didn't have much chance to remain overnight within our perimeter.

Other Weapons

We had an assortment of other weapons and devices. Each track had a pump shotgun, which we sometimes carried on point, especially at night when contact with enemy forces occurred at close range. The shotguns held five rounds, with a sixth one in the chamber. I carried a shotgun on point on several nighttime operations but felt vulnerable because it had so few shots and wasn't lethal at anything except close range.

We also had light antitank weapons (LAWs), which were short, armor-piercing, recoilless rifles with fiberglass barrels. After being fired, they were discarded; they couldn't be reloaded. They were excellent for blowing bunkers. When we anticipated coming in contact with enemy installations, we made sure to have a few LAWs with us.

Each squad also had an M14 rifle, usually stored inside the track. The longer barrel and increased rifling provided greater accuracy than the M16, so the M14 was used for long-range firing such as that of a sniper.

Along the side equipment rack inside our tracks, a few of our squads carried a 90mm recoilless rifle. Because we hardly ever used them, they were largely ignored. An incident that occurred in January, however, forever ingrained this weapon in my memory.

___

Stand-down

In late January, we were given a stand-down in Tay Ninh, one of our larger division base camps. After an extended stay in the field, our officers were concerned that we might get rowdy and cause trouble. So, to keep us busy, they gave us classroom-type blocks of instruction. One of the blocks, taught by our platoon sergeant, covered how to disassemble and reassemble the .50-caliber machine gun. It was a painful and boring class for me to sit through; I could have taught the lesson just as well, thanks to how I distracted myself following my Dear John letter of two months before.

We were also instructed to take everything out of our tracks and pile it in neat, orderly stacks, then clean every piece of equipment and every weapon. Plans were made to test-fire all company weapons the next day.

While in the field, I had been designated the 90 gunner for our squad. I was responsible for finding and deploying the 90mm recoilless rifle, better known as a bazooka, in the event that our perimeter was attacked by a large force. I had never fired one of these guns before, but I found it and cleaned it the best I could, using a brush and diesel fuel.

The next day, we loaded several of our larger weapons, including the 90mm, in a vehicle and set out for a field, which we would use as a firing range.

My assistant gunner for this exercise was a blonde kid named Roger Wilson. He had the color of hair that required that he wear a hat at all times in the field. When he removed his helmet, his bright blonde hair stood out immediately. He also wore glasses, which fogged up with regularity in the humidity. Although he was not one of my best friends, we got along well and hung around together occasionally.

During combat, we would have done away with the formalities and I would have fired the 90mm recoilless rifle by myself. But here in the rear, we did it by the book, with Wilson kneeling at my right side, facing me. His role as assistant gunner was to load the round, then tap me on the helmet to signal that it was okay to fire.

I had been aiming at a barrel in the field. When he tapped my helmet, I took a deep breath and slowly squeezed the trigger. There was a whooshing noise, and I was propelled violently forward. The front end of the gun, which looks like a big tube, was now protruding several inches into the ground before me, and smoke was coming out of the weapon. Several of our platoon members who had been watching ran up, grabbed Wilson and me, and pulled us back to safety.

When I squeezed the trigger, the round had started to fire but became lodged in the end of the barrel, which is what had thrown me forward. In addition, a five- to six-inch crack had opened on the right side of the gun, and a flame about six feet in length shot out, hitting Wilson squarely in the face. Although he was twenty years old, he suddenly looked as though he had a receding hairline. All the hair was singed off his face and arms, which blistered for a few days. After he recovered, we kidded him about his lack of eyebrows and receding hairline.

THE ENEMY

Body Count

The first enemy soldier I had a good look at was dead, lying at the side of a road, apparently where he had fallen. He had been there for several days and looked and smelled like it.

When they could, the enemy removed their dead, presumably so we could not tell how many of them we had killed and, more importantly, how many of them remained. For better or worse, the measure of success in this war with no front lines became the number of casualties inflicted by either side. If we killed more of them than we lost, we were winning. If not, we were losing. Accordingly, after battles, the surviving enemy soldiers dragged their dead with them when they retreated. Usually they buried them in mass graves, some of which had been prepared in advance by the soldiers themselves.

Preparing graves, possibly their own, beforehand must have had an effect on the morale of our enemy, but it also served to demonstrate their commitment. They had to believe in what they were doing to dig graves for those who might not survive.

Enemy Tactics

Over the course of our tour, we developed a healthy respect for our enemy. It was inconceivable to us that they could hold up their end of a battle against a force that obviously had more firepower. And they performed this willingly. The average Viet Cong soldier that we would see, usually post-mortem, wore only a pair of shorts, a button-down short-sleeved shirt, thong sandals (shoes were rare among the Vietnamese), and some type of hat to ward off the sun and rain. Many of them wore the familiar black pajamas and conical straw hat. Canvas backpacks were common.

Three plastic bags were tied to the belts of quite a few of the dead Viet Cong we encountered. One contained about thirty additional rounds for their AK-47, enough to reload a magazine. Another held a rice ball, the VC's version of C rations. The third held marijuana, which we understood the enemy smoked like Americans smoke to-bacco. We supposed that the drug provided battlefield courage and possibly, as with our own troops, a diversion from the stress of life in the infantry.

We couldn't begin to fathom how these troops, with so little am-munition and equipment, would dare to take on the U.S. Army or the U.S. Marines in combat. We would not choose to trade places with them under any circumstances.

Most NVA regulars wore olive-drab uniforms and were much bet-ter equipped than Viet Cong soldiers. They carried more ammuni-tion and usually had more access to mortar rounds, rockets, RPG rounds, and grenades. They often had web gear with pockets hold-ing three additional AK-47 magazines strapped to their chests. This would have been unusual for the VC.

Our enemy compensated for their inferior firepower and often lower numbers with cunning, which we would have admired had we not so often been its recipient. They excelled in guerrilla warfare, the art of engaging superior forces. Their philosophy was to avoid knockdown, drag-out battles, which, of course, favored the side with the most soldiers and higher technological ordnance.

A common tactic was the hit-and-run attack. The objective was to inflict as much damage as possible in a time span short enough to preclude effective response on our part, then get out of Dodge.

Something I learned in training, which was reinforced by Jimmy Sutton, is the importance of knowing your enemy. The lesson was not lost on the VC and NVA. By watching us, they learned several tactics that they could turn to their advantage.

With only a few exceptions, we operated in relatively large groups. American forces could be found clumped together in perimeters that were spread far enough apart to avoid endangering our own forces when we opened fire. Once the Viet Cong and NVA determined the location of our forces, they traveled unhindered through the large areas between our forward base camps, company perimeters, and ambush sites, at least at night.

More often than not, it was more advantageous for the VC and NVA to pass through our areas rather than engage us. This allowed them to prepare for large campaigns, such as the 1968 Tet Offensive, or to mass their troops for attacks on perimeters or installations that offered the best tactical or political advantages. Doing battle with us would result in casualties and expenditure of ammunition that they could ill afford.

While preparing an attack against one of our perimeters, they had plenty of room to maneuver their forces to take advantage of the most tactical terrain, or even surround us entirely. We gave them this advantage by keeping within the perimeter almost all our forces, except for ambush patrols and LPs, both of which were insignificant against a force large enough to sustain an attack.

Of course, the enemy always knew where our company was by the sound of our diesel engines. And it was easy for the enemy to follow us on operations that we conducted on foot. In order to avoid booby traps, we moved in single file. A column of GIs wearing lug-soled combat boots, in a country where thong sandals were the preferred daily wear, left a trail that a child could follow, especially during the monsoon season. Although we were seldom attacked from the rear, as one would expect, VC scouts probably followed our trail when they could, to determine the location of our perimeters when we operated without our tracks. They most likely also waited for our ambush patrols to depart, then followed. It was this knowledge that gave them free movement through the remainder of the countryside.

American forces took pride in never leaving their own dead or wounded on the battlefield. Our enemy quickly learned this and used it against us by placing snipers or establishing ambushes where they could watch the bodies of our dead or wounded comrades and wait for us to retrieve them. Too many times we obliged them; in doing so, we suffered even more wounded and killed. This enemy tactic inflicted additional casualties on our forces with little expenditure or effort on the part of the VC or NVA.

Often it is more effective to wound soldiers than kill them. A wounded man must have his wounds treated and must be transported, which removes at least two additional unwounded soldiers from the ranks, at least until the wounded man is dusted off or placed in the care of medics.

The term "dust-off" is slang for medical evacuation by helicopter. The nickname came from the dust that was picked up and blown throughout the landing zone, obscuring vision and getting into everything.

A lesson we sometimes failed to remember involved land mines. They usually appeared in groups. On February 1, we were going down a road in the jungle and the Charlie 6 track, the captain's track, hit a mine. Nobody was hurt, but the track was destroyed. While they worked on it to get it good enough to tow, about a dozen people were standing around watching. As another track was being backed up to tow the captain's track, that one hit a mine. Two people who were standing nearby were injured.

THE YEAR OF THE MONKEY

With the approach of the lunar new year, known as Tet in Vietnam, our contact with the North Vietnamese Army increased. Their troops passed through or gathered in our area of operations—War Zone C, of III Corps—as they prepared for the major offensive, and some of their main targets were in the Saigon area, within a day's march to the southeast. The heavily wooded area between Tay Ninh and Cu Chi, with a lower population density than their target areas in South Vietnam's capital, afforded an excellent base from which to assemble troops and stage operations.

Tet is a celebration lasting from three to seven days in Vietnam during which families and individuals celebrate a new beginning by forgiving others for past wrongs and preparing and consuming special foods to mark the new year. It occurs during the first new moon after the sun enters Aquarius.

The 1968 Tet Offensive was chosen by the Viet Cong and the NVA as the final big operation that they hoped would build sufficient momentum to win the war. They anticipated, planned for, and attempted to stimulate a general uprising similar to those that the Vietnamese people had used in attempts to overthrow past oppression by French colonialists. They hoped and expected that the general population would come out of their homes and places of business to join them in suppressing and overthrowing the South Vietnamese government and expelling us Americans.

In that respect, the Tet Offensive did not succeed. More than a hundred military targets were attacked during the three-day holiday and the days that followed it. The people did not rise up or come to the assistance of the Communists, who could not hold the meager installations and territory they had won. In the end, the offensive was a military defeat. But it turned into a psychological victory because of the effect it had on U.S. citizens back in the world.

During the offensive, a squad of Viet Cong soldiers gained access to the U.S. embassy grounds in Saigon. The soldiers were quickly killed, but this act in a supposedly impenetrable installation shocked the folks back home, resulting in a marked increase in antiwar fervor and a further eroding of political support for the war.

After Tet, the Viet Cong were never again a major force in Vietnam. They suffered many casualties during the Tet Offensive and never fully recovered their former strength. NVA officers and senior NCOs had been dispatched from Hanoi, the capital of North Vietnam, to "help" VC units. This served to further erode the military and political power of the Viet Cong while implementing the hidden agenda of the Communists in increasing the north's influence in the south.

When the offensive began, we were operating out of the Tay Ninh area and had moved almost every day for the past two weeks. We were tired of setting up a complete perimeter, only to tear it down the next day, move, and do it all over again.

We heard that Cu Chi had been mortared twice in the past few days and that five VC battalions were in the Saigon area, three of them in the city itself.

In a letter to my mom, I told her that on this day, February 3, our 3d Platoon found and killed a VC soldier. In the next sentence, I said, "I don't know when I'm going on R&R. In the summer probably." The sudden switch of topics exemplified my state of mind at the time. Warfare had become a normal part of our world. It was not considered unusual to discuss incidents of war in one sentence and something innocuous in the next.

Wildfire Incident

Around this time, I made one of the dumbest mistakes of my career as a soldier in Vietnam. Our company was on a sweep in a grassy area where a wildfire was burning. We stopped to take a break downwind from the fire and, as usual, we took off our web gear harnesses, which were weighted down with ammunition, grenades, ponchos, C rations, and other supplies. The harnesses could weigh well over thirty-five pounds, depending on the amount of stuff being carried.

In addition to being heavy, usual web gear, equipment, and ammunition blocked free air movement, making us hotter. When we stopped for a break, we took all of this off. The sudden free circulation of air under our jungle fatigue shirts produced a refreshing cooling effect as some of the sweat which soaked into our uniforms began evaporating. As soon as it was removed, we felt as light as a feather and immediately cooler.   We sat or lay down to rest for a few minutes.

"Okay, saddle up, you guys," our platoon sergeant commanded. "We're moving out."

I put my stuff back on and took my place in the column. The company moved out.

About thirty minutes later we had not moved very far, having moved slowly to check for mines and booby traps, when shots suddenly rang from our rear. The company dove to the ground, and we all wondered what was going on. The shots were coming from the area behind us, near where we had taken our break. We wondered if the enemy had sneaked in behind us and, if so, how they did it without detection.

The shots sounded funny, though. It didn't seem as though they were coming through a rifle barrel; they didn't have the characteristic pop. After months of combat, we could tell.

All of a sudden, a thought struck me and I patted my chest where my bandolier should have been.

"Uh-oh."

I had left my bandolier back where we had taken our break, and the brushfire had caught up with it. The rounds inside my seven magazines were cooking off.

"What is it, Hayes?"

"Um, I think that's my bandolier back there." I thought I might as well admit it; someone was sure to notice that it was missing.

We stayed put for a half hour until the 126 rounds stopped firing. My bandolier and abandoned ammunition had the entire company pinned down. Word got around about whose bandolier it was. Although I received some good-natured kidding from my buddies, I sensed that some of our guys were rolling their eyes at the thought of what I had done. It was not my best moment.

Meanwhile, the increased action associated with the Tet Offensive continued to affect us.

On February 5, we were set up about a mile from Nui Ba Den, the Black Virgin Mountain. We received reports of nine hundred NVA soldiers moving toward and possibly preparing to attack our division's base camp at Tay Ninh. The next day, we moved our perimeter about a thousand meters, speculating that the new position had something to do with the reported enemy activity. Of course, as infantrymen, we relied on rumor and were never sure what thought processes were occurring within the higher ranks. Our officers weren't obligated to share them with us. In their defense, it was probably good logic to withhold tactical information from us. We might speak out of turn with civilians or Vietnamese base camp employees, and the word might eventually reach the enemy.

A few days later we moved again. This time we set up on the opposite side of the town of Tay Ninh from our forward base camp. Never having established a perimeter there before, we moved during the afternoon with insufficient time to develop a fully protective perimeter.

That night I had LP. Our lieutenant took us to our position, which had never happened before, and he didn't carry a weapon or wear a helmet. We figured something was up.

He took us to the inside edge of the concertina wire, just beyond our tracks, and said, "Here you are."

I guess he felt sorry for us after we had worked hard all afternoon establishing our perimeter, which wasn't nearly complete. We set up on the inside of the wire but took the precaution of digging a hole to sleep in.

Later that night, the perimeter at our Tay Ninh base camp was mortared, and we could see and hear the rounds hit. We stayed inside our hole.

A day or so later, we moved again, this time back near Nui Ba Den, but not in our usual location near the rock crusher. Our platoon's sector of the perimeter that night faced an ARVN compound. During my stint on guard duty, our .50-caliber machine gun was pointed directly at our allies.

At 0200, shots rang out as four snipers began firing at us from the opposite side of our perimeter. We could hear the rounds zing past us for about half an hour. We all crowded into a bunker and listened as our guys on the opposite side of the perimeter returned some of the fire.

In one of our platoon's other bunkers, Jose Mohica was being shaken by one of the new guys, who was known for getting excited while in contact with the enemy, and for falling asleep on guard. He was jumping up and down, shaking Mohica and yelling, "We're being attacked, we're being attacked."

"Go away, man," said Mohica. "Wake me up when they're fighting on our side [of the perimeter]."

Mohica was hard core.

Our area of operations was crawling with NVA units. We received reports several nights in a row that we might be attacked. On February 7, four hundred enemy soldiers were seen crawling along a stream toward our perimeter. They didn't attack. It's possible that they were en route to another location and simply had to get past us.

The next day, toward evening, a battalion of heavily camouflaged VC or NVA were spotted crawling toward our position. Artillery was called in, and the next morning we found twenty dead soldiers where the rounds had impacted. We were prepared for attack with eight Claymore mines in front of my bunker and eleven hundred rounds of .50-caliber machine-gun ammo inside the bunker and ready to fire. We were also armed with LAWs, a case of grenades, two hundred rounds for a grenade launcher, and five thousand rounds of M16 ammo. We were ready to do battle, but no attack materialized.

On February 8, it was reported that we'd be moving again, but we didn't know for sure where. Having heard that Cu Chi had been attacked almost every night for the past ten nights, we thought we might be used to strengthen the main base camp's perimeter.

Heavy contact with enemy forces throughout our division's area of operations was beginning to affect the delivery of mail and supplies. Convoys to and from Cu Chi were being ambushed. This was the heaviest enemy activity since my arrival in Vietnam. It was going to get worse.

On February 10, we went to Cu Chi but didn't get to stay long. As we moved through the base camp for our first visit since Thanksgiving, we didn't see any damage from the recent numerous mortar attacks—that is, until we arrived at our battalion's area. Although our company area wasn't hit too badly, the other company areas were flattened.

We unloaded all the tracks and ate chow. Just as we were getting ready for some much needed sleep, we were told to prepare to move out. There was some grumbling, but everyone understood that there was a war going on and something big was happening throughout much of South Vietnam.

As soon as we finished reloading the tracks, the company moved out with Bravo Company and headed south. We ended up just outside Saigon but were told we wouldn't stay there. Nobody knew where we would go next.

The next day, February 11, we entered the suburbs of Saigon. We were driving on city streets, the first we had seen since we arrived in Vietnam. The battle scars from the recent offensive were everywhere. Only a few buildings remained standing, and those were severely damaged. It reminded us of footage from the World War II movies we had grown up watching.

All of a sudden, we received sniper fire from the roof of a two-story building. My squad went up to the roof and found the shells from where the sniper had taken aim at us, but there was no sign of the shooter. About the same time, Bravo Company drew M79 and automatic weapon fire.

While continuing our movement through the area, picking our way around the debris in the streets, we spotted some enemy web gear with four grenades and ammunition for an AK-47. It was lying outside a shot-up building. We searched the area and found an RPG, more ammunition, web gear, a toolbox, and a makeshift gas mask made out of a plastic bag with cloth over the breathing opening. Apparently we had surprised an enemy unit, which was unable to retrieve its equipment before fleeing.

That night was one of the more interesting evenings I spent in Vietnam. We had moved to a less damaged neighborhood and our tracks roamed the streets all night, with several guys on the top of each one in the event that they received fire or ran into large enemy units. The rest of us occupied the roofs of buildings in the area where we were to act as snipers if NVA or VC soldiers were spotted below. This was an unusual combat mission for us.

Our lieutenant pointed at a building that he wanted each squad to occupy. When he pointed out ours, we took off, entered the building, and climbed a narrow staircase to where it ended at the third floor. A Vietnamese family lived there, and several kids were playing in the hall outside the apartment's open doorway. We made sure that the parents saw us, then watched for their reaction. When they didn't lunge for a weapon, we figured we were relatively safe, so we entered the apartment. Through signs and body language, we let them know we were no threat, then we looked around. A window led onto the roof. It would suit our needs perfectly. We climbed out and established radio contact with the lieutenant.

"Two-six, this is Two-one. Over."

"This is Two-six. Over."

"Two-six, we're in position. Over."

"Roger that, Two-one. Two-six. Out."

"Two-one. Out."

We took up positions where we could see the street three floors below but also had some cover. We couldn't see the other squads and didn't know which buildings they were on, but we could hear them on the radio. Occasionally we heard or saw one of our tracks pass nearby.

I was sitting on the roof closest to the apartment window and overheard the man of the house say something in French. I leaned in the window and said, *"Pardonnez moi, monsieur. Vous parle francais, n'est-ce pas?"*

"Oui, et vous parle francais aussi?"

"Oui, mais un peut."

He smiled and said, *"Tres bien."*

Once we decided that we shared a common language, we spoke for an hour. He asked about my family back home and told me about his. He excused himself for a moment and came back bringing me a cup of tea. He told me that his son, who had turned twenty-one the day before, was a student. His school was closed, though, because of all the action.

We slept on the roof and took turns on guard duty. When it was my turn, I sat near the radio so I could see below. The family was asleep or was quiet. The breeze felt good up this high in the air. It was a pleasant change from sitting in wet grass, as we usually did.

The next morning, the French-speaking head of the family brought us bread and coffee. I gave him a box of C rations.

On February 12, we moved ten miles north of Saigon to Hoc Mon, a large war-torn village, and established a company perimeter. The next day we found an NVA base camp. We called in artillery and air strikes on the base camp, then moved in, expecting a major battle. But the enemy had evacuated. My track passed within three feet of a dud five-hundred-pound bomb, which we blew in place when we left so that the enemy couldn't use it against us. They were known to saw through large rounds such as this one, then use the explosives inside to create smaller bombs or booby traps that they could carry more easily.

Inside the enemy camp, we found about seventy-five bunkers, eight weapons, several grenades, and an assortment of mines and mortar rounds. Four dead enemy soldiers were inside the base camp along with an American soldier who had been dead for two to three days. He was tied to a tree and his head had been blown off by an RPG round. The fins of the rocket were protruding from the tree trunk where his head should have been. We later found out that he was a sergeant who had been reported missing in action by another unit a few days earlier.

The Tet Offensive was still going strong. We were soon to be caught up in the war and the offensive in ways that none of us would forget.

On February 14, we were still near Hoc Mon, searching the outskirts of the large village. Our mission was to find antiaircraft positions from which the enemy had been shooting at American aircraft. The search for the antiaircraft guns ended in failure, and our platoon was remaining to cover the withdrawal of the company.

Sutton and I were off exploring bunkers when we heard an explosion followed by small-arms and machine-gun fire in the direction of our platoon. We decided it was time to turn back.

From the sound of the firing, we could tell that some of it came from AK-47s. We weren't sure about the machine guns, but we knew that the AKs had to be the enemy. We headed toward the sound of the M16s.

Our platoon had broken into two teams of two squads each. Our platoon leader, Lt. Ralph Williams, was with the same group as I was. The area we had been searching was a recently abandoned enemy position, or so we thought. We found some mortar positions—areas dug a few feet below ground level—with marks made by the gun's base plate and where rounds had been stored. There was a large amount of ammo for a .51-caliber machine gun in some of the firing positions. That should have tipped us off that the enemy was nearby, but we didn't pick up on it. We had seen many hastily abandoned enemy positions prior to this day, and we thought little of the fact that the enemy had left ammunition behind. But these weren't Viet Cong soldiers; they were hard-core North Vietnamese regulars who had probably been underground when our entire company was present.

There were bunkers all over, and we were intrigued by them and were checking them out. We had wandered some distance away from the rest of the platoon by the time the battle started. Actually, we were lucky that we hadn't run into enemy troops.

When we arrived at the source of the M16 fire, we found five or six of our fellow platoon members lying near a low rice paddy dike in an open area. We looked at each other, shrugged, and ran and dove behind the dike with them.

"The lieutenant and some of our guys are in that hootch over there," explained one of our comrades, pointing directly across the dike. "They were searching it and Charlie threw satchel charges or grenades in on them."

The heavy enemy fire continued, and we—as well as those in the hootch—were pinned down. We could hear the lieutenant calling to us that he had a bullet wound in one of his legs but was otherwise all right. His plan was to call in an air strike of jet bombers to drop napalm and five-hundred-pound bombs. He planned to throw a smoke grenade to mark the enemy position for the air strike. He said that a few of the men were unhurt but he wasn't sure about the others.

Just as Lieutenant Williams pulled the pin on a purple smoke grenade, another explosion rocked the hootch. NVA soldiers had thrown another grenade or satchel charge and it landed near him. The explosion killed him and the smoke grenade released purple smoke, which poured from the hootch.

A lot of confusion ensued and we didn't know what to do. Unseen NVA were throwing grenades at us, so we decided to get out of their range. The few of us behind the dike backed up to another dike farther behind us; we moved in two groups, with the alternate group laying down covering fire. Bullets zipped over our heads and all around us, but we avoided getting hit. We lay there for about an hour and a half before another of our platoon's squads ran up and joined us.

Whenever one of us moved, which we had to do to return fire, bullets struck the dike near our heads or zipped past. As far as we knew, only two of the men in the hootch were still alive. We could hear one of them yelling that he was hit and needed help. The other, a medic, was waving a flag to let us know he was okay. With the heavy incoming fire, all we could do was return fire where we thought there might be enemy soldiers.

To make matters worse, the enemy began lobbing mortar rounds at us. It looked as though they had us zeroed in, because the rounds were coming closer with each impact. Just when we thought the next one would reach us, the rounds stopped. We surmised that a tree or other obstacle prevented the enemy from aiming at us just right. Or maybe they ran out of rounds.

We lay behind the low dike for a few hours. Because I was exhausted and relaxed by the warm sun, I fell asleep for a few minutes. I was teased about that later.

Dupres Whittington, a likable black guy from Michigan, raised his head in an attempt to identify a target or see what was going on, and a bullet struck his ear, splitting it in two pieces that flopped together. He was in tremendous pain.

"Whitt, do you want me to get you back to the tracks?" I asked him.

"Yeah, I can't stand this," he replied.

"I'll help you," a voice said.

I looked to see who had spoken. Dennis Hackin, better known as Hack, had been lying on the other side of Whittington and also felt badly about the pain he was experiencing.

I glanced in the direction of our tracks. They were across open ground, and I wondered how visible we would be to the enemy during the retreat. If they were lying down, we might be okay. The dikes would provide some cover. Otherwise, we'd be prime targets.

Whittington was lying on his back, holding his head slightly to one side to keep his wound out of the dirt. Hack and I low-crawled a bit in the direction of our tracks, away from the enemy, then reached back, grabbed onto Whittington's fatigue shirt, and pulled. He helped by kicking with his feet. Hack and I continued to low-crawl, with our chests never leaving the ground, then reach back and pull Whittington as far forward as we could, then crawl some more and repeat the process.

It probably took us close to an hour to cover the two hundred or so meters between the dike and our tracks, which were out of immediate danger from the incoming rifle fire. Our medics bandaged

Whittington's ear, gave him something for the pain, and called a dust-off chopper for his medical evacuation.

In the meantime, the medic in the hootch had run to join the others behind the rice paddy dike. After seeing that we had made it back to our tracks, they followed us.

A few guys from Bravo Company joined us at our tracks, having returned when the battle started. Together, we all went back to the rice paddy dike in an attempt to get to the bodies in the hootch, and were once again pinned down by enemy fire.

We had not heard from the one soldier remaining alive in the hootch in some time, and we assumed that he was either unconscious or dead. It was late afternoon, and there wasn't much daylight left. After dark, we would be vulnerable to enemy forces. If we were going to recover any of the bodies, it was now or never.

We decided that four of us, including me, would run up to the hootch and drag back the dead. The others would place heavy covering fire on both sides of the hootch. If we ran directly toward the hootch, we wouldn't be hit by our platoon's fire.

On a signal, we ran as quickly as we could while staying low to avoid being targets for enemy snipers. The fire from our platoon and the soldiers from Bravo Company behind us was deafening.

Upon reaching the hootch, we crashed inside and looked around. There were supposed to be five bodies here but we could see only three of them. Two had been killed by the explosion and the other had been shot in the chest. Lieutenant Williams was inside the door on the left side. The smoke grenade that he had been in the process of throwing when he died was pointed toward him when it went off. From the shoulders up, he wore a purple death mask.

I wondered what had happened to the other two bodies and went through a back doorway to search for them. I had just found them, not too far from the door, when the sound of a machine gun broke the silence and bullets crashed through the thatched walls of the hootch behind me. The enemy machine gunner had been waiting for us to attempt to retrieve the bodies. I dove back inside the hootch. One of my companions was still there, hugging the ground as was I; the others had run back to the dike when the firing began.

Bullets continued passing through the walls over our heads and we lay there among our dead platoon members until the gunner paused in his firing. We then got up and ran back to the dike, successfully rejoining the platoon.

After another half hour or so, we concluded that we would not be able to retrieve the bodies and withdrew. We would have to leave them overnight.

That night, we were uncomfortable knowing that we were safe inside the perimeter while five of our platoon members were lying dead out there in the darkness.

The next day we returned to the site of the battle to make another attempt to retrieve the bodies. Returning to the site of a battle always produced a feeling of dread. The spirit of the enemy somehow lingered there, or that's what it felt like this day. We anticipated receiving heavy enemy fire once again.

We were afraid that the enemy had mutilated the bodies in our absence. We had found mutilated American corpses before. We had been told, although we were not sure if it was true, that some of our enemy believed in reincarnation, and that if someone lost an arm in the trauma that induced death, he would appear in his next life without that limb. We thought that maybe the enemy chopped arms off corpses so that they would be less effective soldiers in their next life.

The morning was calm and quiet, and as we approached we knew instinctively that we were alone. The enemy had gone. We found the bodies just as we had left them.

In addition to Lieutenant Williams, who was twenty-seven when he died, there was my friend Roger Wilson. He had been my assistant gunner on the day that the recoilless rifle I was test-firing blew up. He was twenty-one years old. David Keister was nineteen. Richard Vellance, a sergeant, was twenty. I had thought that Earl Mack was a lot older than I, maybe because he had been in Vietnam longer. He was twenty-one.

We remained in the area for the next two days, blowing up bunkers and policing up weapons, equipment, and supplies. Among the highlights were thirty M16s that the enemy must have taken from American bodies during past battles, two .51-caliber machine guns, and numerous brand new AK-47 assault rifles.

We made contact with a force of undetermined size later in the day, and Solly, who had inherited an M60 machine gun from Sutton, was firing it when he was hit by shrapnel in an arm. He told us later that he thought that the enemy may have been attempting to silence his machine gun and had fired an RPG in his direction.

Lieutenant Marschewski

Lieutenant James Marschewski was working in a battalion staff position when Lt. Ralph Williams was killed by the explosion in the hootch. Marschewski had previously served as a platoon leader with Alpha Company (A Company) and spent some time with us before rotating back to his battalion job. For a while, Hack had served as his RTO. Our current platoon RTO was Lynn Pruitt, from Texas.

The officers in our battalion were aware of how fast our platoon was losing its leaders. During my tour, seven different lieutenants served as our platoon leader and three of them met their death while with us. Because the battalion was running short of officers, Lieutenant Marschewski volunteered to take over our platoon. He joined us in the field shortly after Lieutenant Williams was killed.

Marschewski had played football in college and looked the part of a combat leader. We had become accustomed to brand new second lieutenants arriving to lead our platoon. Because the war in Vietnam was unique, it was normal for new lieutenants to go through a learning and adjustment period before being trusted by the guys. Lieutenant Marschewski was different, having already served six months in the field—considerably longer than most of us.

The first day, it became apparent that he knew what he was doing. He was also nice, stopping to chat with a few of the platoon members when time allowed. He was immediately trusted, liked, and admired.

Shortly after joining our platoon, he wrote a letter home telling his family of his new assignment. He advised them not to worry about him because he felt that his level of experience would help him survive. Through no fault of his own, he lasted five days with our platoon.

Calm Under Fire

During my high school years, I learned that I am seldom startled or panicked. I discovered this one day while I was riding in the back-seat of a friend's car with several other people. My friend was showing off to some of the girls with us and wanted to impress them with how fast he could negotiate corners. He lost control of the car on one corner, and we slid sideways on a collision course with the back end of a black '66 Chevy.

While everyone was screaming, I sat calmly thinking to myself: Yep, we're going to hit the back of that car. Here we go. *Boom.* There's the impact. Is everyone all right? Yeah, it looks like it.

The trait of remaining calm through a crisis served me well in combat. As a result, I could use logic to figure out the best course of action in a battle. In some ways, combat seemed to occur in slow motion.

On February 17, 1968, our company was dispatched to an area where enemy activity had been reported. As we moved out that day, our track was the last in line. We pulled into an assembly area from where the search was to be launched shortly after dawn. The first track pulled off the road to the right and parked at an angle. Each of the other tracks pulled in successively and parked facing in the same direction.

As we pulled into place beside the others, there was an explosion on the side of the track opposite from where I was sitting. Everyone else jumped off and ran to join the remainder of our company at the rear our track, where they had taken cover behind a log in a small depression. I jumped down and stood between our track and the one next to it. I figured that whoever had thrown the grenade, or whatever it was, wouldn't throw another, because everyone except me was gone and they could not know that I remained. I was out of sight.

I reached up, grabbed my web gear from the top of the track, and put it on. I then retrieved my rifle and helmet and began walking toward the others. They were gesturing animatedly for me to hurry and join them. Suddenly, my peripheral vision picked up movement to my right. I glanced over and noticed the head of a man who was standing in a tunnel or spider hole. He was looking directly at me. I was in eye contact with an enemy soldier!

I swung my weapon in his direction and he ducked below ground level. I fired several rounds in his direction and motioned for more guys to join me. Several did, including our platoon sergeant. I walked a little closer to the man as they opened fire, at the same time removing a grenade from my web gear and pulling the pin. I tossed the grenade into the hole, and we joined the others.

I was greeted with slaps on the back. "Way to go, Hayes. You got one."

It sounds strange but we congratulated each other on taking a life. The logic was that each enemy soldier we put out of action increased our chances, and those of our buddies, of returning home safely. Some veterans say that they fought for the flag or for their country. Not so in our unit, or in others where I knew some of the guys. We fought for one another and for our own survival.

In a conventional war, a line separated the two armed forces. Success meant capturing enemy territory and extending the front line forward. Defeat meant losing ground to the enemy and having to retreat. In Vietnam, where there were no front lines, success was measured in terms of how many of them we killed versus how many of us they killed. We counted or estimated bodies after each engagement, under orders, and the number of enemy casualties was reported upward. This data was known as body count. A dead body or the act of seeing an enemy soldier and shooting him was referred to as a confirmed body count. Too often, we simply fired where we knew the enemy was and didn't know the outcome until we inspected the area after the engagement ended.

We spent the remainder of that day in combat. Two more tracks were hit with RPGs, and the enemy threw tear gas at us. The gas was dispersed quickly by the wind, though, and constituted only a minor nuisance. We had a good body count by the end of the day. When we left, phantom jet bombers took over.

That night, we set up in a large ARVN compound. The ARVN unit was shorthanded and was expecting an attack. We had come to reinforce their compound for the night. Our company was dispersed throughout the perimeter, and I ended up sharing a large, comfortable, cool bunker with a Vietnamese soldier. At first, because of the language barrier, we fumbled around with hand signals trying to communicate with each other. Then I heard him say something in French.

"*Vous parle francais, n'est-ce pas?*" I asked.

"*Oui, je parle francais.*"

For the remainder of the evening, we shared stories of our families, using mostly French with a little English, Vietnamese, and hand signals thrown in. He was born in Hanoi and had moved south with his family when the war began because they were Catholic and sympathized with the political views of the south. He showed me his personal weapon, a Thompson submachine gun, an American weapon from World War II. It was the first one I'd ever seen, and he taught me how to load it and break it down. The evening passed peacefully and enjoyably.

After several days in continuous contact with the enemy, our platoon suffered quite a few casualties. We were borderline combat ineffective and thought we would take it easy for a while until replacement troops arrived, but it was not to be.

FIRST BLOOD

On-Line Assault

February 19, 1968, stands out in the memory of our platoon. It coincidentally marked the date of my first wound. By this time, we had been in contact with the enemy for ten consecutive days. The 2d Platoon was down to twenty-two men standing. With two people for each track, that left only fourteen of us available for combat.

Our mission this day was to check out an area where our battalion reconnaissance unit had recently run into a significant enemy force. It was a huge rice paddy with several large wooded areas. As we approached the reported enemy area, we began receiving small-arms fire from a tree line in one of the wooded areas. It was the dry season, so we took cover behind a rice paddy dike and watched as air force jets bombed the wood line.

Time after time, an F-4 Phantom roared in low just above treetop level and dropped a five-hundred-pound bomb or a canister of napalm. The latter would slowly tumble end over end, then erupt in a fireball with reddish orange flames and black smoke rising a hundred feet in the air. We could not understand how anything could live through that. For two hours the bombing continued. We "smoked and joked" behind the rice paddy dike and enjoyed the air show.

When it was over, the company commander, Captain T, sent in our platoon to mop up, or check out what was left. We entered what remained of the woods on line, with the usual ten meters or so separating each of us, with no one too far ahead or behind. If it became necessary to fire, we would be in position to engage the enemy without shooting one another. This also spread us out and allowed us to get a quick look at the entire area.

We stepped over smoking trees that had been knocked down by the bombing, looking for bodies or signs of human activity. We found nothing. The bombing had saturated the area from where we had received fire but had actually covered only about a third of the woods. We approached the end of the bombed area and still didn't find any weapons, bunkers, bodies, equipment, or any other sign of human activity. Lieutenant Marschewski called back to the company commander and told him our status.

The captain's reply consisted of two words, "Keep going."

We continued on line for fifty meters or so beyond the bombed area. I was on the left flank in a small clearing along with Jim Slagle and Billie Barnett when Gallagher, one of the well-liked members of our platoon and one of our veteran soldiers, saw the enemy soldiers we were seeking.

"I see 'em; I see 'em," he said, turning to those near him. "Do you see them?"

And then louder as he opened up with his machine gun, "There they are, there they are."

Heavy enemy fire, including RPGs, machine guns, and small arms, erupted from the woods to our front. Barnett, Slagle, and I knew that remaining in a clearing during a firefight could mean death, so we moved forward to a dike that we could use for cover and concealment.

Gallagher, who was one of the few to identify targets and was firing a machine gun, was one of the NVA's primary targets. He was quickly hit and killed.

During the initial outburst of fire, Lieutenant Marschewski and Pruitt, his RTO, were wounded by what appeared to be a recoilless rifle or an RPG. They were both down, lying in a pool of blood to my right rear, and were not moving.

Slagle, Barnett, and I were wondering what to do when a machine gun began firing from somewhere close to our right. I looked over and saw dust being kicked up by the rounds coming from the barrel of a machine gun about five feet from where I was lying, along the same dike we were using for cover. A well-camouflaged bunker had been dug from the opposite side of the dike against which we were positioned. It was a good thing we had moved forward; otherwise, the machine gun would have been shooting at us, at close range.

I wondered what it was shooting at and looked to the rear. I watched as machine-gun rounds entered the chest of Sam Stewart, who had remained in the clearing where we were when the firing erupted. He took about eighteen rounds in his chest, then stood up and began walking to the rear, toward the rest of the company. He didn't make it; he collapsed to his knees and fell to his left. He was most likely dead by the time he hit the ground.

Another bunker, just like the one to my right, was about fifteen feet farther to the right. These two bunkers had the platoon pinned down, and the three of us were the only ones we could see, and the only ones who could move.

I fired several magazines at the bunker, then reached for a grenade. By this time I had been in quite a few enemy bunkers and had some idea of where I thought the entrance was. Most of the ones I had seen had an L-shaped, trenched entrance in the rear, which allowed access but reduced the chances of shrapnel entering. I pulled the pin of a grenade, got up on my knees, exposing myself to whatever firepower existed from behind or beside the bunker, and tossed the grenade to the other side of the berm where I thought the entrance was.

When the grenade went off, the machine gun stopped firing for about a minute, then resumed. Perhaps the bunker's occupants wondered what the explosion was, or perhaps it had wounded some of them. I couldn't know which.

I pulled the pin on a second grenade and once again aimed for the rear door. This grenade struck some bamboo growing on the top of the bunker, then fell on top of the dike and rolled back down toward the front of the bunker and near us. Fortunately, it came to rest near the firing port of the bunker, but when it exploded it wounded all three of us.

When I saw where the grenade came to rest, I dove to the ground between Barnett and Slagle and the grenade. When it went off, I was hit in the upper right arm and left lower leg. The first sensations I felt were heat and numbness over my entire body, possibly a result of shock to my nervous system. I'll never forget the feeling as the heat and numbness slowly but steadily dissipated from the rest of my body and centered on my arm and leg. It was a weird sensation. Without looking, I knew where my wounds were. Barnett was struck in the wrist and Slagle received an ankle wound.

We yelled that we were hit, but no one came to our assistance or called to us. One of our medics was already dead, and we didn't know if there was another one with us. Moreover, as far as we knew, the other members of our platoon were still pinned down. We looked around but couldn't see anyone except Marschewski and Pruitt, who we assumed were dead. We found out later that our company's executive officer, a first lieutenant named Miller, who had taken charge of the platoon when Marschewski was wounded, had moved the platoon slightly to the right, not realizing that we were over on the left. We were stranded, and there was no sign of the rest of our platoon. The battlefield was momentarily silent.

Because we were almost inside the enemy perimeter and would probably be killed if we stayed there much longer, we decided to try to make it back to the company to get medical attention. We discovered another smaller dike, about thirty feet to our left, running back toward the company. We decided to crawl along it, using it for cover.

Barnett had trouble crawling with his wrist wound and gave me his M79 grenade launcher. As we moved, I fired a couple of grenade rounds. They hit the front of the bunker, but I couldn't tell if any damage had been inflicted. At least it might keep the enemy's heads down long enough for us to get away.

As we made our way toward the low dike, I heard a distinct thump.

"Grenade," I warned the others, and we hit the dirt again.

The grenade didn't go off. Chi-Com grenades were susceptible to damage from moisture. I rose to a crouch and fired a full magazine from my M16, scattering shots over the entire enemy area in hopes of placing a bullet close to whoever had thrown the grenade to discourage them from tossing another one. We then resumed our retreat. We crawled along the small dike until we reached the bombed area, where some of the downed trees provided a bit of cover. We then stood up and hobbled back to the rest of the company, who had stayed put during the contact.

After our wounds were bandaged, we rested against a large rice paddy dike with a few more wounded and waited for the dust-off chopper to come get us. I went into partial shock and felt light-headed from either the shock, loss of blood, or both.

We found out later that, during the battle, someone else had been wounded by a recoilless rifle and was later finished off. A medic named Zale, who had come to his aid, was killed next. One of our sergeants had a little finger shot off. Ordy, who had been taking cover behind a well, was shot in the chest.

Ted Chadwick, from Georgia, whom we called Chad and who would later become one of my best friends in Vietnam, had been to Gallagher's right when the firing began. He ended up near Lieutenant Miller, lying in a ditch with several others. Chadwick was firing his M79 toward the enemy positions when Lieutenant Miller suggested that he fire more to the left, where the heads of some of the enemy troops were popping up. Chad placed several rounds where Lieutenant Miller indicated.

It takes a few seconds to remove the spent shell from an M79 and reload it. Chad was reloading and firing as fast as he could, but he had established a timing pattern that our enemy recognized. After firing for a few minutes, Chad was ready to aim and fire another round. He lifted his head to identify a possible target when a round zipped past, just missing his ear. Chad continued firing but timed his rounds differently.

Some of our tracks had moved up to our right where they could provide supporting fire from behind the berm against which Barnett, Slagle, and I had been lying. Unfortunately, the machine gunners on the tracks didn't know where the rest of our forces were, and some of their rounds hit one of the bunkers or the ground, then bounced and rolled through the ditch where Chad and the others were.

Chad and two other guys crawled through the foliage toward our tracks. When they reached the clearing, they stood up. So they wouldn't be mistaken for the enemy, they yelled profanities toward the tracks. Chad found Captain T and told him that some of our forces were directly in front of the firing tracks. Captain T directed the tracks to cease firing, then he and one or two others went forward to a large termite or anthill. From there, they could apparently see our guys and could place more effective and accurate fire. The captain's RTO was coming forward to the commander's position when he was gunned down and killed.

That day we learned a valuable lesson about the folly of attacking an enemy stronghold with our forces on line. Lieutenant Miller, who had been the platoon leader for our 1st Platoon, realized the danger inherent in this alignment and taught us to go in single file along the sides of open areas rather than walk abreast through them. The unfortunate aspect of attacking in single file is that the entire firepower of the platoon or company can't be engaged without maneuvering into position on line, facing the enemy. The advantage, however, is that only the first two or three men in the column are in serious danger, not the entire unit, if a superior enemy force is met. It was along the sides of open areas where the enemy placed their bunkers. We found that it was much safer to crawl along the bunker line, taking them on one at a time, lobbing grenades in them, rather than assaulting them on line, head on. This would serve us well in the near future, but there would still be times when we would attack on line.

Our remaining platoons retrieved the wounded and the dead, and the company retreated.

By the end of this day, our platoon was down to five men who were combat effective. I would be out of action for a month because of my wounds.

RECUPERATION

The dust-off chopper flew us to Cu Chi, where we were taken to the emergency room of the 12th Evacuation Hospital. We were told to wait our turn. The doctors and staff were attending to wounded soldiers from another battle that had occurred that day. Those who were wounded more severely than we were naturally received higher priority for medical attention. We could afford to wait a while; some of the others could not and may have died without prompt attention. The ones who the medical staff thought would die anyway, were worked on last, if they survived.

We waited for four hours. Slagle and I found crutches and hobbled around a little. Of the three of us, Barnett was operated on first. As a doctor worked on his wrist, Slagle and I stood nearby, leaning on our crutches.

"Does it hurt much?" I asked Barnett.

"It hurts only when I laugh."

So Slagle and I proceeded to make him laugh for the rest of the time he was being operated on.

While we were standing there, we couldn't help looking around at others who were having wounds cared for. Behind Barnett was a soldier lying on a narrow bed with a tray, similar to those that hospital meals are served on, over his lower body. He had an abdominal wound, and the doctor treating him had spread out his intestines on the tray and was sorting through them.

The doctor was humming to himself. When he found a damaged section, he would say, "Here's a bad part," and make two exaggerated chops with an instrument that looked like a meat cleaver, one on either end of the damaged section. Then he dropped the chopped-off portion into a bucket on the floor and sewed the two good ends together. He repeated this four or five times. We were astounded to see that the GI was conscious and was calmly watching the doctor work on his own intestines. He was probably drugged up as well as locally anesthetized.

Another soldier had been wounded in the penis and a doctor was operating on him. This was a wound that all soldiers hoped to avoid. Legs, fine, but not that!

The process of having my wounds treated was more painful than the initial infliction, which had been a little worse than that of an intense bee sting. None of my wounds, however, had broken any bone, and all were superficial or non-life threatening.

To begin the process, an x-ray was taken to determine the location of any shrapnel, but they were taken from only one angle. Accordingly, the doctor and medics knew which portion of my anatomy held shrapnel, but did not know how far down it was.

Next, lidocaine, a local anesthetic, was injected right into the raw tissue on the inside of the wound. This really stung badly. After several minutes, in order to test if the area was numb enough to proceed, the doctor poked the tissue adjacent to the wound with a needle, inserting it about a half inch with each jab.

"Can you feel that?" he would ask.

"Yeah, that hurts!"

The doc would leave and return after a few more minutes had elapsed and repeat this process until I couldn't feel the needle any longer.

Surgery would then begin by cutting away dead tissue and removing foreign objects such as fabric from my uniform that would be carried into the wound along with the projectiles. This was performed with surgical scissors and most likely involved cutting away at least some live tissue along with the dead.

Next, a probe, which looked like a knitting needle, was inserted into the wound in an attempt to find and follow the channel created by the shrapnel. This was usually unsuccessful because shrapnel tends to turn corners and often breaks into several pieces, which mine had done. The individual pieces took different paths. In all, according to the x-rays, I had five small pieces of shrapnel between my upper right arm and left lower leg.

If the shrapnel could be found, it was removed. If not, it stayed put. The latter was the more frequent occurrence; one of the doctors told me that three-quarters of all shrapnel stays in. Digging a new hole in my arm or leg would, in effect, be the same as wounding me again, more severely, so my shrapnel stayed put.

The last step of the operation was to clean the wound as thoroughly as possible and try to eliminate any bacteria and/or fungi, not an easy task in the tropics. This was accomplished by inserting a sterile bandage or cloth that had been soaked with hydrogen peroxide into the wound, then twisting it, which wrung out the bandage like a dishrag. Despite the anesthetic, that hurt the most.

Finally, the wound was bandaged. Stitches were not used in this tropical climate, with its huge population of bacteria and fungi, until about three days after initial treatment, as a precaution against infection. If the wound was clean and sterile after three days, it was assumed that the wound would not become infected and could be safely closed.

As the injury on the back side of my upper right arm was being worked on, I was lying on a metal operating table on my stomach. Barnett and Slagle weren't around anymore. Barnett was probably done by that time, and Slagle was undergoing surgery elsewhere. To take my mind off the discomfort, I tried to engage the doctor in conversation.

"How long have you been in-country, Doc?"

"Doc? I'm not a doctor; I'm a mechanic. I just came over to help out because they're busy."

Nice guy.

Later he asked, "Know what I'm doing now?"

"No." I couldn't feel anything.

"I'm sticking my finger in the hole in your arm."

I looked over my shoulder and saw that his index finger was inserted into the small hole on the back of my upper arm up to his first knuckle. He was twisting his hand, rotating his finger back and forth inside my arm. I guess doctors had to have a sense of humor too. And mechanics, or whatever.

I was on the operating table for four hours. When I was patched up, I was returned to our company area about ten o'clock that night. Twice a day for the next two days, we returned to the medical facility to have our bandages changed and our wounds cleaned. On the third day, our wounds, which were uninfected, were stitched closed. After that, the dressings were changed daily until our wounds were healed.

During our recuperation, the Cu Chi base camp was mortared often. During the first two weeks we spent there, mortar rounds fell as many as six times on many nights. We assumed that these were harassment rounds fired to interrupt our rest and make us less effective soldiers. They didn't do much damage, but each time they fell, GIs dashed from their hootches and dove into bunkers built for protection during such attacks.

A few guys slept in the bunkers and made them their homes, so there were bunks to sit on during the mortar and rocket attacks. Usually the bunkers held so many people that some had to sit on the dirt floor or stand until the incoming rounds stopped falling.

Most of us preferred to sleep aboveground in the platoon hootches. The bunkers were damp and smelled like mildew. Aboveground, at least there might be a breeze, and it was usually less humid.

Because of the location of my wounds, movement was slow and painful. Rising from a prone position took several minutes. Not having the use of my lower leg and arm muscles made me realize how much I normally depended on them. I had to do everything with my left hand, and little things such as buttoning my uniform shirt became a major chore. Getting around was worse. I couldn't walk because of my leg wound. I couldn't use a crutch under my right arm because of that wound. The only option was to move about by using a single crutch under my left arm and hopping on my right foot. The going was slow. It took me twenty minutes to reach the mess hall, normally less than a five-minute walk. As for mortar attacks, they were usually over by the time I got on my feet or was just barely out of our hootch. On one of these attempts to reach the bunker, I moved faster than I knew I should and felt my wounds rip open. During my recovery, when mortars fell and the troops would run out of the hootch on their way to a bunker, I was left to fend for myself. One friend, however, stayed with me to help get me to the bunker. He would hold on to my left, unwounded arm and shoulder and help me walk. He did so without regard for his own safety. It was a display of bravery and friendship.

A few weeks later, that friend was heading to Sydney, Australia, for rest and relaxation (R and R). Because he didn't have any civilian clothes, he borrowed the set that I kept in my duffel bag, and we said good-bye. R and R lasts a week, but that time elapsed and my friend had not returned. After a few days, he was reported absent without leave (AWOL). We never saw him again. But we received a report from a fellow soldier who also took R and R in Australia that my friend was driving a jeep for a kangaroo hunter and shacking up with his daughter. We had no way of confirming the rumor, but we liked to think it was true. Because he had helped me in my time of need, I didn't mind losing the only set of civilian clothes I had.

23 Feb 68

Dear Mom,

My arm and leg are still sore but getting better. Yesterday I got stitches. The only thing that hurt was the pain killing shot. They put it right in the wound. The doc said, "Here comes a little needle." Then I felt all that pain & said, "Little?" He said, "Well, it's the smallest we've got." I said, "Then you're putting that stuff in like you're pumping gas."

Us 3 guys who were hit together haven't stopped laughing since we got hit.

Whenever you hear of the 25th Division northwest of Saigon, that's us [in response to a question]. When I was hit, 14 of us were going in against an unknown size which they didn't think would be in fighting condition after the air strikes, but there were 400 of them waiting for us. Well, I got 4 of them that I know of.

A friend of mine got a bullet between the eyes. He was lying down reloading his M-16 and a bullet hit the 16 and split. Part of it lodged in the gap between his eyes & the rest in his temple. He's pretty lucky he's alive. Another guy in here was

firing a 50 cal. machine gun & it wasn't timed right. It tried
to put 2 rounds in the chamber at the same time and one
went off & got him in the leg. He's hurt about as bad as me.
    I guess I better sign off. Write soon, Love, Roger

The Company Area

Our company area was located in the northeast corner of the base
camp at Cu Chi. It consisted of two rows of hootches used as barracks, an outdoor shower, the headquarters or charge of quarters
(CQ) room, a motor pool for the tracks, and a mess hall, which we
shared with the other companies in the battalion. One of the
hootches was used as our supply room.

The hootches were tents placed on wooden platforms raised
about a foot above the ground. The lower portions of the walls were
built of wood. The upper portions were canvas, which could be
rolled up to increase air circulation when there was a breeze.
Around each hootch was a low wall of sandbags, which provided
some protection from mortar and rocket fire for anyone lying on
their cots. While standing up, we were above the level of the sandbags.

Wooden walkways provided access to the hootches, company
headquarters, supply tent, and showers. Placed by some of the soldiers when the division established the base camp in 1966, the
walkways allowed access to facilities without having to tramp
through the mud during the rainy season. The soldiers who chose
not to use the walkways had gooey mud packed to their boots and
tracked it inside the hootches.

Our company did not spend a lot of time in Cu Chi during the
year I was in Vietnam. While we recuperated from our wounds, we
did not see much of the company. They were working out of smaller
battalion or brigade base camps at Tay Ninh or Dau Tieng, or were
out in the boonies operating from a company or battalion perimeter. Charlie Company set an all-time division record during this period for time spent in the field. In all, they were out for 170 days,
close to six months, from around Thanksgiving until May. We had

been in Cu Chi for a few hours prior to being ordered down to the Saigon area, but because we hadn't spent the night, I guess that didn't count.

Our company was still making contact with the enemy. A major battle occurred on February 27 during which one of our platoon's squad leaders, Sgt. Patricio Maldonado Jr., was killed. He was twenty-four years old.

During the month we spent recuperating from our wounds in Cu Chi, we settled into a temporary life in the rear. We didn't have electricity in our hootches, so I bought a kerosene lamp from a Cu Chi street vendor. Afterward, my bunk became a gathering place after dark because I had the only light in our hootch, and my footlocker became a center of activity for card games and rap sessions. We didn't have kerosene, so I scrounged diesel fuel from the motor pool. It worked fine in the kerosene lamp.

Another favorite evening activity was attending a movie at a nearby artillery unit. The movies were shown in an empty field next to the unit. We sat on the ground in front of the screen, a bedsheet stretched across two poles inserted into the ground. The movies were old and not terribly exciting, but they attracted a large crowd. They provided a good diversion and helped pass the time. After dark, it cooled down enough to make these evenings at the movies an enjoyable experience. The projector whirred into action and the screen showed images of a world that we had almost forgotten. The movies were mostly whodunits with a few romantic comedies. It was a good form of escapism, although it sometimes exacerbated the feeling of homesickness.

Bunker Guard

When our wounds had healed sufficiently to enable us to move around a little, we were placed on perimeter bunker guard. We were trucked out to the base camp's perimeter with all of our combat gear and crutches. We performed guard duty in the two-story sandbag bunkers along the fortified perimeter, just as I had back in October during the week prior to joining the company in the field.

We began around suppertime, remained all evening, and were picked up the next morning about seven o'clock and taken back to our company area.

Three of us would be assigned to each bunker during the evenings and we would sit and talk until we got sleepy, then took turns on guard duty throughout the night.

The huge perimeter bunkers at Cu Chi lasted only about a year. The sun and pounding rain weakened the fabric of the sandbags, and they eventually began to leak the soil they were filled with. The bunkers were then knocked over with a bulldozer and new ones were built on top of the rubble.

The bunkers were made by building a heavy wooden frame that looked like two cubes stacked on top of each other, then surrounding the frame with thousands of sandbags placed row upon row in layers, four or five sandbags or more in thickness at some points. I was sure that the bunkers could survive a direct hit from mortar or rocket rounds. A ladder provided access to the upper level, which was used during the daytime because it afforded a better view and was more apt to catch a breeze.

Rice rats, the world's largest rats, some as large as domestic cats, lived in the underground spaces and air pockets created by the debris from previous bunkers. Being nocturnal, the rats came out at night. They sometimes walked over our feet, brushing against our pant legs as we stood peering through the firing port. The first time that happened to me, I had no idea what it was.

"What the hell . . . something just brushed against my pant leg."

"That's just a rat," one of my bunker mates explained.

There were stories of guys being bitten by these rats. One account, the veracity of which we never determined, was that a rat jumped from above onto the chest of a GI while he was sleeping.

When there was a full moon, some of the guys sat on top of the bunker with their M16s and waited for the rats to come out, then shot at them. I did this myself on a few occasions, but the rats never showed themselves. Unfortunately, rifle fire from the perimeter produced calls on the field phone from the base camp's interior. Officers and senior NCOs got nervous, wondering if the camp was under attack when they heard firing.

"Hey, what's going on out there? Are you under attack?"

"Naw, we're just shooting at rats."

"Well, cut that out."

We were told that we could shoot only at the enemy. To us, the rats *were* the enemy.

A dirt road headed east from the back side of Cu Chi. About a half mile out, the road crossed a bridge that had been built over a creek. The enemy must have previously booby-trapped the bridge or blown it up, because two bunkers intended for security guards had been placed near the bridge. The GIs called the place Ann-Margret, who had visited Cu Chi with Bob Hope's Christmas show. I didn't understand the connection, unless it had something to do with the similarities in topography between the two bunkers and Ms. Margret. In any event, some of us were periodically assigned guard duty at Ann-Margret.

Slagle, Barnett, and I spent a few nights out there in one of the bunkers while two of us were on crutches. Our orders were that if we sustained an enemy attack and couldn't hold them, we were to delay them as long as possible, then make it back into Cu Chi as best we could. On crutches. We made a lot of jokes about not surviving a retreat to the main camp. Hobbling along on crutches, we would have been gunned down in a matter of moments. I guess that's the humor of men at war. We couldn't do much about the predicaments in which we often found ourselves, so we might as well laugh about them. It helped relieve the stress. Making Barnett laugh while his wrist was being operated on was probably prompted by the same reasons, even though laughing had caused him pain.

About a week after I was hit, I got a jeep ride into the village of Cu Chi, where I bought a guitar from a street vendor. I paid only twelve dollars for it, but it played well and sounded only a little tinny. It gave me something to do.

On February 24, I took my first shower since being wounded, and I had been without a good bath for some time prior to that. Showering was difficult because of my wounds, but I felt great afterward.

The next day, Barnett went on R and R to Taipei, leaving Slagle and I to make cracks at each other. Also in the rear was my friend Bob Ordy, who had taken a machine-gun round in the chest on

February 19, during the same battle in which Barnett, Slagle, and I were wounded. During his recovery, he was a regular at the card games at my bunk, and we went to a few movies and the PX together.

On February 26, my first squad leader, who had been transferred to another platoon, was killed by a mortar round. He had been sleeping outside the bunker, and the first round landed close enough to mortally wound him. We always assumed that we would hear the rounds exploding before any of them landed close enough to injure or kill us. This attitude of "it can't happen to me" led to high-risk behavior, such as sleeping aboveground without protection in a war zone. We all did things like that, though. It was partly our age and partly human nature. My friend died in the hospital the day after he was wounded.

By February 28, I could put some weight on my left leg and had almost full use of my arm, although it was a little stiff and sore. My leg took a lot longer to heal, perhaps because walking on it hampered the healing process. The wound would still be open when I returned to the field.

The enemy began to mortar our division base camp more frequently. Upon arriving back in October, I was told that mortars dropped into Cu Chi only once or twice a month. This had changed, probably due to the ongoing enemy offensive. We were mortared five out of the first nine days we spent during our recuperation period. On some of the nights, the enemy dropped in three or four rounds, then waited a bit and did it again. One night we were mortared five times; on another, we received two mortar attacks and two rocket attacks. Most of the mortars were 60mm, smaller than those used by the American forces and more easily moved from place to place. The rockets, which didn't require a heavy mortar tube and base plate, were significantly larger, up to 122mm. Mortars and rockets made a different sound coming in. Mortar rounds had a telltale whistle caused by air passing over or through the fins on the back of the round. The larger rockets made a whooshing whine. When rockets landed, the explosion was much more forceful than the *crump* of the smaller mortars.

1 Mar 68

Dear Mom,

This morning my buddy with the wounded foot said, "Hey Hayes, there's blood running down your leg." I looked & he said, "April Fool!" Then he stopped and said, "Wrong month." He's from Tennessee and named James Slagle.

Yesterday I had my stitches out. My arm healed up nicely but they goofed when they sewed up my leg. When they took out the stitches, the wound was just like it was before they put any in. It will heal, but not as fast. They're not going to do it over again cause it's a little infected. In 30 minutes I'm going to go get the dressings changed. This afternoon, I'm going with Slagle to the PX.

We were chased out of bed by mortars 3 times last night. At least here in Cu Chi we get 3 hot meals a day. Always some kind of meat & potatoes with vegetables & usually cake or ice cream.

I just got 2 letters from you, so I'll answer them. I got the kerosene lamp today. I'm writing by it now.

They didn't sew me up the night they operated in order to wait & see if infection would set in. I had 5 stitches in my arm & 4 in my leg. They're both about an inch long. The one on the leg is a little shorter. It never did hurt except when they gave me the pain killing shots before operating. Then when they were done they poured hydrogen peroxide in the hole and pressed it in with a gauze pad. That hurt! The next few days I could hardly raise my arm. Then I got it up far enough to play guitar. Now I can do almost anything with it except reach all the way up and on the left side by my shoulder. There was no bone damage, I don't think.

The wound on my right arm is about halfway between my elbow and shoulder. The one on my left leg is on the back side just where the top of my boot comes, in fact, it went through my boot about ½ inch from the top. When we started out fighting we had 29 men. But some were already back here taking care of financial matters & some slightly injured

& some on R&R. We had 5 left after I got hit. All in all, there were 10 of the old ones left, I think.

The Vietnamese guy I made friends with in Saigon didn't invite me back, but he knows that I can't come drop in on him any time. I'll stop by if I'm ever in the area. Besides, he has a real cute and nice daughter.

I don't know very much Vietnamese, just a few words. Us GIs know barely enough Vietnamese words, & the people here, especially the kids, can speak some English.

Write again soon. Roger

Base Camp Details

While not on bunker duty, we found that it was advantageous to learn routines of the company in the rear. At about the same time each morning, a sergeant walked through the hootches looking for men to whom he could assign details. Most of the guys learned to stay away from the company area during these times. A walk to the PX, for example, at ten in the morning was good timing. Someone had to do the work, however, and none of us escaped it indefinitely.

One of the daytime duties to which we were periodically assigned entailed what was referred to throughout all American installations in Vietnam as shit burning detail. There was no sewer system in the villages and hamlets, and even had there been we would not have been able to take advantage of it. Our base camps and perimeters were intentionally established away from heavily populated areas.

The civilians in larger villages and towns maintained a sewage trench running along the outer borders of their backyards, some with feeder trenches extending toward their dwelling. People would defecate in these trenches, and the monsoon rains would wash it away. During the dry season, they collected some of it, along with dung from their livestock, to fertilize their rice paddies.

We did things a little differently in our base camps. Latrines consisted of freestanding wooden structures with hinged openings that flipped up on the lower back side. Fifty-five-gallon drums were cut in half, and each portion was inserted beneath one of the holes.

Many of the latrines had three or four holes. Every few days, the drums would become full and the contents would need to be disposed of. Because of the hazards of contamination and/or pollution, and because there was nothing else to do with human waste, it was burned.

On several occasions, I and a fellow assignee would be sent to "burn the shit." We would lift the hatches in the back of the latrine; fasten them with the hook and eyelets on the side of the building or, more commonly, prop them up with a stick or two-by-four; and slide out the drums. It was especially tedious if they were full.

For some reason, all of the latrines had a raised floor that held the drums. There was no good way to pull them out and negotiate the six-inch or so drop while keeping the stuff from slopping all over us. Most GIs developed a technique that consisted of hunching over, then pulling out the drums while simultaneously scooting backward, out of the way of the spillage. If this maneuver were pantomimed away from the latrines, even years after the war, most GIs would recognize it instantly.

Once the drums were safely outside, it was time to light the fire. A five-gallon drum of diesel fuel was kept near each latrine. Some of the fuel was poured onto the fetid mixture, then set on fire with burning toilet paper. The tubs often contained maggots, which emitted a high-pitched squeaking noise as they burned. Pillars of black smoke rose high into the sky on days with little wind. From a helicopter these smoke trails could be seen for miles. I wondered if some of the pilots ever used them for navigational purposes. Our enemy certainly could use them for aiming their mortars and rockets.

Once the fire was well under way, we stood out of the way of the smoke and odor and waited for the flames to die down. Then we approached from upwind to judge how much of the waste had been disposed of. One burning was never enough, so we waited for the remains to cool a little, then stirred them around and poured in more diesel fuel. This process was usually repeated two or three times, until there was sufficient room in the tubs for a few more days of use.

There was a legend about a couple of guys on shit-burning detail who let the tubs get so full that they couldn't be hauled out of the back of the latrine without the contents spilling on them. The men solved the dilemma by burning the latrine to the ground. Sounded logical to us.

During our recuperation period in Cu Chi, our company commander, who was processing out of our company, stopped by our hootch, sat on the end of one of the bunks, and chatted with us for about twenty minutes. We liked Captain T, whose real name was John Theologos. All of us had been wounded while he was our CO, and he expressed gratitude for our service under his command. We were sorry to see him go. He was admired by the troops of C Company, both for his leadership in battle and because he seemed to care about the GIs under his command.

Captain T transferred to a battalion staff position, where for a short time he was our operations officer, or S-3. In a previous assignment, he was a G-3 (brigade operations officer) and coordinated air forces. Because of that, he served for a short time in Phu Bai as part of the Provisional Corps Headquarters, which was formed to support the Khe Sanh operation. From there, he was assigned to the air force 3d Tactical Fighter Wing at Bien Hoa, near Saigon, to coordinate army tactical air support operations.

Captain T had served previously in Vietnam, in 1963. During that time, he adopted a baby Vietnamese girl from an orphanage in Saigon. While he was our company commander a few years later, he kept an eye out for medical supplies or other material that we captured or discovered after overrunning an enemy position. If he thought that they might be useful to the orphanage where he had adopted his daughter, he policed them up and stored them inside his track. When he had a few free days, such as during a temporary stand-down, he would borrow a deuce-and-a-half truck and, with the help of several of Charlie Company's soldiers, would load the supplies and travel to Saigon to deliver them to the orphanage.

During one such visit, the folks at the orphanage talked him into adopting a second baby girl. He picked one out and began the paperwork process.

Enter the 1968 Tet Offensive, when an NVA regiment utilized the orphanage as its headquarters. The women who operated the facility rushed into the streets carrying children and handing them to passersby with quick instructions to either keep them or deliver them later to another orphanage. The women had concluded that the orphanage would become engulfed in the ensuing battle and feared for the children's lives.

When things calmed down a little and Captain T was able to return to the orphanage, his new daughter was gone, and no one knew where she had ended up. After returning to Bien Hoa, he searched orphanages in the Saigon area and surrounding villages during his free time while serving with the 3d Tactical Fighter Wing. He eventually found his daughter, Lien, in the dust on the floor of an orphanage and was successful in getting the adoption process back on track. When he left Vietnam, she went home with him.

Captain T served a third tour in Vietnam in 1973. As such, he was one of the first as well as one of the last Americans sent to Vietnam, and was there during the height of the military buildup and the time of the most intense fighting. Quite a record.

By March 12, the wound on the back of my right upper arm had healed nicely and no longer required a bandage. My left foot had swollen up when I was hit and it remained so. The wound on my leg remained open for quite a while. My mom had asked how long I was in the hospital after having my wounds treated. I explained that I hadn't been in the hospital at all. I never even saw a nurse. A half hour after leaving the operating table, I was back in our company area.

Barnett, Slagle, and I continued to be assigned bunker guard on the perimeter and often performed that duty on successive days or nights. Usually, we were in the same bunker, which was good. We were all hardened combat veterans and felt confident that each of us could hold our own in a firefight with the enemy. In addition, we were friends and we continued to make one another laugh, which was a pleasant way to pass the time.

A few guys on guard in some of the other bunkers had been caught asleep and, according to the rumor mill, were receiving courts-martial. We didn't worry about falling asleep, though. Compared to time in the field, during which we never received enough sleep, we were fully rested here in the rear. It was easy to remain awake during our shifts.

On March 12, it was determined that I would return to the field in another four days. The decision was based on how my wounds were healing and how I felt. Because the wound on my leg had still not closed, I remained in the rear a few days beyond the estimated return to my company.

After a month, to the day, of recuperation, my wounds had healed sufficiently for me to rejoin the company. It was operating east of Cu Chi, near the Saigon River, an area that I had not yet seen.

When I returned to the company, I was placed in a different squad. I was now in 23, meaning 2d Platoon, 3d Squad. Our squad leader was Andy Gimma, a dark-haired, good-looking, and experienced Nam soldier from Connecticut with ten months in-country. He was a patient and understanding leader, and we had a lot of respect for him. Everyone in our squad got along pretty well, and we were a tight, effective unit. Each of us knew what had to be done, and we all pitched in.

I was named the second in charge of the squad, the Alpha Team leader. Supposedly, each squad was to have an Alpha Team and a Bravo Team, but in actuality we didn't use the two-team system. It was designed to enable more effective movement while under fire. One team would lay down a base of covering fire and the other would maneuver, moving either forward, to the rear, or toward one of the flanks. Once that team was in place, it would begin firing while the other team moved. These were some of the World War II tactics that we were taught in training but didn't use. We functioned usually as a platoon and utilized these tactics to some extent, but with squads rather than fire teams doing the maneuvering.

For some reason, we kept the designation of Alpha Team leader as the squad's second in charge. A more appropriate term was "assistant squad leader."

On March 22, we were in the Hobo Woods east of Cu Chi near the Saigon River. We remained in our perimeter throughout the day. My leg wound, which was slow to heal, was infected, and I had it cleaned and bandaged.

The next day, I received orders promoting me to specialist fourth class. I was no longer a private. Two more of our platoon made it too; one of them was my buddy Jim Slagle, who was the Alpha Team leader on 21, my old squad. Barnett, due to go home any day, was already a specialist fourth class.

The rumor was that we would go to either Cu Chi or Trang Bang within the next few days. This rumor turned out to be true. The company moved out on March 24 but maintained the perimeter. Those of us who were on LP the previous night stayed behind to man the perimeter. I spent the day cleaning our squad's area and several of our weapons, including the .50 and its tripod. During the day, we heard VC or NVA over our platoon's radio frequency.

The company made contact near Trang Bang beginning on March 25 and was engaged in combat for three days straight. During that time, I remained in the company perimeter in the Hobo Woods.

Billie Barnett completed his tour and left Vietnam about the time that Slagle and I returned to the company. Jimmy Sutton, who I considered to be my teacher, also went home in March. We were glad to see them make it out of the country. When Sutton left, Solly took over his squad.

My first wound had been inflicted on February 19. I was wounded three more times, the last injury occurring on August 19, exactly six months to the day after my first. As a child I had repeatedly dreamed that I would be killed in a war when I was twenty-one. I turned twenty-one three days after my first wound. I thought this was bizarre until one day I thought about world events that were transpiring when I was a child. I remember playing on the floor with my brother and sister in the living room and our parents imploring us to be quiet when the news came on the radio at the top of each hour. The newscasts during some of those years included coverage of the Korean War. My mother probably told me that the war was fought by young men who were twenty-one, which perhaps manifested itself through my dreams. I felt better after making that connection.

The Purple Heart is the oldest American military award. Because I had been wounded, I received one. The medal was initiated by Gen. George Washington during the Revolutionary War as an "award of merit." It was not until World War II that it became a medal for wounds received in contact with the enemy. The wound did not have to be inflicted directly by the enemy, just while in contact with them. There are several interesting stories describing incidents that led to the award of a Purple Heart. My favorite story involves a mortar attack.

Once while the company was in Cu Chi on a two- or three-day stand-down, a time for rest and replenishing supplies and equipment, a Vietnamese man who had been employed by the army and who worked inside the base camp was observed pacing off the distances between buildings and hootches in our company area. The man was suspected of making a map of our area for use by our enemy in aiming mortars or for an attack of some kind, and he was apprehended. To be safe, though, in the event that the suspect's handiwork had already been turned over to Viet Cong forces, the company was moved to temporary quarters, which consisted of an open field. We dug several bunkers for protection in case of incoming mortar or rocket rounds, and slept on the open ground.

One soldier from our platoon didn't want to have to rush into the bunker in the event of an enemy attack, and chose to sleep in one of the bunkers. Because it was stuffy underground, he slept on an angle with his head near the corner entrance where he could get a breath of fresh air on occasion. The remainder of the company slept outside, where it was cooler with a better chance of a breeze.

In the middle of the night, mortar rounds began dropping nearby, and the guy sleeping inside the bunker did not hear them. Eight soldiers dove into the bunker at the same time, landing on top of the poor GI sleeping inside. He received a brain concussion and awoke the next day in a field hospital. He was awarded a Purple Heart. To my knowledge, this was the only occurrence of someone earning the medal without being conscious during the attack or while sustaining the injury that made him eligible for the honor. We thought it was great.

On March 28, the company returned from Trang Bang with a body count of more than 240. The three-day battle had been intense. There was still enemy activity in the area, and we had been designated as a reaction force for one of our sister companies that was in light contact not far from our location.

We were approaching the end of the dry season and were anticipating rain beginning sometime in April. We had become accustomed to being dry, but the rain would cut down some of the dust. On the negative side, it would also produce more mud than we liked.

The Animal Inside

Phil Strittmatter, a buddy from another squad in our platoon, became our most trusted and relied upon M60 machine gunner. He had a quick wit and an easy laugh, and he got along well with all members of our platoon. We could rely on him in combat and as a good friend. On evenings when we were inside the perimeter, while not on an ambush patrol or an LP, and when there was a bright moon, several of us—including Stritt, as we called him—played cards on top of one of the bunkers. The moonlight was bright enough to enable reading, writing letters, cleaning weapons, and lots of other activities that can take place in low light conditions. We played cards for money, but the wagers were kept small enough to avoid hard feelings, which we could ill afford. During these games, between 9:00 and 10:30 P.M. or so, the heat of the day would have dissipated, leaving us more comfortable. We would play cards with friends and enjoy a soft drink or beer. These were relaxing and enjoyable evenings.

One day after setting up a new company perimeter, Stritt and I were returning from a daytime patrol and noticed the body of an enemy soldier in a gully not far outside the wire. We decided to cut off the dead guy's head and display it dangling from a stick in front of our track as a warning signal the next time we drove through a village that we suspected of being a "VC village," one that aided or housed the enemy. What can I say? War brings out the animal in each of us.

A few days later, we spent the afternoon inside the perimeter rather than out on an operation. We decided this would be a good time to execute our plan. Stritt retrieved the asbestos gloves that he kept for handling machine-gun barrels, which would occasionally get so hot that they were in danger of bending and had to be changed. We armed ourselves with our weapons, a bayonet, and Stritt's large hunting knife, the latter two of which we planned to use to detach the head.

One of our company's brand new second lieutenants noticed us walking through the perimeter. We made an unusual sight, with Stritt wearing big, heavy gloves in the tropical heat and humidity, and both of us carrying large knives. The lieutenant was new but wise enough to figure out that we were up to something unusual, and he followed us.

We crouched over the body, with Stritt on one side and me on the other, not sure whether we wanted to go through with this gruesome task. Stritt placed the blade of the hunting knife on the neck of the corpse and began a slow sawing motion. He didn't exert enough pressure to break the skin, only enough to make it move back and forth under the blade. We were going to go slow and see how distasteful this procedure would become, leaving open our option to change our minds.

"Hey, what are you guys doing down there?"

We looked up to see the lieutenant watching us from above the gully.

"We're cutting this guy's head off, sir," I replied, as if it was an everyday occasion and completely normal.

"Get away from there," he ordered.

I'm not sure if we would have gone through with our grizzly act had the lieutenant not broken it up, but we returned to the perimeter relieved that the decision had been made for us. I never found out what the lieutenant thought of our actions, but, being new, he must have wondered just what type of unit he had been assigned to.

On the last day of March, a week and a half after I rejoined the company, we were providing security for a unit of the Corps of Engineers, which was bulldozing a large portion of the tropical rain forest in the Iron Triangle, an enemy stronghold southeast of Tay Ninh and north of Cu Chi dating back to the 1940s and the days of

the Viet Minh. The engineers' mission was to knock down the cover
provided by the forest to rid the enemy of its use as concealment.

Hack, who had been in the platoon when I arrived, was now our
driver. Like the other good drivers, he had developed a knack for
selecting the safest course. But on this day, we were driving in a cir-
cuit, traveling in large ovals around the bulldozers for the purpose
of providing a buffer between the engineers and any enemy who
happened to be around. Because the bulldozers were moving, our
route changed with each revolution, and we couldn't employ our
usual method of following the tracks made by the vehicle ahead of
us. It was uncomfortable riding on the tracks, bouncing over the un-
even terrain, but it could have been worse. It beat sweeps that we
conducted on foot over long distances in the heat.

During late morning, we heard the boom of an explosion. We
heard radio transmissions that indicated that track 22, 2d Platoon,
2d Squad, which had already hit eight mines, just hit another one.
We also heard that there were wounded. Because the guys in that
track were all close friends of ours, Hack made a beeline for the
source of the explosion so we could aid our comrades. When he did
so, he abandoned all caution.

I was riding on the top of the track on the right side just behind
the large, open cargo hatch, with my legs dangling inside. Andy
Gimma had jumped down inside to get something and was in the
process of climbing out when suddenly there was a tremendous explosion. My view became completely filled with dark smoke; orange
flame protruded upward into the smoke and illuminated it from the
inside, making it appear more brown. I had the sensation of
floating through the air; after a few seconds, I landed hard on the
ground. Shortly afterward, Andy landed on top of me. Andy
thought that he had landed on a corpse, because my muscles were
relaxed and my body was soft. We grabbed each other, stood up, and
made our way to fresh air, blinking out the smoke. Hack came out
next. Two more emerged from the dense smoke on the opposite
side of the track.

Guffey was a thin, blonde member of our platoon who looked
younger than the rest of us; because of this, we considered him al-

most like a little brother. He had been riding in the turret behind the machine gun when we hit the mine, and he took a wild ride as the turret flew straight up into the air and landed about fifteen feet away, miraculously never turning over. After landing, Guffey stood up and walked away, complaining of nothing more than a sore butt. Had the turret rotated in the air, Guffey would have been in trouble.

Some of our guys were wounded, including Hack, who had been driving from inside the driver's hatch. He was momentarily disoriented and lost his hearing for a while. Everyone who was on the track was stunned.

As we were evacuating our wounded, the engineers for whom we were providing protection stood nearby and watched. They wouldn't come over to help, presumably because they were apprehensive about another mine detonating. We didn't even consider this possibility, though, because the mine we hit was an antitank device, not capable of detonating under the weight of a man. We could have jumped up and down on it without setting it off. Nevertheless, the engineers, most of whom were NCOs, did not come near. We were not very fond of them after they refused to help us. Our wounded had to evacuate the other wounded while the engineers watched from a safe distance.

As I was helping someone limp away, someone else said, "Hey, Hayes, there's blood running down your left arm."

I hadn't felt any pain, but after helping my wounded comrade get to a comfortable position on the ground where the medics could treat him, I rolled up my sleeve to inspect the damage. I found a small, clean laceration near my elbow. I had been wounded.

As a result, I was evacuated by dust-off helicopter, along with eight others from the 2d Platoon, and taken to the rear once again. The wound was x-rayed but showed no shrapnel, and my elbow was bandaged.

After I and the other eight soldiers were evacuated to the rear, only eleven of our platoon members were left in the field. Fortunately, some of us returned to duty a few days later. Andy had received a cut over an eye. The other two members of our squad were shaken but otherwise unhurt. We were fortunate.

We were lucky that our track was powered by diesel fuel and not gasoline. Otherwise, most of us, especially Hack, who was inside the driver's hatch, would not have survived.

Whenever one of us showed up in the rear, someone took the opportunity to examine our shot records, a card that shows what inoculations we received and the dates they were administered. It was discovered that I needed two shots for plague and I received another one for cholera.

I flew out to the field on April 3 in a helicopter. Hack, who still couldn't hear out of one ear, remained in the rear a few days longer.

That afternoon, our company went out on maneuvers, but I was kept behind in our perimeter. Our lieutenant thought there might still be something wrong with me. I explained that there was never anything wrong with me except for a scratch on the elbow. But I was left behind anyway with the drivers of the tracks and one other fellow.

Later that day, the word came down that we would be heading to Cu Chi in a few days for an inspection. We were to get everything cleaned up. It was difficult fighting a war and at the same time getting everything ready to stand inspection.

A few days later, during the first week of April, while on a roving platoon patrol, we found twenty-five butterfly bombs. These devices were about the size of a grapefruit and extremely sensitive. We didn't want to move them, so another guy and I blew them in place using C-4.

The plans for our inspection in Cu Chi must have been changed. We remained where we were for a few days and continued providing security for the engineers who were bulldozing the tropical rain forest.

Friendly Fire

A few days after hitting the mine, I was preparing for an ambush patrol on which I would be walking point. We were set up with an attachment from a tank unit in the Hobo Woods, near the Iron Triangle. The best place for our patrol to leave the perimeter, where we could reach vegetative cover and concealment the quickest, was in front of one of the tanks. That afternoon, I approached the tank commander, an E-6 staff sergeant who was playing cards with some of his guys, and told him we were taking out a patrol in front of their tank.

"Do you have any Claymores or trip flares out?" I asked, indicating the area of the perimeter in front of his tank with a sweep of my arm.

He glanced up at me from his card game and responded, "Naw, we never put out any of that stuff."

Just after full dark, our patrol gathered near one of our tracks for the ambush mission. Being on point, I led them in front of the tank, then excused myself for a moment and walked over to the tank sergeant, who was still playing cards, and tapped him on the shoulder.

"We're going out now."

"Hey, good luck out there."

Shortly afterward, while working our way through the three strands of concertina wire that made up part of our perimeter, we hit a trip flare, right in front of the tank. We immediately dove to the ground. Charlie might have been watching, and it would have been stupid to stand there and wave to make sure the guys inside the perimeter realized that we were Americans. We would have been rewarded with shots in the back from the enemy outside the perimeter.

When the tank crew heard the pop of the trip flare, they glanced up and saw movement as we dove to the ground. The sergeant I spoke with apparently had not advised his crew that we were exiting the perimeter immediately to their front, and they apparently were not paying attention and didn't see us go.

Thinking that we were VC in the wire, they opened up on us with small-arms weapons. M16 tracers shot over us, and a round from an M79 grenade launcher landed just a few feet from my head. Fortunately, at night folks have a tendency to aim high, and the round sailed over me. Perhaps the momentum of the round resulted in most of the shrapnel being propelled in the direction of travel, away from me. We got on the radio and told someone to go over and tell them to cease fire.

When the firing stopped, someone from the tank crew came out to us.

"Hey, are you guys okay?"

"Yeah, we're fine, but that was close. Do you have any more trip flares out here?"

"No, that was the only one."

I wondered why we hadn't been told that before, but I shrugged it off. When we started moving again we hit a second trip flare. We dove to the ground once more but received no fire. We remained on the ground until the flare burned out, which took a few minutes. Hopefully, none of our enemy was around.

We didn't spend the entire night at our ambush site. We were to join the company on an operation the next morning and were to be back inside the perimeter by first light. On the way back in, at 0100, we hit another trip flare and once more dove to the ground. For the second time, the tank crew opened fire on us. Once more, we called in to have someone tell them to stop firing. When we began moving again, we hit yet another trip flare, but we were so disgusted at this point that we just kept walking. We set off a fifth one before finally making it back inside the perimeter.

The tank sergeant and I had a brief conversation about trip flares and the importance of not firing at soldiers on your own side, during which I mentioned that the next time we might consider shooting back. I emphasized that we were much better shots than he and his crew, and it would not be to his advantage to test us. I wasn't invited to stay and play cards.

RAIN AND BLOOD

The detail of providing security for the engineers in the Hobo Woods ended in early April, and the company moved near Trang Bang. Our new mission was to provide security for an ARVN compound that contained a Vietnamese basic training center.

Except for the recent battle, we had not been near Trang Bang in months. When we began operations and started coming in contact with some of the civilians, I ran into a "Coke girl," our name for one who sold Coca-Cola. I bought a bottle from her.

"Hi, Roger."

I didn't wear a name tag and had no idea how she knew who I was.

"What did you say?"

"Hi, Roger." She repeated.

"How do you know me?"

She explained that she knew my girlfriend from Trang Bang. I was astounded by the realization that although I had spoken to my "girlfriend" only a few times back in October, her friends, whom I had not met, could recognize me on sight after a period of six months. I saw my "girlfriend" shortly after that but didn't have a chance to talk to her; I only waved as we passed through town mounted on our APCs. If the girls had a communications network like this, the Viet Cong and NVA must have had an extremely comprehensive one.

On April 10, our platoon received two new tracks, replacing those that were lost on March 30 when they hit land mines.

Andy Gimma was in Hong Kong on R and R, and I was the temporary squad leader in his absence. I was considered most likely to be the squad leader after Andy went home.

The rumor mill said that we'd be operating near Trang Bang for the next six days, after which we didn't know where we would be or what we would be doing.

During April, I became close with our platoon sergeant, Jackie Polk. Sergeant Polk was riding on our track for a while in April when the entire platoon shared two vehicles, and we compared notes and discovered that he had been a drill instructor at Fort Leonard Wood, Missouri, where I had received basic training. He was there while I was going through training, and we were even in the same battalion but in different companies. It's a small army.

I was also developing close friendships with Dennis "Hack" Hackin, who was the driver of our track, and Ted "Chad" Chadwick, who was in our squad. We and a few others, including Gimma, Solly, Stritt, Ordy, and Slagle, formed close relationships that would last beyond our tours in Vietnam. We had became important to one another.

The cut near my left elbow had healed, but it was still bruised and a little sore. My leg wound had finally closed after a month and a half.

After five months without a drop of precipitation, it began raining again during the first week of April. The monsoon season had begun. By April 12 it had rained every day for ten days in a row. By June it was raining hard several times during the day and night, a pattern that would continue until late October or November. We forgot what it felt like to be dry. The rice paddies once again filled with water and reflected the sky, and the tropical vegetation took on a lusher shade of green and sprouted new growth. In spite of the inherent danger in Vietnam, I was in awe of the country's beauty.

We were pulling platoon ambushes almost every night from our base camp in the soccer field at Trang Bang, with company-sized sweeps during the daytime. During almost every ambush patrol, I took up my usual position as point man.

27 April 68

Mom,

Sorry I haven't written for a while. We had ambush almost every night, or else LP.

I almost have a year in the Army. We're securing artillery for a large ARVN compound and training center. We were set up by Trang Bang. I talked to my "girlfriend" a few times.

Did you hear on the news of B-52 strikes northwest of Saigon in the Tay Ninh Province? I took a picture of it.

Nothing exciting has been happening. I was squad leader for 2 more days while Andy went to Cu Chi to get some checks cashed.

I put in for R&R last night. In another 2 weeks I should know where I'm going and when. We wear khakis [on R&R] with rank and all our ribbons. I'll have 5 ribbons including 2 purple hearts.

I better go. Love, Rog

On April 30, we were conducting one of our company sweeps in which we lined up with about ten meters between us and moved through an area searching for signs of the enemy. We began receiving sniper fire, which was often a sign that we were getting close to an enemy encampment. We hit the dirt if the fire was close; otherwise, we usually ignored it. We came upon a series of bunkers and found three VC in one of them. We took them prisoner. Whenever that happened, a chopper came in and transported the prisoners to Cu Chi, where they were interrogated to learn about the enemy's size, strength, plans, weapons, unit designation, and so forth. After the chopper left, we found numerous bunkers. The place looked like our battlefield at Hoc Mon.

On May 1 we replaced a company that was moving elsewhere and took over its perimeter. Before the soldiers left, we spoke briefly; they advised us that they had been mortared every night for the past two weeks. That afternoon I was told that I would be in charge of an LP that night.

Because LPs didn't dig in, I was concerned about being unprotected during a mortar attack. I conducted a brief reconnaissance during the afternoon, looking for a spot that would provide a good view of the countryside and offer protection from mortar rounds. To avoid having the enemy know what I was doing—in case anyone was watching—I acted as though I was nonchalantly taking a stroll outside our wire. I found a ditch three to four feet deep and about eight feet wide just the right distance out from the wire. It was perfect.

The two guys who were going to be with me on the LP, both of whom had less time in-country than I did, were relieved that I had found a safe spot. When the last flicker of daylight left the sky, we negotiated the wire and trip flares and made our way to the ditch. We placed our poncho and radio in the bottom of the ditch and checked out our site. We found that we could see the area in question only if we were perched on the slope with our heads protruding above the ditch. It was an uncomfortable position, because we kept sliding downward, but we would be difficult to spot, because only our heads protruded above the ditch. In the bottom of the ditch, we were completely out of sight and didn't have to be careful with our movements. That was a pleasant change. Another concern was that the ditch was a likely avenue of approach for enemy troops. They could move undetected through it. So, as well as watching the open area to our front, we kept an eye out for movement on either side of us.

Sure enough, mortar shells began dropping on us later that night. We laid flat on the ground in the bottom of the ditch throughout the shelling. Several mortar tubes were involved in the attack, and one of them was walking rounds in our direction. The gunner was probably attempting to scatter rounds from one side of our perimeter to the other, but his rounds were falling short and landing outside the wire on our side of the perimeter. Judging from the whine and whistle of the fins as the rounds dropped in, we thought that each successive one would land in our ditch, but fortunately none of them did. The last one sounded as though it exploded just above our heads at the edge of the ditch.

When the mortar attack ended, we scooted up the sides of the ditch to watch for attackers. Mortar attacks often preceded human wave attacks. Fortunately, no one was moving about.

We usually counted the mortar rounds that were fired at our perimeter. This had been a big attack involving more than fifty shells. Sometimes we could hear the tubes fire, and that gave us a few seconds to call "incoming" and take shelter. This time we didn't hear the tubes, and three men were seriously wounded—one from our platoon and the other two from the mortar platoon.

After the excitement died down, we called in a sit-rep and resumed our normal routine, with two of us going back to sleep.

The next morning we found a small crater a foot or so away from the edge of our ditch. We had escaped another close call; the ditch had saved us.

May 1 was a Vietnamese holiday, their version of Labor Day. We were told that there would be parades in the large villages and towns. For us, though, it was business as usual.

On May 2 we made heavy contact. We fought all day and all that night. Our lieutenant was killed. An enemy round had creased his forehead, and he died of what we think was shock while waiting for a dust-off chopper to arrive. One man from another platoon was also killed.

So far during my tour, we had gone through five lieutenants. Three of them had died and one, Marschewski, was in a hospital back in the States.

During the battle, which occurred on the outer fringes of an NVA battalion base camp, Solly was walking down a road when he spotted a freshly made *punji* pit. These booby traps consisted of a rectangular hole dug to various depths along a trail or other avenue that the enemy thought we might walk. Into the bottom of the pit the VC would embed sharpened wooden stakes protruding upward, the tips of which were coated with excrement or another toxic substance. Small twigs, usually bamboo, were placed over the hole, which was then camouflaged with soil and vegetative matter in order to blend in with the surroundings. The enemy hoped that we would step on these traps, fall through, and become impaled on the sharpened stakes.

We had seen a few *punji* pits, but most of them were pretty old and the stakes were no longer sharp. I had once intentionally stepped down into one of these old pits and jumped up and down on the worn stakes. The pit that Solly found, however, was new. He assumed that there were more of the dangerous traps along the road he was on, so he moved off to the side. But in doing so, he stepped into a brushy area and tripped an explosive booby trap. The force of the explosion somersaulted him along the roadside, and he received fragmentation wounds to his right leg, his face, an eye, an arm, and his chest. The man behind him was wounded by a large portion of the grenade that had composed the booby-trap explosive charge. They were both evacuated by dust-off. Solly was within a month of rotating home; this, his second wound, provided the means for an early trip back to the world. He recovered fully in the States.

The next day, we moved our perimeter back to the soccer field at Trang Bang, where the company was when I arrived in Vietnam.

Useless Blood

On May 3, shortly after arriving in Trang Bang, we received word to load up the tracks in order to move out in a hurry. Another unit was in contact with the NVA several klicks east of Cu Chi, and we were going to reinforce them. Darkness fell while we were en route. Traveling at night always made us nervous. Because we never used headlights, we couldn't see far if the moon wasn't out. If the sky was overcast, we couldn't see beyond the edge of the road. We could have been within feet of entire enemy regiments without knowing it.

We arrived at 2200. There were four wood lines covering about twenty acres, and the area was filled with NVA. That first night, we were placed in position as a blocking force while artillery and jets pounded the wood line to our front.

At about 0500 the next morning, Ted Chadwick had just climbed down from the turret control (TC) hatch behind the .50 caliber where he was pulling guard. Andy Gimma woke up shortly thereafter and noticed that nobody was in the TC. He arose, took a short walk, and was relieving himself near a small hootch when he heard movement. Glancing around the corner of the hootch, he saw VC or NVA soldiers trotting one after another through an open area in front of our position. He crouched over me where I was sleeping on my poncho a short distance from the track and touched my arm. I awoke instantly, as I always did in Vietnam. He silenced me by placing his finger to his lips. He pointed and I followed his gaze and saw thirty-five or so VC trotting slowly past our position, from right to left, only about a hundred feet to our front.

Chad had seen the movement also from the left side of the track. Because most of the rest of the guys were asleep, we would not engage them. But I was frustrated because for the first and only time that I was in-country, my weapon was not within arm's reach. I had been exhausted the night before after pulling guard duty and had left it leaning against the track about ten feet away. We watched in fascination as the enemy force, all of whom carried weapons, entered a small woodlot to our front. Of course, they knew that we were there; our tracks were parked in a line out in the open. I scrambled to retrieve my weapon.

A few minutes later, a track two down from ours observed a VC soldier sneaking toward them with three hand grenades. They got him. The company interpreted that as a possible sign of impending attack. To discourage further attempts, the men fired toward the wood line until dawn.

Shortly after full daylight, an unarmed man came out of the woodlot with his arms raised. Sergeant Polk, a few tracks to our left, saw the man and screamed to us over the radio, "Kill him, kill him, kill him."

We were not used to this cold-blooded action, and I didn't want to watch. I stood behind the track and heard several shots. When I came out, the VC was lying on his back with his feet toward us. Not sure whether he was dead or suffering, I aimed for his chin with my M16 and fired twice. His body was still there when we left the area the next morning. There were two entry wounds below his chin, and the top of his head extended upward a few inches, with large exit wounds several inches in diameter. The M16 did not make neat, small wounds.

This day was not one we were proud of. Andy considered it the low point of his tour. We were, however, following orders. We did not have a lieutenant at the moment—having lost our last one during the action of May 2, two days previously—and our platoon sergeant was in charge. We did as we were told.

Andy thought that the man we had killed was a local farmer. I thought that maybe he had come from the group that we saw entering the woods. My guess was that the men wanted to surrender but were not sure how they would be treated, so one man came out to see. If we had taken him prisoner, I think the others would have followed. Instead, our actions may have increased their desire to continue fighting. It was impossible to know for sure.

On this day, May 4, we were joined by several soldiers from our rear. The night before, in order to maximize the number of troops in the field for the upcoming battle, our company commander had called back to the first sergeant, who was in our Tay Ninh base camp, and told him to send out all of the slackers and other men who, for one reason or another, were in the rear. Among them was Kellum "Kelly" Grant, who had been in the rear processing out of the company. He had received another assignment in the rear, and his time with us was over except for turning in his equipment and processing the paperwork that would remove him from the roles of the company. We were surprised to see him emerge from the chopper.

Our first sergeant, a man named Grey, had been in the army for twenty years but had never served in an infantry unit. No one liked him because he seemed to enjoy asserting his authority and hassling the guys. He never set foot in the field, a fact that did little to increase his credibility with the troops.

In an apparent misinterpretation of the captain's orders, or being overzealous in an attempt to follow them to the letter, Grey sent out everyone who was in the rear, including Grant. So, with only a few days left in our company, Grant was back out for one last battle.

Later that morning, our company, along with another from our battalion, organized a sweep covering the area where the group of VC had been spotted. We advanced on line and received some small-arms fire. We then called in mortars and air force jets. An hour later, after the completion of the bombardment, we moved in again and swept the area, tossing grenades into bunkers.

On the other side of the woodlot was another patch of woods; it was surrounded by a five-foot dike. This would be our next objective.

The platoon was upset that Grant was back out in the field. We wanted him to make it out alive. If someone completed his tour and went home, that meant that maybe we would too. That morning, we were joking around before kicking off our assault of the second enemy position.

"This is the last time I'll be able to help you guys do this," Grant said, kidding us. "After today, you're on your own."

That made us laugh, and we kidded him back good-naturedly. Grant had been with the company since the previous summer and commanded respect. He was the center of attention during this brief social exchange.

There was an open space to cross before getting to the enemy's perimeter, and we assaulted on line, throwing as much lead as we could. We had at least one track with us, so the firepower from the .50-caliber machine gun could be added to the assault.

We didn't know it, but most of the enemy had retreated during the previous night, leaving one man, possibly mortally wounded, in a bunker to slow us down. When the man thought we were close enough, he rose up and squeezed the trigger of a recoilless rifle.

Grant, who was fifteen to twenty feet to my right, was hit in the chest, and the shock of the explosion among our ranks halted the assault. Grant was killed instantly. Five others were wounded with shrapnel from the explosion, including Sergeant Polk and Andy Gimma, who was to my right between Grant and me.

Andy was wounded in one foot and received minor wounds to both legs. His left arm, however, was injured severely. He later described the wound by saying that the blood was shooting out of his arm like water from a fountain.

Polk, our platoon sergeant, received a serious leg wound. His time in combat ended on that day, and we lost a good leader.

I was hit, too, but it was only a nuisance, not a major wound. One small piece of shrapnel entered my jaw and came to rest on the outside of the bone, just under the skin. Another went through three ammunition magazines in the ammo pouch on the front right side of my web belt, and a third entered the trigger mechanism of my rifle, rendering it useless. I was given a replacement, which had belonged to one of our casualties.

The company backed up, leaving Grant's body lying where it had fallen. Another air strike was called in, and once again we watched the air show as F-4 Phantoms dove in at treetop level to bomb the enemy position. Afterward, we made another assault with a secondary objective of recovering the body of our fallen comrade. When we approached the same spot, another recoilless round was fired, but this one sailed over our heads and detonated harmlessly behind us. The company once again retreated, leaving one track with the engine still running up by the berm at the edge of the enemy perimeter. Nobody wanted to go back to get it.

While the platoon was figuring out its next move, Jim Bell sprinted toward the abandoned track, jumped on top of it, and dropped into the driver's compartment. He pulled backward on the levers, and the track backed into position in our line. It was an act of bravery on Bell's part. He was held in higher esteem after that day.

Chad and a medic we called Tiny were helping one of our guys who had taken a bullet in one of his legs. He was lying down in the path of the retreating track, and they pulled him to safety.

Our wounded soldiers, including Andy Gimma, were dusted off. Because of the severity of his wounds, Andy didn't return to the field. I was appointed to temporarily replace him as squad leader of the 3d Squad of the 2d Platoon. The plan was that because I was only a specialist fourth class, not a sergeant, I would act as squad leader only until a higher-ranked individual came along. There were only three of us now in the squad.

Staff Sergeant Polk was eventually replaced by SSgt. James Cattrell, who became our new platoon sergeant. He was a sandy-haired man probably thirty-five to forty years of age. He, too, turned out to be a good leader.

That night, we again functioned as a blocking force and on the following day we assaulted four more woodlots. We fought our way through the first two, finding an occasional body, a large amount of web gear, ammunition, and other enemy equipment.

In the third woodlot, we found four or five weapons and two live VC in bunkers. We cleared the bunkers with hand grenades. After resting for about forty-five minutes, we began receiving fire from a marsh on the opposite side of a hedgerow. No one was hurt, and we called in artillery on the marsh.

Our next assignment was to attempt to take the same patch of woods where Grant had been killed, but we were delayed by the enemy in the marsh. Another company was sent in to assault the stronghold in our place.

They maneuvered on line and began their assault the way we had, with everyone firing as fast as possible as the company moved over the open area toward the tree line. Once again, the enemy fired an RPG, killing two Americans. The company backed up as we had, and that was the last attempted assault of the day.

That evening, we operated once more as a blocking force, probably to preclude enemy withdrawal. Of course, if there were tunnels under the enemy camp, our attempts to prevent their escape would be useless.

The next morning, we were right back at it, attempting to fight our way into the enemy stronghold. We called in an air strike, which must have done the trick because we finally made it inside. We spent the rest of the morning in the enemy base camp searching and clearing bunkers. Our platoon found seven AK-47s. I found three of them but gave them away. There were fifteen bodies in the enemy perimeter. We presumed that the rest of the VC had somehow eluded our attempts to entrap them and had withdrawn.

Before we left the area, I walked with Hack, who had been good friends with Grant, to the site of the battle where Grant had died. His helmet was still lying where he had fallen. Hack picked it up and inspected it for a while. It was unmistakably Grant's helmet; we recognized his handiwork. Most of the guys decorated their camouflage-cloth helmet covers with slogans and drawings made with a ballpoint pen. It was an emotional moment for Hack, conducting a silent memorial service to say good-bye to a good friend.

A few days later, a unit of ARVNs discovered a mass grave containing NVA soldiers. Our enemy had dug it to prevent us from knowing the extent of their casualties. We took credit for the kills, which raised our body count for the action near Hoc Mon to three hundred.

Hoc Mon

Later in the day, we were moved back to within sight of Hoc Mon, arriving after dark. We'd had only a few hours of sleep each night for more than a week and were exhausted. Before the day ended, however, we heard drums beating and saw flickers of light filtering through the trees from a bonfire in the woods. We guessed that it was an enemy force working up the nerve to attack us.

Later that night, during an intense thunderstorm, our perimeter was attacked by a small force carrying RPGs and AKs. We were sure that it was the same people who were at the bonfire. We assumed that they had been smoking marijuana to gain battlefield courage. During the assault, an RPG round streaked over our track with a whooshing noise, and the flame and orange sparks from the rocket were clearly visible as it passed within a yard of our heads.

Our mortar platoon answered with several rounds, which were fired without the usual charges added for longer ranges because of the closeness of the enemy troops. The enemy assault was silenced.

At first light we sent out a patrol to see if any sign of the enemy remained. It was on our platoon's sector of the perimeter, and I joined the patrol. On the opposite side of a berm that the small force had used for cover during their assault, not too far outside our perimeter, we found four dismembered bodies. Our mortar platoon had determined the exact location of the small enemy force and had fired well.

In the heat of the momentary battle the night before, with lightning and small-arms fire flashing around us and the *whoosh* of the RPG right over our heads, I had called our platoon sergeant on the radio.

"Two-five, this is Two-three. Over."

"Two-three, go ahead. Over," Sergeant Cattrell answered.

"Sit-rep normal. Over."

"Roger, Two-three," he replied with a chuckle. "Two-five. Out."

"Two-three. Out."

I guess a sense of humor during a battle means that things are going pretty well, considering.

Because we were so exhausted, it was easy to fall sleep that night. We didn't unload the tracks but slept on top of the equipment. I found a comfortable place on top of a pile of duffel bags containing extra uniforms. They were piled so high that I was just under the top of the track and could reach the roof. It was the most comfortable sleeping position I had found in the field. I considered that I would die instantly if an RPG round struck our track, but I was so tired that the idea passed quickly. I drifted off to sleep thinking that no spot offered complete protection in this dangerous place; one place was as good or bad as the next. Might as well relax while I can.

SQUAD LEADER, BOBCAT CHARLIE 23

I would remain a squad leader for the rest of the time I spent in the field. For the first few weeks, there were only three of us in my squad: Hack, Chad, and me. Everyone else had been wounded. I didn't have much in the way of responsibility. It was important, however, that someone be in charge, mainly so that our platoon sergeant and platoon leader would know who to summon to squad leader meetings, where they gave us our orders and decided what each squad would do during upcoming operations. It was important also that they know who to go to for the numerous small things that required coordination among the squads, such as determining who would go out on LP or ambush patrol. Decisions within the squad's authority had to be made by someone in charge, but all three of us were seasoned veterans and could do that. We all knew what needed to be done and would probably reach the same conclusions. Although our squad was small, we were a good, tight unit.

Hack was the driver, so of course he remained with the track at all times. It was just as important that someone remain in the turret behind the .50-caliber machine gun so that the track was protected at all times. That was Chad. As a result, when our platoon dismounted to conduct an operation, I hopped down to the ground, and that was it for the 3d Squad. Until we received replacement troops, I usually attached myself to another squad and hung out with them.

Over the next few days, each of us in the 3d Squad pitched in and accomplished the many small tasks that needed to be performed, such as filling the water cans, cleaning the .50-caliber machine guns, monitoring the radio, and pulling guard or watch. Unfortunately, with only three of us, each stayed awake a third of the night to be on guard on top of the track. None of us got much sleep through this period, and we functioned in a constant state of exhaustion. We were operating on adrenaline and not much else.

On May 5 we were on a company sweep, and our operation included a village. North Vietnamese Army soldiers were reported to be moving into the area, and our mission was to put on a show of force and secure the area in an attempt to prevent an enemy buildup. It didn't work.

The next morning, we swept another area and found five NVA soldiers hiding in a clump of brush. We killed one and captured four along with two M16s, an AK-47, and two pistols. The butt plate of one of the pistols, a .38, was stamped "St. Louis Police Department." We had no idea how the NVA got that gun, but several possible scenarios came to mind. They could have found it on a dead GI or one they had taken prisoner. We had heard that several antiwar organizations in America had sent weapons to North Vietnam to aid them in ridding themselves of us foreign aggressors. We didn't understand how American citizens could do such a thing, but there was a lot about the feelings of our fellow countrymen that we failed to comprehend. We didn't, however, have much time to worry about it.

We completed the sweep at 1530 that afternoon. We then received word that a unit we were working with was in contact and we had to help them. By this time everyone was plain beat. We had been in contact with the enemy for several days in a row, and none of us had slept more than three hours a night for well over a week.

We mounted up and headed off to provide assistance to our sister unit, arriving about 1600. They had called in artillery, gunships, and an air strike, after which we were to go in. But the NVA had other ideas. They put out enough sniper fire to keep us out until dark. At 0115, we moved in. It was one of our rare battles during hours of darkness outside of a company perimeter, except for contact made during ambush patrols.

I was the only one on the ground from my squad; it was still just Chad, Hack, and me. I attached myself to the 21 squad, whose squad leader was a sergeant who had just arrived in Vietnam. There was a good moon and we could see fairly well. We were sweeping across an open area, an action that made me uncomfortable.

I got the attention of the new squad leader. "Wait a minute," I said. "I've seen too many guys get messed up by doing this. Let's head over to this hedgerow and move down it in single file." I had learned that from Lieutenant Miller, who had left our company in February.

I thought that the sergeant might appreciate advice from someone with a little more experience than he had. He seemed to like the idea. We headed to our left and moved along the tree line adjacent to the open field. We held in place for a few minutes to wait for a unit on our right flank to move up on line with us. While doing so, the squad's machine gunner watched an NVA soldier fire an RPG at us from a bunker right in front of the open area that we would have been crossing. We would have walked right in on him. The round went high, missing us.

After giving away their position and missing us, the three NVA troops scrambled out of their bunker and ran. Our machine gunner opened up on them, killing at least one and wounding the others. We swept the rest of the area without incident.

When morning came we were still in there. I was given a new man for my squad that morning and he joined us as we continued sweeping for the rest of the day, without making contact. For my new man, this was an inopportune time to join the company. He had been thrust into combat on his first day.

We heard that every infantry unit in the 25th Infantry Division was making contact now with the NVA. Our enemy was making a big push, but we felt that it wouldn't last long.

Since the Tet Offensive, we hadn't run into many VC units and wouldn't do so for the remainder of my tour, possibly for the rest of the war. During Tet the VC lost a significant portion of their forces, which were then bolstered by NVA troops, especially among the higher ranks.

After clearing the enemy position, we returned to a company perimeter. Over the next few days I would begin breaking in my new man, but now my highest priority was to get some sleep.

After a week or so, we were given a few more new guys. I broke them in and taught them as best I could how we did things in the 2d Platoon. When one of them walked point on an operation, I went with him to show him what to do and what to look for. I tried to explain not only what we did but the reasons why we did them. After a few weeks, I was told by our platoon sergeant that the lieutenant liked the way I had broken in the new guys. I was told I would be the permanent squad leader.

It was customary in mechanized infantry units for the driver and the squad leader to sleep inside the track. My days of sleeping in bunkers had come to an end. Also, as squad leader, I wouldn't be expected to go out on LPs or OPs; I would stay with the majority of the squad. Of course, my presence would be required on all combat missions as well as my usual share of the ambush patrols.

Inside the track, there were two narrow benches, one along either side, covered with a thin foam rubber pad. If used with a little imagination, the benches could serve as beds. My shoulders were wider than the bench, though, so to lie comfortably I stretched one arm over my head, which prevented my arm from flopping to the floor. I became accustomed to that position and still often lie that way when I sleep or rest.

During the evenings when we were not out on ambush, the members of our squad and a few other friends from the 2d Platoon gathered inside the track, and we wrote letters, cleaned weapons, and chatted, enjoying one another's company. Someone's transistor radio was usually tuned to Armed Forces Vietnam Network (AFVN). The music of the '60s played softly and accompanied our chatter. We grew close during these evenings, and the bonds we formed led to a deep sense of trust among the members of our squad. We knew we could rely on one another—in combat and during these peaceful evenings inside the track.

A red light mounted along the right inside wall of the track provided enough illumination to see. But red light does not emit streaks of light the way white light does, so it didn't give away our position because the enemy couldn't see it. In addition, red light doesn't destroy night vision the way other colors do.

One day I received a letter from my mother that had been written in red ink. I opened the letter after dark, inside the track. The red light made the pages appear red and the ink didn't stand out. I thought that Mom had mixed up her pages before sealing the envelope, and I remarked to the others that my mom had sent me four blank pages. We laughed about that. I didn't realize that there was writing on the pages until the next day, when I happened to glance at them on the floor where they had fallen the night before.

Chad became my assistant squad leader and served as my right-hand man and trusted adviser. He was excellent in combat and completely reliable, and we thought alike. I never had cause to question his loyalty, credibility, or dependability. And depend on him I did. I had a lot of confidence in him; when I wasn't around, he was in charge. He did what I would have done and made the decisions I would have made, given the same circumstances. It was almost as if I had been there. When the squad was split, he was always in charge of the half I wasn't with. On several occasions during the remainder of our tour, he refused offers to have a squad of his own, preferring to stay with us. I don't think that was because we were the best soldiers. But being close made us operate as a tight unit, which perhaps increased the chances of our survival. And I guess he felt comfortable with us. We certainly didn't want to lose him.

During the evenings, just before going to sleep, Hack and I talked of the day's events and the operation coming up the next day. We had a similar sense of humor and got along well. He became a mentor to me and was in many ways much wiser, more worldly, and more experienced about life than I was. He had a slightly different way of looking at things than I did, and I learned by listening to him. It was obvious that he liked and cared about me too, and he listened to whatever I wanted to tell him.

When the company went into combat without the tracks, Hack monitored the radio, listening for signs that we were in trouble and looking for ways he could help us. When we returned from battle, after periods when he wouldn't hear our voices on the radio, I would see him standing next to the track anxiously looking for us. He visibly relaxed when he saw us coming. We had become like a family.

The new soldiers I had broken in became dependable members of the squad and the platoon, and I was glad to have them with me. One of the highest compliments I have ever received came from two of these men. One day they pulled me aside and asked to talk with me for a minute. I had no idea what was coming. In a solemn and sincere manner, they told me that they were not afraid to go anywhere or do anything in Vietnam as long as I was leading them. I was deeply touched and honored, and I cherish the memory of that conversation.

The members of the squad surprised me one day with a jeep seat that they had scrounged from one of the rear-echelon units. They strapped it to the top of the track on the left side of the cargo hatch, and for the remainder of my tour that's where I rode when the track was in motion. The seat was olive-drab canvas and contained sponge rubber mounted on a springed frame. I sat in it with my M16 across my lap and enjoyed the ride as we bounced along, sometimes at speeds close to thirty-five miles per hour.

A radio headset was used for communication among squad leaders and our platoon leader and platoon sergeant, as well as the rest of the company. The headset didn't fit under my steel pot, so I placed one earpiece on top of the helmet and the other on my left ear. A microphone swung into position near my mouth. A switch on the cord extending across my chest was used to transmit. Hack also had a headset, and we had an intercom channel that permitted private conversations between the two of us, which we mostly limited to discussions concerning directions or the day's activities.

My jeep seat was the first to appear in our company as far as I know, but soon other tracks were sporting them. We never saw jeeps without seats, so I guess they weren't missed too much. In any event, we would not have been too concerned if they had been.

Eventually, more replacements were assigned to our squad. One of them was an E-5 sergeant named Kirkham, who was on his second Vietnam tour in the same squad. He explained that he had re-upped (reenlisted) and received orders back to Vietnam. No surprise there. Because this was his second tour, he was given the opportunity to choose the division with which he would serve. Because he was with the 25th Infantry Division the last time, he said he might as well go back there. When he arrived at the 25th, he was allowed to choose which battalion he'd like to be with. This was repeated all the way through the company and platoon levels. Two separate tours with the same squad in the same unit must have been a rare occurrence, if not a record.

Our squad was now composed of Hack, Chad, Bo, Big John, Little John, Giant, Ski, and a few others. John Lewis earned his nickname of Big John when someone else named John joined our squad. The man with the most time in-country was thought of as the oldest and most experienced, so he became Big John even though he was the smaller of the two. The other one became Little John. Time and experience in country were more important than physical stature. Bob Smith became Bo, and Harry Nissen, the biggest, was called Giant. We used first names, but not on a regular basis.

Little John was the only soldier I ever had in my squad who gave me trouble. Because we seldom received a full night's rest, a lot of soldiers were difficult to wake up in the mornings. Little John was one of them.

The process of waking up the company consisted of a radio call from the commanding officer (CO) or his RTO to whoever was on guard with instructions to wake up the squad leader, who was then responsible for waking the rest of the squad at the appointed time and ensuring that they were prepared for the day's activities.

One morning we were to move out at dawn, and I woke everyone early enough so they could get ready, have something to eat, and be prepared to leave at the assigned time.

Little John preferred to sleep rather than eat breakfast, which was fine, and I woke him again after breakfast. He said he would have plenty of time to get ready, then he fell asleep again. When it became apparent that he would still be sound asleep when it was time to move out, I shook him pretty roughly. This was about the fourth time I attempted to rouse him, and he came up swinging, striking me in the face and knocking me down. He felt badly about it and apologized later.

Chad was a tall, thin, good-looking blonde from Georgia. His friendly drawl and easy manner made him a well-liked member of the platoon. His calmness under fire made him an invaluable asset. Because we arrived in-country at about the same time, we often fell into the same social groups. Accordingly, we were already friends, but when we ended up in the same squad, we became very close.

By May 10, we were still down near Hoc Mon conducting company-sized sweeps but not making much contact. It was pleasant to walk through the villages again without VC or NVA in them.

We had a new lieutenant named McDonald, who we felt was going to be a good one. He had been in Vietnam almost as long as I had and was scheduled to go home five days after me.

That afternoon, I helped the new guys in my squad prepare for an ambush. The night passed quietly.

Two nights later, on May 12, we made contact once again with a force of forty-five enemy soldiers. We called in mortars and an air strike, then moved in. Just inside the wood line we found a .30-caliber antiaircraft machine gun and a loaded RPG.

There were numerous bunkers, and we dropped grenades in all of them. I saw a man's leg and an AK-47 in one bunker and tossed in a grenade. After it went off, I reached in and pulled out the weapon. It was a little messy, but I cleaned it up and decided to keep it. I carried it on operations for the next month or so. I found rounds for it when we overran enemy positions or came upon one that had been hastily abandoned as we approached. The AK-47 also fired M60 ammo, which is the same as that for the M14, a few of which we had because of their greater accuracy. My captured AK-47 had been made in China, as we could tell by the rosy color of the wood that made up the stock.

Near the same bunker where I found the AK, I also found a document inside a backpack that had been left behind when the enemy hastily withdrew. It turned out to be a membership certificate in the National Liberation Front, the Viet Cong.

While moving through the area a little later, I spotted what I thought was a bunker to my front, and pulled the pin on a grenade. It turned out to be a well, but I had already tossed away the grenade's pin, so I dropped the grenade in the hole and walked away. After it detonated, Lieutenant McDonald, who was following along behind me, glanced in the well and noticed a body floating in it. The soldier must have been hiding underwater, perhaps breathing through a reed. McDonald congratulated me on finding the enemy soldier. I told him what happened and that it was just a coincidence.

A little farther on, I was leading my squad along a path when we heard excited Vietnamese chatter coming from a dense, shrubby area.

I said, *"La dai"* (we were told that this means "come here"), and a soldier emerged with his arms raised. I directed him to lie on the ground, where I searched him to ensure that he was not armed. Someone else tied his hands behind his back, and I had him stand, then took him back to our tracks. On the way there, he was visibly frightened and shaking, afraid that he would be executed or beaten. I placed my arm around his shoulders in an attempt to calm him. He responded with a smile.

I was grateful that he did not decide to go down fighting, as did many of his comrades. I or some of my friends probably would not have been around much longer if he had. I turned him over to the guys from our headquarters, who formed an entourage for our company commander, and returned to my squad.

After I caught up with them, we continued our sweep and came to the end of the woods. A trail along the top of a rice paddy dike connected to another patch of woods to our right front. It would be our next objective. We could not afford to leave it unsecured; it was too close and could hold a large enemy force.

On the way to this patch of woods, we followed the trail on top of the dike. One of our new guys saw a VC lying in a hole. He went over to see if he was dead, and the guy turned his head and looked at him. He ran back startled, and our machine gunner shot the VC.

A little farther along, as Chad and I were leading the squad, I found a VC in a fighting position that was about a foot deep, several feet wide, and long enough for someone to lie down inside. Unsure whether the VC was alive or dead, I shot him in the chest. He was very much alive, and I fired several more times to finish him off. When we got closer, we discovered that he was unarmed.

This event has become the one incident that I participated in that I would like to relive. I am confident that I could have taken him prisoner, as we had with the other VC only a few minutes before. But in the brief instant I had to evaluate the situation and decide on a course of action, I concluded that if I had called to him, he might have come up shooting, or he could have tossed a grenade at us. All of these things flashed through my mind quickly, and I shot him to ensure the safety of my squad. Later, however, the fact that he was unarmed weighed increasingly on my conscience. I knew that if I had called to him, he might be alive today.

On this same day, I received a radio call advising me that I had two new replacements for my squad. I went to the rear, introduced myself to them, and led them back to the front, some distance away. As we passed through our recent battlefield, moments after the conclusion of hostilities, the new replacements' eyes grew wide as they took in their first glimpse of the effects of war. Trees were scarred by shrapnel, smoke drifted from destroyed bunkers scattered here and there, and an occasional dead body littered the area. About halfway back to our squad, shots rang out to our right and slightly to the rear. The new men dove to the ground for cover.

"You can get up," I told them. "That's an M-sixteen. He's on our side. He's over there about a hundred and fifty meters, and shooting that way." I pointed in the direction of the fire, then off in the direction the shots were going, and continued walking. They hurried after me.

After hearing gunfire for months, we had learned to distinguish the different sounds made by various weapons. The M16 has a high-pitched *pop*. An AK has a deeper *crack*. We also learned to tell which direction someone was shooting by listening to the direction of the echo. The relative volume of the fire told us how far away the shooter was.

After months of combat, we learned to instantly recognize and ignore friendly fire and dive for cover at the sound of enemy fire. My two new replacement troops would learn this, but not for a few months.

That evening, I heard that our headquarters people had beaten the prisoner whom I had turned over to them. This upset me terribly, and I confronted them about it. I was thankful that the prisoner hadn't killed me, and told them so. I also told them that what they did wasn't right. These soldiers, who had not experienced combat firsthand, had used violence against an unarmed man. I detested their actions. It seemed to me that the ones who were not doing the actual fighting were the ones who could be the most cruel. In my view, if they wanted to kick butt, they could have strapped on some equipment, grabbed a rifle, and joined me and the others up where the fighting was rather than stay back within the safety of the perimeter formed by the tracks. I had little use for these people, and less respect.

It seems that the most glorious war stories I heard in Vietnam were told by guys wearing clean fatigues and black boots in an NCO club way back in the rear. I doubted whether some of these men had ever been outside the perimeter, not to mention experienced combat.

COMBAT OPERATIONS

Turkey Shoot

On May 16, we were assigned to act as a blocking force for an ARVN operation. The plan called for a South Vietnamese airborne battalion to parachute into an area to our front, on the opposite side of an area suspected to be occupied by the NVA. They were to sweep toward us, pinning any enemy forces between their forces and ours.

Once we were in position, we looked forward to seeing the parachutes descend from the sky to our front. This was different than our usual operation. We watched as the parachutes glided to earth, but we didn't see or hear any of our allied forces once they were on the ground. We never learned what happened to them. Speculation was that they made their jump, loaded up on waiting trucks, and went back to their base.

While we waited, a squad to our right saw six VC in civilian clothing carrying weapons. A while later the squad reported spotting an RPG team. After failing to make contact with the ARVN unit with whom we were supposed to be working, it was decided that our company would conduct a sweep to our front in the direction of the reported enemy and also toward the ARVN drop zone.

After walking for half an hour, with the tracks behind us, we came upon a series of dried-up rice paddies over a mile in width extending to our front. As we approached the edge of the open area, a group of VC emerged from bunkers and began running. Because our company was spread out in sweep formation, the enemy had nowhere to go except into the rice paddy. Three of them ran into the open and one paused to fire an RPG-7 at one of our tracks. The round missed. We opened fire and the VC took cover behind a rice dike, where we eventually killed them.

We left by driving our tracks across the huge rice paddy. When we were almost to the other side, someone pointed behind us. We looked back to see about half a dozen people, presumably the enemy, dragging away the dead. They must have been in well-concealed bunkers or tunnels while we were near. We covered such a wide area that we would not have missed them had they been aboveground. It always amazed us that we could be so near our enemy but not be able to locate them. It was a tribute to their ability to construct camouflaged tunnel entrances and bunkers.

We referred to the action that occurred on this day as a turkey shoot.

Tan Son Nhut

Our next stop was just north of Saigon at Tan Son Nhut Air Force Base, for which we were to provide security. We set up a company perimeter on the outside of the wire and conducted ambush patrols every night but relatively few operations during the day. It was a pleasant change from the heavy combat we had been experiencing.

After several days, a few of us at a time were allowed to go into the base to look around. Hack, Chad, and I and a few others walked in early one evening. We were surprised by the sights inside. There were real city streets with curbs, the first we had seen since leaving the world.

We ate at a cafeteria just like those on U.S. bases. After a steady diet of army food, we devoured hamburgers and French fries and drank malts. We looked unusual in our dirty, faded fatigues when compared with the air force guys, who looked as though they broke starch each morning and even polished their boots. Ours had never been shined. After a month or so in the field, the constant moisture we endured and the friction from vegetation had rubbed off all the black dye. Most GIs who spent time in the field had whitish boots.

After eating the American fare, we walked around for a bit and found an honest-to-goodness, air-conditioned movie theater. Dinner and a movie, just like home. We went inside. Most of us had long ago become used to the oppressive heat and humidity of Vietnam and this was the first air-conditioned structure we encountered. We froze.

The movie was the recently released *The Green Berets,* starring John Wayne. It was largely a World War II movie format but supposedly set in Vietnam. We sat in the back and laughed at how unrealistic the film was. It was so far from reality that it was hilarious to us and we had trouble containing outbursts of laughter. Quite a few of the airmen stole glances at us. I'm not sure what they thought of us, but we might as well have been of a different species or from another planet, judging from their expressions and reactions. Of course, they couldn't know how ridiculous the film was.

Afterward, in good humor because of the movie, and with our bellies full, we walked back across the air force base to our company position outside the base's wire. The evening had been like a *Twilight Zone* episode and we were returning to normality.

The duty at Tan Son Nhut was like a four-day vacation, except for the extremely long ambush patrols we conducted. The surrounding countryside was composed of numerous, huge, open areas covered with rice paddies. In order to be effective in hampering enemy activity, our ambush patrols needed to hump considerable distances to get to the areas where enemy activity was likely. We set up so far from our position that we were not in place until well after midnight, and it took us most of the morning to get back to our company perimeter.

On May 23, we went back to Cu Chi for the first time in 170 days, a division record for time spent in the field. A mile or so out, we pulled over in an open area near the main roadway and tied purple pennants to the radio antennas on our tracks to identify ourselves as the 1st of the 5th (Mech) Infantry. We never flew the pennants in the field. To do so would alert the enemy to our identity. We thought we were being sneaky, but they probably knew who we were, where we were going, and what we were up to most of the time, anyway. They probably sometimes knew before we did.

We entered the main gate of Cu Chi proudly and felt as though we were in a parade. It was great to be back. The rear-echelon troops had heard of our exploits in the field, and for a day or two we enjoyed celebrity status in the huge base camp.

Upon arriving at our company area, we lined up the tracks and spent several hours taking everything out and cleaning the interiors. Several items of preventive maintenance were performed on the treads and motor of the track. Some of these tasks were performed by Big John, who had taken an interest in our armored personnel carrier. Later in our tour, Hack let him do some of the driving, and when Hack went home Big John became our driver.

24 May 68

Dear Mom,

We're in Cu Chi after 170 days in the field. It's a Division record. We got here yesterday. We've been busy cleaning the tracks and weapons since we've been here.

Today, we're just cleaning equipment and taking it easy. Tonight, the PX and a brand new snack shop will be open for us.

Somebody found a VC document that said that the VC were out for the 1/5 (Mech).

We'll have an awards presentation Sunday afternoon. This is Friday. Last night there was a movie for us. It was pretty good.

We got our shot records checked today. I needed & got 2 shots.

Last week we spent 4 nights in the Air Force Base at Tan Son Nhut. They have just about everything in there that they have back in the states, hamburgers, cheeseburgers, fries, malts, steaks.

Today my platoon sergeant [Cattrell] told me he was putting me in for sergeant at the end of the month. He says I did an outstanding job breaking in my new men.

I got 4 new guys in my squad about 2 weeks ago. I taught them how to walk point & gave them all a chance to be point man when we were out on sweeps. Two are from the south, both married. One's 26. The other 2 are from Boston and California. Ted Chadwick from Georgia is my alpha team leader [assistant squad leader]. I've got one guy who's been here 4 months. He carries the M-79, pretty good with it too.

I don't know what we'll do tomorrow, probably sit around all day like we did today.

Last week we were on a sweep and Bob Ordy, squad leader on 21, found an empty VC bunker. He threw a grenade in it to blow it so it couldn't be used by the VC again. It didn't do much damage so he came over to me and asked if I'd look at it. I told my men to stay put and get down, then followed Ordy. I looked at the bunker, then unfastened a grenade from my web gear and dropped it in the bunker without pulling the pin. Then I pulled the pin on another one and placed it beside the first one. Then I ran. The explosion blew out the top of the bunker.

I guess I'll get some sleep now. I went to a movie but it wasn't any good so I came back here. I'm sleeping in the track cause in the hootches, they party it up all night & it's hard to go to sleep.

Bye for now & write soon. Roger

We spent about a week in Cu Chi, taking daily walks to the PX just because we could, and watching movies when they were available during the evenings. Some of the guys spent considerable amounts of time in the enlisted men's (EM) and NCO clubs, consuming beer.

I think most of the guys drank beer as a form of escape. Unfortunately, it didn't always work out for them. Because alcohol is a depressant, some of the guys began grieving for our fallen comrades after a few beers.

Sergeant Cattrell was going through similar stress-related problems, though they were not induced by alcohol. Sometimes we heard him crying out orders in his sleep to some of our fellow platoon members who had died. It was sad to witness. While awake, however, Sergeant Cattrell was fine and provided good leadership.

After a week, we were sent back out to the field. The stand-down was over, but the minivacation continued with our next duty, which was our favorite. It was the beginning of June, and we were once again assigned to perform road security between Tay Ninh and Dau Tieng.

We left our perimeter each morning at 0600, swept the road for mines, set up, and guarded the road until shortly before sundown. We began the minesweeping operation from the Tay Ninh end of the road, and another unit did the same from Dau Tieng. After sweeping and reconning by M79 fire in the undergrowth of the rubber plantation for approximately three hours, we met in the middle. The business part of the day would then be over. The remainder of the day, except for rotating a guard on top of the track, was a relaxed time of cleaning weapons or bantering with the civilians. The unit that we replaced had been here for forty-five days. We hoped we could stay that long.

During the morning minesweeps, a squad provided flank security by walking inside the tree line on each side of the road, slightly ahead of the team checking the road for mines. The squad performed reconnaissance by fire, shooting rounds from M79 grenade launchers into areas offering possible enemy cover. Enemy activity in this area had remained high since the Tet Offensive, and the recon fire was a precaution against ambush or attack.

I did some of this myself, carrying a huge medic's bag over my shoulder filled with rounds, most of which we fired during the road-clearing operations. I learned about how high to aim the grenade launcher to hit targets at various distances. If a clump of vegetation appeared to our front, we lobbed rounds into it, firing perhaps thirty rounds per hour apiece. This was enjoyable, and I became proficient with the weapon, although not nearly as accurate as those who carried it full-time. Some of them were amazing with this weapon.

On a few occasions, I operated one of the mine detectors. We wore headphones and listened for telltale, high-pitched beeping noises as we moved the disk-shaped head of the detector back and forth above the surface of the road.

We also looked for signs of fresh digging, footprints on the shoulder of the road, or anything else out of the ordinary. Tread imprints from the tanks and APCs that traveled the road the previous day remained in the dust or mud of the road, but that didn't mean that nothing had been planted underneath them the night before. The VC carried a link from the tread of a tracked vehicle, so after they dug a hole, planted a mine, and replaced and tamped the soil, they made an impression in the road surface with the link to camouflage their work. It would appear to us as uninterrupted vehicle tracks. Likewise, they erased their footprints, presumably with a branch or something else that removed all signs that they had been there.

If constant preparation for attack was our mainstay, theirs was stealth. Their attention to detail, camouflage, quiet movement, and other military skills could make the difference between life and death. They were excellent soldiers.

Once, during a road-clearing operation, a truck coming along behind us hit a mine. I was operating the minesweeper that day and I felt bad, but it was understood that this happened occasionally. Perhaps there was nothing metal in the mine that could be picked up by the mine detector. There was no way to know.

Once, a truck hit a huge mine, sending the driver straight into the air for a distance of almost a hundred feet. It was rare that someone was killed by one of these mines, but this soldier didn't survive.

Each day there were at least two convoys carrying equipment and supplies between the bases at Tay Ninh and Dau Tieng. The first convoy began as soon as it heard over the radio that the road was cleared, usually around noon. The last convoy passed in late afternoon or just before dark. After it passed, we closed up shop and headed back to our night defensive perimeter. After darkness fell, the enemy came down from the Black Virgin Mountain or wherever they hid during daylight hours and planted more mines in the road. The next day, the whole thing was repeated. We did our job; they did theirs.

On a few occasions, the afternoon convoy ran late, and it was fully dark by the time we returned to our nighttime position. It was dangerous at night, especially on the tracks, even for a fully armed infantry company. We couldn't see or hear the enemy until an ambush was popped. Although we felt vulnerable during these times, we always made it back safely. Perhaps the enemy didn't have the manpower or adequate prior notice of the late convoy to set up an effective ambush.

Unlike previous times when we were assigned this duty, during which we set up our perimeter around the engineer rock crusher installation at the base of Nui Ba Den, this time we spent the nights in the base camp near Tay Ninh.

On June 2, I bought a Timex watch for ten dollars from Jerry, the boy from Tay Ninh who sold Cokes and had become a friend. He visited us in our position from which we guarded the road often during this period, and I looked forward to spending time with him.

Sergeant Cattrell told me that around the first of June he had put me in for sergeant along with a letter of recommendation to the captain. I was the only squad leader in our platoon, possibly the company, who was not a sergeant; I was still a specialist fourth class. The promotion, if I received it, would mean almost a hundred dollars more each month. In those days, that was a lot of money, and I was impressed.

Revenge on Sergeant Grey

Our arrival in Tay Ninh in early June marked the first time since May that we were around First Sergeant Grey. Everybody was still upset with him for sending Grant to the field while he was in the rear processing out of the company. We blamed Grey, whether justified or not, for Grant's death, and he showed no remorse or regret for his decision.

Grey usually spent a lot of time in his private hootch, which was actually a huge bunker constructed by new replacements whom he got to work for him before they were sent to the field. It was built below ground level, with a steel roof and several layers of sandbags all around and on top. The rest of us slept in tents on raised platforms, like those in Cu Chi, with only a small, low wall of sandbags for protection. The steps that Grey took to safeguard himself while the rest of us slept aboveground added to the animosity and resentment that the company felt toward him. We interpreted his actions as an indication that he thought he was better than we were or, worse, that he was a coward.

One morning shortly after we arrived in Tay Ninh, Sergeant Grey, while getting dressed, found a grenade with the pin pulled stuffed into one of his boots. The fabric of his jungle boot held the spoon in place. If he hadn't noticed it, it could have fallen out and detonated, wounding or possibly killing him.

It was a silent message. He made a huge fuss over it and demanded an investigation. Everyone heard what had happened but few were concerned. We saw it as a form of frontier justice. Nothing ever came of it, because there was no evidence indicating who had planted the grenade. Not even the rumor mill provided any clues. Grey got the message, though. He didn't emerge from his bunker for weeks and left us alone after that.

No one ever admitted placing the grenade in Grey's boot, and we were stumped as to who could have done it. After everything settled down, however, a Vietnamese Kit Carson scout-interpreter named Sergeant Long, who was attached to our company, dropped a subtle hint one evening that led Stritt to think that he may have planted the grenade.

Sergeant Long

Sergeant Long was a former Viet Cong soldier who defected to our side after the Viet Cong killed several if not all the members of his immediate family. He had no love for the VC and was almost anxious to help us kick the enemy's butt. He kicked a lot of butt himself, and the Viet Cong had set a high price on his head, which became for him a source of immense pride.

Long lived with us and accompanied us on operations, serving as both a guide and an interpreter when we needed information from any Vietnamese we encountered. He also performed the initial interrogation of VC prisoners or suspects.

Because he was a former Communist soldier, he knew how our enemy operated. He knew the terrain and the areas that would be likely locations for booby traps or high enemy activity. He was of invaluable service to our company.

During an afternoon that we spent in the base camp at Tay Ninh, a few of us visited Sergeant Long in his private hootch. We were drinking Coca-Cola, chatting, and listening to the sergeant's stories. He had experienced years of combat; in comparison with him, we were FNGs. We were intrigued by this man.

The peaceful afternoon was disrupted by the impact of several mortar rounds within the base camp's perimeter. We got up and were running out the door on our way to the nearest bunker, as was the norm, when Sergeant Long yelled, "No. Stay here. No sweat."

We were not used to enduring a mortar attack outside of a sandbag bunker, or lying flat on the ground and pulling the buttons off our shirts to get lower, but we stayed. Somehow we felt that we would be safe if Sergeant Long wasn't concerned.

The sergeant stood in the center of the room and said, "Next one, over there," extending his arm and pointing. From the direction he indicated came the crunching impact of a mortar round.

"Next one, that way." Again, Sergeant Long extended his arm, and from the direction he indicated came the crunch of another impact.

He proceeded to call three more rounds, each time indicating correctly the location of the explosion. Then he said, "No more."

We looked at one another in amazement as the mortar rounds stopped. Either Sergeant Long knew the enemy so well that he could predict their actions, or he had called in those rounds himself. Either way, we were sticking close to this guy.

Back to Tan Son Nhut

We were told that we would remain in the Tay Ninh area for at least a month, performing road security, and we liked that idea. But as often happened, that didn't turn out to be the case. We heard rumors on a regular basis about where we were going and what we would be doing. Some of them turned out to be true, but there was no way of knowing. The war was much bigger than our platoon or company, and we had no choice except to roll with the punches.

6 June 68

Dear Mom,
　　Here we are back in Tan Son Nhut. We were supposed to stay up by Tay Ninh for at least a month. After 5 days they moved us down here.

One day just after we finished sweeping the road the captain put down the word that we had to go back to the mountain and load up bags and everything cause we had a change of mission.

We got down here at 12:00 midnight, night before last. Yesterday we went on a dismounted sweep [without tracks]. We got back at 1:00 and worked the rest of the day on a bunker. We finished the bunker at 7:00. At 7:30, they told us to tear down the bunkers & load up bags and baggage cause we were moving inside the wire of Tan Son Nhut.

We moved out at 9:00 p.m. We could see Tan Son Nhut from where we were, but we had to go all the way around it to a gate. We got here at midnight.

Now I just got up. It's 7:30. We don't know what we'll do today. Hot chow is on the way over to us.

We've had 2 instant NCOs come over. They go to a 6 month school to be a sergeant. Only thing is they don't know anything. We have another sergeant who's been in the army 17 years and is E-5. They're all squad leaders in our platoon.

I'm the lowest ranking squad leader, but the most experienced. Almost everybody who comes over PFC like I did, if they become a squad leader, it's in their last few months. Andy made sergeant right after he was hit.

I heard about Kennedy yesterday. It makes us feel kind of foolish over here. Trying to show these people how to run their country & we can't run our own.

Anyway I'd better go. Bye for now, Roger

It was hard to explain how we felt when we learned of the death of Bobby Kennedy and Martin Luther King, both of whom were assassinated while I was in-country. Vietnam was supposed to be the most dangerous place to be, and we infantrymen were the ones with the shortest life spans on earth, supposedly only a little more than three weeks. It was disconcerting to learn that our political leaders were being killed for no apparent reason. The United States—the world, as we called it—was supposed to be the safest place on our planet. We were hoping to survive so we could return to it. Once there, we thought we would be secure. The deaths of these two men upset that balance.

Bob Ordy went home to Pennsylvania on emergency leave for a while; when he returned, I was a squad leader. He was, too, for a month or so, but was then replaced by an instant NCO, someone who had attended a leadership course after completing basic training and AIT back in the States. At the conclusion of the course, the attendees—who were brand new in the service, had conducted no missions other than training, and had no practical experience— were promoted to sergeant and subsequently assigned to positions of authority over experienced soldiers such as Ordy. It wasn't right, but the army must have had a shortage of NCOs, and this was an intermediate corrective measure.

The instant NCOs, whom we called "shake & bakes," received their rank quickly but did not receive the experience necessary for effective leadership in Vietnam. Some of them turned out pretty well, provided that they took the time to learn what was going on from those with more time in-country. Those who preferred to throw their weight around impressed no one.

We thought that Ordy made a much better squad leader than the new instant NCO who had bumped him. Ordy had a good head, was excellent in combat, and knew what the war was about and how to fight it. He had a fine sense of humor and was liked and respected by those in our platoon. He was a leader whether he was a designated squad leader or not.

Our company ran two ambush patrols per night while we were near Tan Son Nhut, with each of the three line platoons going out two out of three nights. We didn't like this schedule. We had been spoiled by road security duty and had grown to enjoy remaining inside our perimeter at night.

By June 11, there were seven members in my squad. When not out on ambush, we spent the evenings getting to know one another better. When new arrivals joined our squad, we learned what was happening back in the States. We had been separated from home now for quite some time; I felt as though I had spent my entire life in Southeast Asia and would spend the rest of my life there. Home seemed to be only the subject of a dream I once had. So, when new guys fresh from the world joined our squad, they were a source of information about our country and served as confirmation that it still existed.

Some of the news they brought was good or neutral, such as the development of ten-speed bicycles, which became popular that summer, or descriptions of new-model cars. There was also bad news, such as political assassinations and the antiwar movement, the latter of which gathered steam during our year in Vietnam, partly because of the NVA's psychological victory of the 1968 Tet Offensive. By the time we were close to ending our tours, we heard that some of the troops returning home required police protection while getting off the plane. We knew that the war was unpopular, but hearing that the public's anger and frustration was being directed toward us and our fellow soldiers blew our minds. Weren't we the ones risking our lives to serve our country? Why was the hostility directed toward us? There wasn't anyone around who could give us an answer. We didn't have much time to dwell on this matter, but it was there in the backs of our minds.

The evenings we spent in our track were a good diversion from life's problems. Our conversations covered a wide variety of topics, from telling one another what we were like when we first got here—which brought a lot of laughs—to who gets sick when they're drunk, and even to men's cologne, which none of us used even if it had been available.

On June 14, I learned that I'd be going to Tokyo on R and R on June 25. That meant finding my khaki uniform back in Cu Chi. The minivacation was on my mind, and the anticipation helped improve my mood for a few days.

The company stayed at or near Tan Son Nhut throughout the month of June. The day after ambush patrols, we usually stayed within the company perimeter. To gain a momentary reprieve from the heat of the sun, we conducted a few pleasurable squad-sized patrols for the purpose of exploring the area and enjoying the cool shade of villages. It was pleasant walking along the main paths, which were lined with tall trees. We conducted some patrols in one particular village for the sole purpose of patronizing a roadside stand that sold fruit juice. Compared to the warm water from our canteens, this juice was highly prized. With the exception of the high number of long-distance, overnight, ambush patrols, this was a laid-back, enjoyable month.

Almost everyone in Vietnam either drank alcohol or smoked pot. Some did both. On June 17, a minor problem that I had been experiencing came to a head. My track had become a meeting point for guys in our platoon who smoked pot. My policy was that if they wanted to, okay, but not around me. I could have gotten in trouble if they were caught on my track, because I would be seen as condoning, at least through acquiescence, the activity by men under me. If they went to a bunker to smoke, I wouldn't know and would not be in trouble.

Some of the guys in my squad smoked marijuana—not enough to impair their judgment while we were out in the field, but enough to relax. Others in the platoon knew it and came over to join in when the opportunity presented itself. I had kicked them off my track on five occasions within the past month.

Around the middle of the month, our lieutenant, who wore prescription eyeglasses with thick lenses, broke his spectacles. Until a replacement pair was sent out, he was temporarily relieved of most of his command duties and didn't go to the field with the company. He spent some of his time inebriated, and on June 17 he joined the usual crowd on top of my track as they smoked pot. When the pipe was passed around, he took his share of the hits. I was inside the track and knew what they were doing because I could smell it. The rest of the guys assumed that because the lieutenant was there, I wouldn't kick them off.

I stood up in the hatch, turned off the radio, and called for some attention. "I told you about this before," I said when everybody quieted down.

You could have heard a pin drop. I let it soak in a while, then said, "I'm asking you to leave." The lieutenant was the first to move, then the rest slowly got up and left. I didn't have much trouble after that. I didn't condemm anyone for trying to escape the war for a few hours, I just asked that they not do it on my track.

• • •

On June 25, I went on R and R to Tokyo. The minivacation—rest and relaxation—was misnamed. There was no rest involved. Most of us didn't get any rest until we returned to Vietnam. We jokingly referred to our time away as I and I (intercourse and intoxication). I didn't drink, so I just called it "I."

I sat on the plane to Japan with someone from my division, a rear-echelon soldier. We got along well. He said that a friend from home who was in the air force and stationed in Japan was meeting him. If I wanted, I could hang around with them. Because I knew nothing about where I was going and had absolutely no plans, I was glad to do as he suggested.

We spent one night in Tokyo just to say we did, then took a monorail train to Tachikawa, a small town outside an air force base where the pace was a little slower and the cost of living was more reasonable.

On our first night there, I left my friends and headed off to find female companionship. I had walked several blocks along a street lined with nightclubs when I saw a cute-looking girl wearing a dress that came to slightly above her knees walking across the street in front of me. She glanced at me and headed into an alley. I followed. She turned into a doorway, glanced back to see if I was still there, then motioned for me to follow. So far, so good.

The place turned out to be a local drinking establishment that catered to airmen. The girl, I learned later, was what is known throughout most of Asia as a bar girl. She took my hand and led me to a booth. She said that if I wanted to talk to her, I would have to buy her a drink. She suggested that I get her something that turned out to be about 95 percent tea with 5 percent or less gin. It sold for three dollars. To stay in the establishment with this attractive girl, whose name was Mako, she said I would have to drink, too. I ordered a Coke.

The deal was that Mako and other girls who worked there were paid to hang around in the bar and let guys flirt with them. As long as the patrons continued to buy drinks, both for themselves and for the girls, they were allowed to stay. Otherwise, tough-looking bouncers took care of them.

Mako later explained to me that the girls were propositioned every night. The would-be suitors were informed that unless they stayed until quitting time, the girls couldn't leave with them. Most of the guys didn't hang around that long because they couldn't handle the alcohol or couldn't afford to keep buying drinks, most of which the girls wouldn't consume anyway. The guys would stay a while and then leave. If any of them lasted until quitting time, the girls told them that they didn't want their friends to see them leaving with them and directed them to another club a few blocks away where they would meet at an arranged time. Then the girls would leave through the back door and go home by a different route.

Because I didn't consume alcohol and had plenty of cash to keep Mako supplied with fresh drinks, she spent a lot of time with me at my table. I asked her to spend the night with me. By her quitting time, she decided that she liked me and agreed. I took her to my motel, and she insisted that we both take a bath before she'd let me touch her. After spending months without a shower, I didn't mind bathing twice in one day. When I was finished, Mako was in bed waiting for me. She was wonderful.

The next morning, I asked her if she wanted to go sight-seeing with me in Tokyo, and she agreed. As we were getting ready to leave, she said, "Pack your things."

"Huh?" I replied.

She said, "Just pack your things and come with me."

She took me to the front desk and checked me out of the hotel. Outside, she hailed a taxi and gave the driver directions in Japanese, which I didn't understand. The taxi entered the traffic and after a few minutes pulled up outside her apartment. She moved me in, and I spent the remainder of the week at her place. She took the rest of the week off from work.

By the end of the week, I was in love, and she cried for days before I left. I tried giving her money when I departed, but she wouldn't accept it. When I returned to Vietnam she wrote me passionate love letters every day for three weeks. Then they abruptly stopped. I concluded that she had found someone else. It was very nice while it lasted.

Returning to Vietnam was strange after having a taste of the real world. I was back in the land where everything was a lush shade of green and the people on our side wore olive drab.

6 July 68

Mom,

The war is still going on. Tomorrow night we're supposed to have 1000 NVA visitors. There's supposed to be 2 battalions closing in on us now. That's okay. It will be the first time we've ever had a large body count without worrying about losing our men.

We send about half our men out on LP when we don't go out on ambush. Last night we had to pull 2 ½ hours of guard apiece.

We had a paper wad fight that lasted til midnight. Then our track attacked another one. That's what we usually do when we're expecting to be attacked.

I'll mail this in the morning. Roger

The next night, July 7, was the night we were to be attacked by a thousand NVA troops. At 1100, I was on guard under a full moon. We had two LPs out in front of our sector of the perimeter for additional early warning.

One of our tracks had a starlight scope mounted on its .50-caliber machine gun, and while looking through the scope the guard spotted movement in a hedgerow not far away. He called in the movement to our platoon sergeant, who relayed the information to Charlie 6, our company commander. He said he would come down to take a look. With the warning of the attack, we were on heightened security, and adrenaline was flowing along the perimeter.

When the captain showed up, he climbed on top of the track, peered through the starlight scope, and found the movement that the guard had reported.

After studying it for a while, he laughed. "I see four monkeys out there and two of them are screwing."

That caused the mood to lighten up a bit, but it didn't last long. Our next radio call came from our guys out on ambush. They were receiving sniper fire from a hedgerow a hundred meters away. All of our new guys were tense, but the old-timers were more relaxed. They knew that all they could do at this point was wait to see if the attack materialized. There was no need to get excited. We made a living being prepared for attack; if it came, *c'est la guerre.*

I had been out on ambush the previous night, and we were scheduled to go out again the next night. I was as tired as I had ever been and was pulling three and a half hours of guard duty—half the night. Ten of our guys were out on LP and five more were helping the 3d Platoon with its ambush. That left only four men in each squad with two guards posted, one on the track and the other in the bunker.

A little later, the captain, who was new, called the ambush to see how the men were doing. They whispered that they were still getting a little sniper fire but were unhurt so far.

"There are no friendly forces in that area, so stay alert out there and keep me informed. Charlie Six. Out."

The next morning, the ambush patrol made it safely back inside our perimeter. We had survived another night.

One day after an all-night ambush, Chad found an aboveground sleeping position that someone had constructed. It was a sand-bagged structure about twelve feet square with about six pieces of PSP for a top. Chad was curious and poked his head inside. It was cool in the bunker's interior, and Chad crawled in and found a comfortable spot where he slept for the next twelve hours. The owners of the bunker didn't return, and Chad never found out who they were.

In addition to providing security for Tan Son'Nhut Air Force Base, we were acting as a reaction force for several locations in downtown Saigon that were high on the enemy target list. Among them was the U.S. embassy building. Each night, one of our platoons was on alert and standing by in case it was needed.

We squad leaders were taken into town in a jeep to become familiar with the routes we would have to take if we were called. My tour occurred the next day, July 8. We saw the U.S. embassy building, the Saigon River with lots of U.S. Navy ships, and the downtown area. Three or four of us rode in a jeep through the heavy city traffic as our driver honked his horn to clear our path of civilians, who were riding bicycles or small motorcycles and scooters. The air in our faces cooled us off, and we relaxed and enjoyed the drive through the large urban area with its tree-lined streets. The driver and I shared the same last name. He was stationed in Saigon and made a good tour guide.

At one point, a tank rumbled down the street at a high rate of speed. We pulled over to let the faster-moving vehicle pass. But the street was blocked farther ahead by a motorcycle with a cooling compartment on it, from which the owner sold frozen food items. The bike had stalled in the middle of the street, and the driver was attempting to kick-start the engine. Every once in a while he glanced over his shoulder to check how fast the tank was approaching. His kicks became more frequent and frantic. Finally, when it was apparent that the engine wouldn't start and the tank was going to hit him, he dove out of the way. Only a few feet separated his flying legs and the armored vehicle as he landed on the pavement. The tank never slowed down. It drove over the motorcycle, smashing it into a pile of rubble only a foot or so high. As the roaring sound of the tank's engine faded in the distance, the motorcycle owner walked out to the middle of the street and stood there a while with a stunned expression on his face, looking down on what had been his mode of transportation and his means of making a living.

The war affected most American families to some degree, but I don't believe that a single Vietnamese, whether soldier or civilian, on either side, emerged unscathed from the war's devastation. This was most likely not this man's first brush with the war, nor would it be his last.

We continued our tour along the shady streets.

We were never called upon to react to emergencies in Saigon. That was my only visit to the city, although we had fought in its outskirts a few times.

Also on July 15, we received a new platoon leader. Lieutenant McDonald had been transferred, for reasons unknown to us, to another company. Two weeks later we heard that he had been killed while on a combat operation with his new platoon. Our platoon's bad luck with platoon leaders was continuing. Our new lieutenant was a graduate of West Point, and we would soon learn that he was trouble.

On July 16, we headed back to the Black Virgin Mountain for more road security duty. During the rainy season, there was a limited number of missions that were suitable for our armored personnel carriers. There was just too much water and mud for the heavy vehicles. In addition to guarding Tan Son Nhut and road security, we went on several company-sized foot operations, without the tracks, staying out for several days at a time. On some of these nights, we were soaked by the rain and didn't dry out until the sun rose the next morning.

On July 23, while checking for mines during the road-clearing portion of the day, we were confronted with nine piles of rubble that had been placed across the entire roadway for a distance of several miles. Each pile contained brush, rocks, and soil. There were several reasons why the enemy might have placed such barriers. Perhaps they did it to slow us down to provide time for an enemy withdrawal to our front. A more serious threat would be an ambush, with the roadblock to slow us down to produce better targets. Of course, it could have been nothing more than a message that the enemy was still around.

The roadblocks could be booby-trapped. Sometimes a grenade with the pin pulled was found next to an unexploded mortar or artillery round and held in place against a branch or lump of soil with a rock or some other heavy object. Moving or jostling the pile would cause the spoon to spring off the grenade, and its detonation would set off the larger round as a secondary explosion.

Getting rid of these roadblocks relatively quickly was to our advantage. We sometimes did so by tying a long rope between the lead track and a large branch on the pile of debris, then clearing the area and backing up, pulling the structure apart. If there was no resultant explosion, we plowed through the rest of the debris. Sometimes, when in a hurry, we simply went around the piles.

A village that was thought to be aiding a group of thirty-three Viet Cong was near several of the roadblocks. We suspected that if the rumors were true, the VC from the village had placed the roadblocks.

After the road was clear, my track ended up near the suspected VC village, from which we would provide security for the road as convoys traveled back and forth. About 1400, I took two guys from my squad and made a little patrol through the village. We weren't conducting a search but were just looking around.

I wasn't worried about being hit, because if there were only thirty-three enemy soldiers there, they wouldn't attack us during the day-time with so many other GIs nearby; they weren't prepared for a large battle. The village was not hostile but neither was it friendly. No kids came up to us, as they normally did in more secure villages or areas without enemy activity. Not surprisingly, we saw only women and a few children. The women avoided eye contact with us and the kids mostly stayed out of sight, an ominous sign.

We walked back to our tracks and felt safe there, albeit unwelcome, for the remainder of the day. None of the villagers approached us, as would have occurred in normal areas. We increased our vigilance but made it through the day with no incidents.

Once again, we heard reports that we were to be attacked that evening back in our company perimeter. This time, the strength of the enemy was reported to be four battalions. Just in case it was more than a rumor, we placed additional Claymores outside the wire and made sure we had large amounts of ammo and grenades within reach. Once again, the night passed quietly but with higher amounts of anxiety.

I now had less than a hundred days left in country. I was officially getting short.

During the month of July, I talked to Sergeant Cattrell about promoting Chad to the rank of sergeant. He was a good soldier and certainly fulfilled the role of a noncommissioned officer in our squad. He deserved the promotion. I completed a nomination form, and Sergeant Cattrell turned it in for me. Effective August 1, both Chad and I became buck sergeants. We proudly sewed on our three stripes.

Dau Tieng

During the first part of August, the company, and the entire brigade consisting of four battalions, moved its base of operations to Dau Tieng, near the village of that name, located approximately twenty-one klicks (thirteen miles) southeast of the Black Virgin Mountain and near the banks of the Saigon River. For a while in our new location, our daily routine consisted of overnight ground operations in the nearby rubber plantations. Ground operations were another option during the rainy season when we had limited use of our tracks.

We conducted sweeps and searched villages during the daytime and set up an ambush each night. In the morning, we would meet Alpha Company, who came out to meet us on their tracks. They would dismount and we would return to Dau Tieng on their tracks. The next morning, we would drive out to where they were and continue their operation while they returned to the base camp on our vehicles.

We began seeing the first signs of an enemy buildup and what became known as a summer offensive. On August 8, we ran into five VC in the rubber plantation. We opened up on them, but they escaped. That afternoon, we were eating C rations when we received sniper fire. We took cover, and the shots stopped after about twenty minutes.

That evening, en route to an ambush site with my squad on point, we were moving through some dense brush and making entirely too much noise, but we couldn't help it. Someone in the rear of our column saw five VC soldiers following us, maybe to get a fix on our ambush location and to judge our vulnerability for a possible attack.

Suddenly, up on point, we heard Vietnamese voices to our front. We pulled back a short distance and established a quick company perimeter, where we spent the night. We altered our plans because we had enemy to our front and to our back. We assumed that they knew of our presence, and there was little chance of us surprising anyone with an ambush, so we switched to the defensive. With two groups of enemy units of unknown size somewhere nearby in the darkness, we remained on high alert throughout the night.

Early the next morning, we heard mortar tubes firing from where we had heard the voices the night before. Seven mortar rounds landed close to us, but no one was hurt.

Later, we were fired at by some of the VC, one of whom was using an M79 grenade launcher. We learned why this weapon was the small arm that our enemy feared the most. There is a tremendous psychological impact when the *bloop* is heard. Our hearts stopped as we wondered if the round was heading directly toward us. When it exploded and no one was hurt, we resumed breathing. In all, ten rounds were fired at us through the rubber trees. Half an hour later, we were mortared again but with no casualties.

Alpha Company was due to meet us near a village, but we heard on the radio that the company had been ambushed on the way out. They joined us later as we were on our way back to Dau Tieng, where we would spend the rest of the day in the large base camp. On the way we were fired on by about twenty-five enemy troops from a wood line approximately two hundred meters away. Again, no one was hurt.

We knew that our luck couldn't hold out like this forever. We were ready to go back to the boredom and long-distance ambush patrols of Tan Son Nhut.

That day, Alpha Company's luck ran out. They had a lieutenant shot and killed.

Elephant Grass Incident

One day we were assigned a mission of searching an area we had never been to but was suspected of being an enemy stronghold. Upon arrival at the area, our company commander assigned search areas for each platoon. We had not conducted reconnaissance patrols and knew little of the territory. The captain assigned areas to each platoon by pointing to locations on a map.

When we reached our platoon's assigned area, we found that a considerable portion of it consisted of a clearing covered with ten-to-twelve-foot-high elephant grass. Some of us, myself included, felt that this might be an easy search. We were surprised when the lieutenant said we would penetrate to the center of the tall grass. It didn't sound like a smart thing to do.

I was on point that day and Chad was right behind me. Elephant grass leaves clack together when moved. It was impossible to move through the grass without first knocking it out of the way, which produced a noise that could be heard over a considerable distance. Regardless of how cautious we tried to be, we made too much noise. In addition, the grass had sharp edges, which cut into our skin, producing something like a paper cut.

This might have been a good area for the enemy to hide, but it was a difficult place to search using our usual techniques, consisting of the platoon operating a sweep on line. A safer method might have been circling the elephant grass looking for possible access trails, listening for the sound of enemy voices, or watching for any other signs of human presence. Instead, the method chosen by our platoon leader was a mistake.

This was Lieutenant McDonald's replacement, and we found out that he wanted to make a name for himself. I believe that this was common among new, young leaders, but unfortunately it was too often dangerous for the members of these people's units.

The lieutenant told us to lead the way directly into the center of the area dominated by the elephant grass. After moving a short distance, Chad and I approached the lieutenant. We were acutely aware that we would be vulnerable and unable to defend ourselves if we made contact.

"Sir, this is making too much noise. If anyone's in there, they'll hear us coming and we won't be able to move on line."

"The captain wants this area searched," replied the lieutenant, "and by God, we're going to search it. I don't care how much noise it makes."

We had our orders, and we had little choice other than to proceed, although we knew without a doubt that this was a dumb thing to do. The only way I could move through the elephant grass was to hold my M16 out in front of me, parallel to the ground, stiff armed, and fall forward into the dense foliage, landing on my hands and knees. That knocked over some of the vegetation and allowed me to move forward about a foot and a half, trampling down a path for the rest of the guys to follow. I repeated the stiff-armed fall over and over, moving forward only a foot and a half each time and making a tremendous amount of noise. The lieutenant followed us unconcerned.

It was hot, and the sun overhead was unobstructed in its assault on our platoon's patrol. The sweat was soon pouring off me. I became exhausted, and Chad moved past me and took my place. By the time he was too tired to lead, I had recovered somewhat and we switched off again. We proceeded in this manner, taking turns knocking over the grass for about an hour, knowing all the while that any enemy within hearing range was aware of our presence. This situation was best avoided; it could get someone killed.

Suddenly, directly to our front, Chad and I heard Vietnamese voices. The enemy had a small camp in the middle of the large patch of elephant grass, and they had heard us coming. It was a good place for a small Viet Cong unit to hide, except for the possibility of detection from the air. Perhaps they had some form of overhead cover.

We could not maneuver the platoon up on line to engage the enemy because of the difficulty of moving through the grass. Besides, the enemy would know from the noise what we were up to and would fire on us first. We would be mowed down. In addition, visibility in the grass was limited to about six feet, and we had no idea of the size and strength of the enemy unit.

Our lieutenant decided that our best course of action was to head back down the path that we had made coming in. This was his first smart decision of the day.

Everyone turned around and began hurrying down the trail, with Chad and I now bringing up the rear. We had just gotten near the end of the elephant grass when we heard enemy mortar tubes popping out four rounds from the spot where we had heard the voices. *Thuum thuum thuum thuum.* No one knew what to do, including our new lieutenant. Sergeant Long, who had been near the rear of the column and was now near its head, took charge.

He pointed and yelled, "Run. That way."

Because no one, including the lieutenant, had any better ideas, we ran in the direction that Sergeant Long indicated. As soon as we cleared the area, four mortar rounds landed and exploded right where we had been standing.

The sound of four more rounds coming out of the mortar tubes reached us, and once again Sergeant Long pointed and yelled, "That way."

Once again we followed his directions, and more rounds landed where we had been standing moments before when the tubes had fired. The same thing happened a third time, and once more Sergeant Long led us out of the enemy fire.

No one received a scratch that day, and we all became believers in Sergeant Long and his unique abilities. He had been useful to us as a guide and an interpreter, but on this day we fully realized that he could help keep us alive as well.

I didn't know what our lieutenant was feeling at that moment, but he had to have been stunned. He must have realized that he made mistakes that day that had almost led to the death of some of us, if not himself. If it hadn't been for Sergeant Long—the ex-VC—some of us would have died. Our Kit Carson scout's credibility rose instantly, whereas that of the lieutenant, who was still an unknown quantity, plummeted. The military has a saying: "Respect for the rank is automatic; respect for the individual must be earned." Our lieutenant had a long way to go to earn the trust of our platoon.

Around August 11, a Viet Cong soldier who surrendered to us told us about a three-story underground hospital, a prisoner-of-war (POW) camp, two large weapons caches, and a base camp, all of which were nearby. We heard rumors that all three of the companies in our battalion would be sent in to overrun and capture the complex. But we also heard rumors that we would return to Tan Son Nhut. As usual, we didn't know what was in store for us.

Rubber Incident

The most unusual thing that I witnessed in Vietnam occurred during the evening of August 13 while we were on an overnight operation in the large Michelin rubber plantation.

We had been assigned duty as a blocking force for an operation against a suspected VC village south of Dau Tieng. It was the usual operation; another unit was going to land in helicopters at dawn on the opposite side of the village. The men would make their presence known by shouting and firing a few shots, then begin moving toward the village. We would block the escape route for any fleeing Victor Charlies (VC).

We were to be in place before the other company landed at dawn. Our battalion, however, was concerned that we might give away our position if we set up too early. So we moved in the general direction of the village on foot the afternoon before, and when darkness fell we established a company perimeter a few klicks away. The plan was for us to move into place near the village around 0430.

In our overnight position in the rubber plantation, we formed a company-sized perimeter, with everyone facing outward. We did not dig in or put out any Claymores. We wouldn't be there that long.

I had two brand new guys in my squad, and this was their first night in the field and their first combat operation. Because they were both excited and apprehensive, I decided to let them stand the first watch together, thinking that they would help calm each other.

Around 2345, I was roused from sleep by Ski, one of my two men on watch, who reported hearing movement. I crawled up on line with them, and we lay there together for about twenty minutes but heard nothing.

"If you hear anything else, come get me," I said, then went back to my sleeping position, about ten feet to their rear.

Within an hour, I was awakened by a shot and a loud scream. Soon thereafter a machine gun began firing. I quickly joined Ski and the other new man on guard, who reported shooting someone about fifteen feet in front of our position as he walked toward them. They said that after I went back to sleep, they heard movement again, but it was so close that they were afraid to move, so they didn't come to get me. Then they saw him. He was moving between rubber trees. He would pause momentarily at one tree, then crouch and move in a half trot to the next tree, where he would stop once more for a few seconds. He repeated this several times, coming steadily closer.

Eventually he was within about twenty feet of our position and appeared to see the men on guard. He stood straight up and began walking directly toward them.

My two new guys on guard were armed with an M60 machine gun and an M79 grenade launcher that was loaded with a canister round, which fires nine steel balls and is like a 40mm shotgun. One

of the two guards attempted firing the M60, but it jammed. He began pulling the bolt backward in an attempt to clear the gun, an act
which made quite a bit of noise considering that the remainder of
the perimeter was silent. The man approaching our perimeter from
the rubber trees did not say anything. Although he had to have
heard the noise my two men made with the machine gun—and he
had to know what was going on—he continued walking toward
them. Finally the other man on guard grabbed the M79 and fired a
quick shot, hitting the intruder in the chest. That shot and the resultant scream is what awakened me as well as the rest of the company.

Moans were coming from just outside our perimeter. The man
on guard finally got the M60 working, and he stood up and fired toward the moans. In the muzzle flashes, he reported seeing other
men running away.

The entire perimeter stayed awake and on 100 percent alert,
watching and listening for further activity for an hour or so. But we
did not hear or see anything outside our perimeter. Eventually
everyone settled back down again.

I was awakened at about 0315, shortly before the rest of the company was scheduled to get up and prepare to move to our assigned
position for the blocking force. Before waking the others, I decided
to check the body, a common practice. We looked for documents,
weapons, or anything else that could provide information pertain-
ing to the status of our enemy. The presence of a watch, money, and
plenty of ammunition meant that the forces we were facing were
well supplied. Documents such as maps or orders could yield important intelligence information. This knowledge helped us know,
and prepare to engage, our enemy.

I told our guards what I was doing so they wouldn't shoot me,
then walked outside the perimeter. After going about twenty feet, I
located the body; it was lying parallel to our perimeter with his head
to my left and his feet to my right. I began checking him over. The
first thing I noticed was unusual; this soldier did not have a weapon.
And he was wearing rubber overalls. I had never seen that before.
Although the night was dark, I could see that the corpse was wearing American jungle boots. I had never known the enemy to wear

our boots, but I supposed it was not unheard of. That alone would have been no big deal, but there were more surprises. The dead man did not have anything in any of his pockets—no money, no watch, not even a pocket knife. Furthermore, he had no ammunition, no web gear, no military equipment at all. Just a dead guy lying out there. I was stumped.

I returned to the perimeter and called our lieutenant and told him what I'd found. He also thought it was unusual and called the captain, who came over and asked me to take him out to the body.

Upon arrival, we crouched over the body, one of us on either side as we tried to figure out what was going on. There was just a hint of daylight in the eastern sky by this time, and the captain crouched over the corpse, lifted the head to within a few inches of his own, and took a close look at the face.

He lowered the head, then looked at me. "I think this is one of our guys," he said.

I was astounded. We returned to the perimeter, and the captain made a radio call to the other platoon leaders.

"Charlie Six to all units. Are any of you missing anyone?"

Sure enough, the 1st Platoon reported a man missing, an instant NCO named Collins who had been in-country and with our company for only about three weeks.

Ski and the other new replacement on guard had been elated that their first taste of combat produced a confirmed body count on their first night out. When they found out that the person they killed was an American, they were devastated. The incident affected them so much that neither of them spoke at all for about the next three weeks, except for a few absolutely necessary sentences, despite my attempts to convince them that they had done the right thing. It wasn't their fault; their mission had been to watch for enemy activity to their front and stop anyone trying to get past them. They had done exactly what they were expected to do.

The next morning I talked to several other members of our platoon and pieced together what I think was the course of events of that strange evening.

Collins, the new instant NCO, was on watch in the 1st Platoon's sector of the perimeter. He didn't own a watch and had borrowed one from the soldier he was to wake up and who was scheduled to replace him on guard. This was a common practice among those who didn't have a timepiece. After waking up his replacement, he was to return the watch.

Collins was on first watch, and it was relatively early in the evening. Because there were others awake in his platoon's sector, he thought it was safe to leave his station. He came over to my platoon, where he was whispering and chatting quietly with a buddy. It was a dark night and we were under the closed canopy produced by the rubber trees. When he was ready to return to his position, he became disoriented and didn't know which way to go. He woke up someone in my platoon and asked him to point the way he could take to get to his platoon. The recently awakened soldier indicated a direction, and the new NCO headed that way. Upon awaking, however, our soldier had also been disoriented; he thought he was lying in the opposite direction and, as a result, had pointed outside the perimeter. He remembered doing so the next day.

So, Collins had gone wandering outside the perimeter. That much we knew, because he was shot attempting, presumably, to get back inside. Nobody had seen him go. I believe that once outside our area, he was captured by an enemy force. They took his helmet and web gear, his weapon, if he had one, and the watch belonging to the next man scheduled to be on guard in the 1st Platoon. They also took everything from his pockets, including his wallet.

The enemy then devised a plan to get inside our perimeter, using their captive. They would have him lead the way, thinking that we would recognize him and not shoot, then they would simply follow him in. Once inside, they could wreak havoc, and we would be unable to fire at them without endangering our own forces on the opposite side of our perimeter. It wasn't a bad plan, but it didn't work. When our guys didn't recognize the man walking toward our perimeter as an American and killed him, the enemy quickly left the area, which explains the fleeing images seen by our machine gunner in the muzzle flashes.

This also helps explain why Collins did not speak or stop while our men were trying to clear the M60, a noise that he had to have heard. Perhaps he thought we would shoot toward the enemy behind him, or they would shoot him.

Further evidence of this theory is that the next man scheduled for guard duty in the 1st Platoon was never awakened. He never saw his watch again, either. The 1st Platoon spent the remainder of the evening with no guard. Apparently after the shooting, they all assumed that someone else was awake on watch, and they all went back to sleep.

I may have been the only one to gather all these pieces of the puzzle. I tried to explain to my superiors what I thought had happened, but evidently they didn't believe me. In their defense, there were other, more pressing matters that needed their attention. They were busy with the details of our current operation and were more concerned with the living than the dead. In any event, the explanation would not bring Collins back.

The last major battle in which I took part occurred on August 19, 1968. Our brigade was still operating out of Dau Tieng, one of the 25th Infantry Division's forward base camps, named for the nearby village. The camp was built on part of an old French rubber plantation. A house and a large, aboveground, concrete swimming pool, now empty, were inside our perimeter, on the opposite side of the airstrip from our company area.

Every company in our battalion was making daily contact with the enemy every time we went outside the perimeter. The day before, August 18, one of the other companies in our battalion refused to go out. To my knowledge, this was the only time that one of our companies refused to perform. It serves to illustrate the enemy's strength and confidence in this part of Vietnam at the time.

On August 19, Charlie Company and Bravo Company were to search an area of reported enemy activity. We left Dau Tieng on our APCs and drove a mile or two west along the rubber tree–lined route toward Tay Ninh before turning into a large wooded area to the north. Bravo Company continued on to its destination a little farther west.

We set up a temporary company perimeter in an elongated bottle–shaped clearing. The thin neck of the bottle projected to the north of the larger circular clearing in which we had set up. I dismounted my squad and headed into the tree line on our side of the perimeter to provide security for the company.

Upon entering the woods, we found a well-used dirt path, called a speed trail, running parallel to the tree line. It was just far enough inside the lush tropical vegetation to prevent visual detection but still allow its users to see what was going on in the clearing. A speed trail as well used as this one apparently was, this far from any village, meant only one thing: an enemy stronghold with heavy enemy activity. *Oh crap,* or words to that effect, went through my mind.

Within seconds, AK fire erupted from the woods around us. It sounded as though we were in the middle of the enemy soldiers who were firing at our guys. We got down on the path, wondering what to do. Vietnamese voices sounded close enough for us to touch the people who were speaking. Because of the density and lushness of the foliage, though, we couldn't see anyone.

The firing continued for a few minutes, then let up. The firing closest to us ceased. We decided that the enemy didn't know we were there, but to remain would have meant our deaths. In order to survive, we had to rejoin the company. I figured that the voices and AK fire were coming from a nearby bunker whose occupants had taken a tunnel to another bunker with a better view and field of fire. That accounted for why we hadn't seen anyone or heard any sounds of movement. In any event, I hoped that was the case.

It was now or never. We ran from the tree line, expecting to be fired upon from the rear, but that was better than the alternative— remaining in the enemy's camp. We successfully joined the company, and the guys took up positions and prepared to fire.

As soon as we arrived, my platoon leader summoned me to a meeting with the company commander. The captain showed us an aerial photograph of the area we were in, including our clearing.

"We're going to meet up with Bravo Company to our west," the captain informed us. "Your platoon," he said, glancing at the lieutenant, "will be on point."

The lieutenant looked at me. "Your squad will lead," he said.

The captain pointed to the map. "We're taking heavy fire and we've got to get out of here," he told me. "Take this clearing due north as fast as you can go." He indicated with his finger the neck of the bottle-shaped clearing.

"At the north end there will be a road leading off to the west. You can't see it on the map because there's a closed canopy over it, but it's there. Take that road. It will lead us to Bravo Company. Now, let's move out."

We jumped on our track, with Big John in the driver's hatch. In a few seconds we were leading the company straight north, traveling as fast as we could go, which was thirty-five to forty miles per hour. As we moved, we continued to take small-arms fire. But as far as we could tell, no one was getting hit, although everyone was riding on the tops of the tracks.

As we approached the north end of the clearing, I looked for the road leading west. I found nothing except the continuation of the dense tropical trees and vegetation that composed the edge of the forest. We were slowing down as we approached the tree line to our front, and I was in the process of calling the captain on the radio.

"Charlie Six, this is Two-three. Over."

"Charlie Six."

"There's no road here—"

My sentence was interrupted by heavy gunfire that erupted from the tree line about forty feet to our front.

A bullet struck my upper right arm. On reflex, I swung my legs over the side of my jeep seat and jumped off the track, landing lightly on the ground. We never fought on top of the tracks. About six feet above the ground, we would have made good targets.

To my consternation, no one else jumped off to assist me in engaging the tree line. Rather, the tracks began backing up and left the area. In a few moments I was suddenly alone. I learned later that the rest of my squad feared that I had been killed or wounded badly.

I was left lying in waist-high grass in front of at least an enemy machine-gun position. With the company retreating behind me, I was once again in the predicament of being stranded with the enemy, where I was certain to be killed or captured. I got up and began running, keeping low, and zigzagging in order to make as elusive a target as possible. I could feel the concussion of the air from machine-gun rounds that zipped past my head, and I could hear the sharp crack of the gun behind me, which meant that they were shooting at me.

I continued to run as fast as I could in my hunched-over position—until I hit a log in the middle of the clearing. I hadn't seen it in the waist-high grass, and I went down fast and hard. Apparently the enemy thought that they had hit me, because I heard the fire shift from me over to the right, toward the retreating tracks. I remained on the ground catching my breath for about twenty seconds, then jumped up and continued running until I caught up with my track. I grabbed the handhold on the back near the top and climbed up.

Everyone on top of the track was wounded. The round that hit me had ricocheted off the .50 turret, thereby splitting in two. The brass casing that struck my arm penetrated all the way to the bone. The lead portion and some of the brass of possibly the same round hit Chad, my assistant squad leader, in the shoulder. The round traversed through his torso and came to rest just under the surface of his back. Chad was sitting up but was obviously in pain. The others had less serious wounds.

Giant turned out to be lucky on this day. We were still wearing World War II–style helmets, which the army was supposedly hesitant to replace because occasionally a round shot directly at a helmet would penetrate the steel shell but then traverse around the helmet between the outer shell and the inner nylon liner exiting out the back. This is what happened to Giant.

The company re-formed in its original position, in the large circular opening at the southern end of the bottle-shaped clearing. This time, though, the tracks set up in wagon train style, with each track not facing outward but pointed toward the track to the front. I had never seen this before. This position offered the broad sides of our tracks to the enemy RPG gunners. The company was spooked.

Small-arms fire continued from the woods and intensified as more enemy troops joined in the attack. Medevac helicopters were called, and a little later I and most of the other members of my squad were dusted off. We swooped upward and out of the dangerous action below.

In our absence, the company eventually joined Bravo Company, but in the process it was openly attacked in broad daylight by a large, confident NVA force. On this rare occasion, the NVA chose to show themselves and assault our forces rather than snipe at us from the tree line or hit and run. It was the most aggressive enemy activity we had seen during hours of daylight.

Back in Dau Tieng, I once again went through the experience of having a wound treated. It wasn't any more pleasant than the last time. For me, it was more painful than being wounded in the first place, but then I didn't have any broken bones or damaged organs.

The brass casing that had struck my arm made a hole about the size of a quarter all the way to the bone, where it lodged. The procedure to remove it was similar to the one used on my other wounds, except that this time there was no difficulty in locating the path that the round had taken. The hole was large, and when the probe was inserted about an inch and a half, it produced a metallic *clink*. A surgical instrument that looked like a pair of needle-nosed pliers was used to grasp the casing, but it would not dislodge from my bone. When the doc pulled, it felt as though the entire bone lifted in my arm. After a few pulls, something popped, and the casing came out on the end of the pliers. It was rinsed off and given to me as a souvenir. Before the bandages were applied, I rotated my fist and watched the ropelike red muscle move back and forth inside my arm. Interestingly, it didn't hurt.

About the same time, Chad was having his wounds attended to. Afterward, he was sent to a hospital in Cam Ranh Bay, along the coast, to recuperate for two weeks, then was sent back to Cu Chi. After a month or so, his wounds had healed well enough that he was assigned perimeter bunker duty. We had already learned that we didn't have to be fully recovered for that duty.

I later learned what had happened to the company after we were medevacked. On the way back to Dau Tieng the next day, the company passed through a well-prepared ambush. Reports indicated that enemy soldiers were in place, shoulder to shoulder, for a distance of a half mile or so along the main road connecting Dau Tieng and Tay Ninh, the road we had taken on our way out to the battle and along which the company would have to travel on its journey back to our base camp.

When the company entered the kill zone, RPG rounds struck and disabled the first and last tracks in line. Rubber trees near the road had recently been knocked down to improve visibility and reduce the likelihood of such an ambush occurring, but they had not been removed. The tracks couldn't maneuver off the road because of these trees and because the first and last tracks had been disabled. The only option was to stand and fight until the lead track could be pushed off to the side. That process took about twenty minutes, during which the company was exposed to heavy and deadly enemy fire.

An MP guard at the front gate to the base camp told me that when our company finally came through the entrance, arms and legs were lying on some of the APCs and blood was running off the tops. The 1st Platoon suffered the most casualties; its hootch was empty that night.

Sometime during this battle, Sergeant Long, who was still serving with our platoon, was killed. He was wounded and had fallen to the ground at the rear of one of our tracks. He was inadvertently run over when the company retreated, with the tracks operating in reverse. The driver didn't know he was there. It was a sad ending for a brave soldier who had endured the better part of a decade engaged in warfare.

Thus began another month-long recuperation period for me, this time in Dau Tieng. Once again, it took me a good five minutes to rise into a seated position from a prone position. It was surprising to me how much my arm muscles were needed for this maneuver.

Sergeant Kirkham, who had reenlisted only to end up back in the same squad for another tour, had been with us for about a month and replaced me as squad leader.

19 August 68

Dear Mom,

I went out and got my fourth purple heart today. I got a bullet in the arm. Everybody in my squad was wounded except 3 guys. The driver (Big John) was hit in the neck with shrapnel. Another guy got hit in the side. Chadwick got a bullet in the shoulder, same one that hit me. It hit someplace on the track and split.

They took it out today (the bullet) and I'm OK. I was hit on the front of my arm exactly opposite from my shrapnel wound. Everybody in my squad's okay, too.

Don't you worry. I won't be going out anymore. By the time I recuperate from this, it will be almost time to go home.

I better close for now. I'll write again in a few days when my arm feels better.

Love, Rog

Although I was wounded four times, I actually received only two Purple Hearts. I guess the paperwork for the other two was lost in the shuffle or was never submitted. When I had been injured on previous occasions, the company was in heavy contact with the enemy and many troops were wounded or killed. It's easy to understand how the appropriate paperwork could have been overlooked or lost.

This time when I was hit, we were in contact with close to four thousand NVA soldiers. Our battalion had thirteen killed and eighty wounded. The next day, the second day of the battle, seventeen men in my company were killed, most from the 1st Platoon. The NVA were climbing on the tracks during the daytime, so I heard. That was unheard of during most of my tour. During the two-day battle, our battalion had an estimated body count of seven hundred.

Charlie Company had no one killed but twenty wounded, until the second day. Nobody in my platoon was killed. Our company lost six tracks but none from my platoon. Meanwhile, our battalion was still making contact every day.

I found myself back in the same routine as in February and March when I was recuperating. I made trips to the first-aid station every day to have the wound cleaned and the bandage changed. For a few days, I read books, rested, and walked to the PX.

On several occasions during my recuperation in Dau Tieng, while the first sergeant was away, I was the noncommissioned officer in charge (NCOIC) of the company area. Next to Top, our first sergeant, I had the most rank out of those in the rear. Each week during this time period, the battalion commander, Lieutenant Colonel Anderson, held a briefing for the first sergeants of the battalion's companies, or their designees. When Top was away, I occasionally attended these sessions. Enemy activity around Dau Tieng continued at a high level for the remainder of my tour. During one briefing, the colonel relayed reports from the companies in the field of taller Asian soldiers who had been observed serving with the NVA. Their uniforms were a different shade of green than those of the North Vietnamese troops, with more of a blue tone, if I remember correctly, with red stars on the caps. The battalion commander thought that these were Chinese forces who were serving as military advisers for the NVA. China never publicly acknowledged that they had soldiers serving in Vietnam and assisting the NVA, but that is what was believed in our battalion after we heard these reports.

Our company area at Dau Tieng, which was right next to the wire on the east side of the base camp's perimeter, was hit by enemy forces several times while I was there. During one battle when our company was in from the field, a track was pulled up to the wire so that the .50-caliber machine gun could be added to the outgoing firepower. After the shooting stopped, an American was found dead in the turret behind the .50 with a small entry wound in the back of his head. The evidence indicated that the mortal wound was probably caused by some rear-echelon warrior who didn't want to get up on line with the rest of us and instead stayed back by the hootches and fired his M16 from there. We guessed that he had been serving in the rear because few infantrymen would make this mistake. I suppose that the official notification of this soldier's death didn't include that he had been shot from the rear where there had been no enemy soldiers. Or perhaps whoever wrote the notification didn't know what happened and said that the man died as a result of an injury sustained during an enemy attack, which was true.

Hack, who was getting short by this time, received a personal hard blow in the form of a telegram from the American Red Cross a few days after the battle in which I was wounded. His kid brother had been killed in a traffic accident back home. The news was traumatic for Hack. He was the one engaged in a war, and just when it looked as though he'd survive and make it out of the country, his brother back in the States was killed. Hack went home a few weeks early on emergency leave. Because it was so close to the end of his tour, he did not return.

After all Hack and I had been through together, it was an awkward way to have to say good-bye. Because my wound didn't affect my ability to walk, I escorted him to Cu Chi, then to Bien Hoa, where the planes that took soldiers home (called freedom birds) took off. Hack was in a daze throughout this period. I took care of the paperwork for him and made sure he was in the right places at the right times and didn't miss his connections. It was the least I could do for someone who had become one of my best friends.

By August 22, my arm was feeling better, although it was stiff and sore because the bullet had gone right through the middle of the muscle. The doctor was to sew up the wound on this day, but it had been healing so well from the inside out that stitching the hole closed would have caused a permanent wrinkle in my skin.

On one of my visits to the PX, I ran into an old buddy from my high school class, Jim Kline. He was also recuperating from a wound to one of his forearms. We were really surprised to see each other and spent a relaxing afternoon chatting, reminiscing about our hometown and drinking lemonade in the shade of the trees near the PX snack bar. Jim was serving with the 3d Battalion, 22d Infantry (3/22), which was one of the four battalions in our brigade. He was in the same platoon as Oliver Stone and was the medic in the now famous film *Platoon*.

Chad eventually worked his way back to Dau Tieng, where we were pleasantly surprised to see him. After a few days there, he went to an aid station because he felt something under the skin of his back whenever he leaned on something. The doctor he was talking to sent him to a nearby tent, where two lower graded soldiers with no rank insignia examined him, gave him a local anesthetic, and made an incision. They pulled out the lead portion of the round that had hit him a month before.

Tran Ngoc Bich

There were several of us walking wounded in Dau Tieng. Because we had little more to do than recover from our wounds, we gathered in the mess hall every day during the afternoon. It was the coolest place in the company area. Our hootches, which were olive-drab tents, baked in the sun and were stifling during the day. The mess hall had a real roof that was ventilated, which made being in the dark interior comparable to being in the shade of a large tree.

The mess hall operated with civilian employees who came from the village of Dau Tieng. Some assisted our cooks in the kitchen; others set places for officers and served them drinks. The rest of us GIs went through the line and got our own food, cafeteria style on a tray. The officers, who sat apart from us, simply walked in, sat down, and waited for their food and drink to be brought to them.

During the afternoons that we spent in the mess hall, some of the girls brought us lemonade, Kool-Aid, or whatever cold drink was available. I slowly developed a relationship with one of the girls, a cute thirteen year old. We began by teasing each other. After a while, she began saving a chair for me at the table where the guys sat and talked. She often escorted me to my seat, then brought me something to drink. If I wasn't there for one reason or another, she asked about me. Sometimes she wrote me a note and gave it to someone to give to me. Some of the guys told me that they thought she really liked me, and they kidded me about it. She began giving me photographs of herself. Like many Vietnamese, she loved to have her picture taken.

Early in our relationship, she teasingly accused me of being a "*beaucoup* butterfly," a Vietnamese term for someone with many girlfriends or boyfriends. A butterfly visits one flower, then flies off to visit another and another. The term was used in a lighthearted, teasing way but also as a means of checking availability and trustworthiness. Much like interactions between the sexes elsewhere, it wasn't always easy to distinguish between teasing and a serious expression of interest. *Beaucoup* butterflies were usually avoided. The French word *beaucoup* was learned during the ninety-some years during which Vietnam and portions of Laos and Cambodia composed French Indochina.

My friend arrived each morning on the deuce-and-a-half truck that transported the mess hall workers and the other civilian employees from the village of Dau Tieng. Sometimes she produced a note from her pocket that she had written the evening before. I would read it later in my hootch and prepare a response. There was a language barrier between us, but she knew some French and we used a combination of pidgin English and French with a few Vietnamese words thrown in.

I started going to the mess hall to see her, and we would talk for a while when she could take a break from her duties. A few times we took walks together inside the compound. Occasionally she visited me in the company area.

She was called Elizabeth by the GIs, who had a propensity for using American names to replace the ones they had trouble learning or pronouncing. Her real name was Tran Ngoc Bich, and that's what I called her. In Confucian societies, such as Vietnam, family names precede familiar ones as a way of showing honor to the family. Ngoc Bich means emerald; thus she was referred to as the emerald of the Tran family, a wonderful designation. I and her other Vietnamese friends called her Bich (pronounced Bic).

Bich had long, silky, black hair and was very attractive in a petite, feminine way. I held her hand twice, during mortar attacks when we shared the same bunker with the other mess hall workers. I kissed her only once, on the day I left to go home.

After I was home, we exchanged letters for four years. Postage to the United States was well beyond her economic means, but she found a way to get mail to me. She sealed a letter within an envelope, then talked a GI into placing it inside an envelope of his own and addressing it to me. Because GIs were granted free mail service back to the world, Bich's letters came to me at no expense to her.

Besides the good friends I made, Tran Ngoc Bich remains one of my fondest memories of Vietnam. I understand the country much better for having seen it through her eyes.

The Club

My arm wound took about a month to fully heal, the same amount of time it took my February wound to mend. Muscle tissue was involved in both cases, and I guess it takes that long for it to heal. That meant I would have about three weeks left of my tour when I was fully recovered. I was short.

Because I was a sergeant, I was the one assigned to find guys for guard duty and the daily details that needed to be performed. Unfortunately, for a while, the only ones present to perform these unpleasant tasks were my fellow wounded soldiers. On a few occasions, I found myself in the position of being the bad guy, the one the others hid from. It wasn't fun. I couldn't blame them; I had done the same thing early in my tour and while recuperating in Cu Chi back in February.

Toward the end of my recovery period, the first sergeant—no longer Sergeant Grey—offered me any job in the company area that I wanted. I could take an existing position or make up my own, whatever I wanted to do. Because I had only about three weeks left, I concluded that it would have been pointless for me to occupy an existing position. By the time I learned what to do, it would be time for me to leave. I had another idea.

Because Dau Tieng was a smaller base than either Tay Ninh or Cu Chi, it had little to offer by way of entertainment. The PX closed at night when the civilian workers left the base, and there wasn't much to do in the evenings. Because the company didn't spend many nights out in the field during this period but instead returned to Dau Tieng, I decided I wanted to do something to make the men's time in the base camp more enjoyable.

I told the first sergeant that I wanted to open an EM-NCO club, to give the guys a place to hang out, write letters, listen to music, drink beer or soda, and be together. He liked the idea.

I was given an empty tent in our row of hootches, and I set about finding equipment and materials. I made a bar from old planks I found in a pile of debris. I removed the tops from some old tables with broken legs, then nailed the tops to the side of a two-by-four frame, with the planks that were in the best condition on the top. It was serviceable and actually looked pretty good. We scouted around other battalion and company areas within the base camp, looking for something to keep drinks cold.

The company electrician began helping me. We were engaged in what the army calls "scrounging." Because everything in Dau Tieng belonged to the army, and I was in the army, it wasn't stealing. It was just redistribution of military equipment. We located an ice-making machine in a mess tent for some rear-echelon company. Close enough.

The next day we cranked up the company's three-quarter-ton truck, loaded a tarp and some rope, and headed off for the targeted mess tent. We timed it for about ten in the morning, when we figured that nobody would be around. Breakfast was over and it was too soon for lunch. We backed the truck to the tent near the ice machine, went in and unplugged it, loaded it in the truck, tied on the tarp to hide it, and drove away as if we were doing something legitimate. It worked; nobody gave us a second glance.

Back in our tent, which was beginning to fill with tables and chairs, we unloaded the machine, plugged it in, connected a hose to the back, and fiddled with things for a while. Eventually, ice cubes began dropping into the bin. We filled the bin with the drinks we had available, which were sodas in the early days of the operation. The ice cubes made them among the coldest drinks we had tasted in Vietnam.

We stocked the "club" with the company's daily ration of beer and soda, which was two-thirds of a case of each per squad. When the company returned from the field the first night, the men jammed the club.

Meanwhile, the war was still going on. We were reminded of it with almost daily rocket or mortar fire, a lot of which fell inside our company area. The tent we used for the club had shrapnel and bullet holes in the canvas top. The base camp was hit with five rockets and about thirty mortar rounds on September 12 and again the following day.

My wound had healed sufficiently that the bandage no longer required daily changing. I still didn't have full use of my arm, but it was mending nicely.

I was down to thirty-two days left in Vietnam. In a way, I didn't want it to end. After waiting for a year for this time to come, the days seemed to be speeding by. This was, I think, because of two factors: the heavy enemy activity in our area of Vietnam, and the time I was spending with Tran Ngoc Bich, which I enjoyed immensely.

By September 16, rockets and mortars were still falling within the base camp's perimeter; five of each fell within our company area. No one was hurt, but a soldier from Alpha Company, billeted nearby, was wounded. The rockets were big ones—122mm. The sound of the explosions was deafening. Rather than the *crump* made by the smaller mortar rounds, the rockets had more of a bang.

I was eating lunch on September 16 when the first rocket fell. Everyone dove for the floor of the mess hall and held their breath. When no more rounds fell in the next few minutes, we ran for the cover of a bunker. I crowded into a bunker not far from my club, and soon we heard another rocket coming toward us. It exploded only fifty feet away. Just that morning I had been chased from my bunk, which was a cot in the back of my club, by five mortar rounds. I resolved to sleep in a bunker that night.

I eventually placed a wall of sandbags five feet in height at the back of my bunk on the side facing our perimeter. The usual low sandbag walls that extended around our hootches provided minimal protection from the other directions. A direct hit would not have been pleasant.

One of my old squad leaders, Sergeant Hensley, went home that week. He was replaced by one of the instant NCOs, who were becoming ubiquitous in the company. Although some of them had been with the company for four months and had turned into good leaders, I was glad to have earned my stripes the hard way.

During one of the battalion briefings that I attended in the place of our first sergeant, we were told that Dau Tieng and the area immediately surrounding it were the hot spot of Vietnam at that time. It would remain so until after I left the country.

GOING HOME

Bob Ordy, who had arrived in-country before me, departed a few weeks before I did. We said good-bye, and he left our Dau Tieng company area on the back of a three-quarter-ton truck. He remembered later that there were tears in my eyes as the truck pulled out. Most of the guys with whom I had served, soldiers I trusted with my life and vice versa, had survived and were finally going home. It helped give closure to my tour. Later, my departure would do the same for Chad, Bell, Stritt, and my other friends who had only weeks remaining when I left.

23 Sept 68

Dear Mom,

[In answer to the question in your last letter] Yes, I'm the N.C.O.I.C. [noncommissioned officer in charge] of the company. I'm the acting First Sergeant, when he's gone. He's going to Cu Chi tomorrow for 3 days.

Our main base camp is still Cu Chi, but there are only 3 guys from our company there keeping the place til we get back. No word yet on how long we'll be here.

[And finally, after a year's worth of waiting to leave and dreaming of home, it was time to discuss my actual departure. When the time came, however, I handled it rather nonchalantly.]

I have no idea when I'll leave country. It will be between the 8th and the 15th. Sometimes they give guys a week drop so they get to leave a few days early.

Hello again. Today's the 25th. In about another 10 days, I'll get my port call. It tells me when I'll be coming home. I should be leaving in about 5 days after I get it.

The mail is in now, but I don't know if I got any or not, so guess I'll go check.

Love, Roger

When my turn came to leave, I was driven to the airstrip in our company jeep. There I would board a flight to Long Binh, then Bien Hoa, where I had arrived a year earlier and from where I would depart. Bich, who everyone in our company knew was special to me, accompanied me to say good-bye. She was the only person to do so. She went with me as far as she could. If she could have boarded the plane, she would have done so, and I wouldn't have minded a bit. Tears glistened in her eyes as I hugged her and gave her the only kiss we ever shared. I hated leaving her. It was fitting, though, that she, a Vietnamese citizen, was the one to bid me adieu.

A few days later I boarded a freedom bird. It was October 15, 1968, the same day of the same month as my arrival a year before. With me were other GIs who had completed their tours of duty, most of whom were rear-echelon troops. As we rolled down the runway gaining momentum, I scanned the tree line, looking for enemy soldiers or signs of incoming mortars, rockets, or tracers from small-arms fire. I waited for the moment when the wheels would leave the ground, ending my physical contact with Vietnam. When it occurred, the entire plane, except me, erupted in cheers. I continued to watch for rockets or RPGs streaking from the hedgerows toward our plane. Not until a few moments later was I confident that we were above the range of enemy fire and beyond the reach of the Viet Cong and the North Vietnamese Army. I then leaned back in my seat and relaxed.

EPILOGUE

For a long time after returning home, I felt as though I still belonged in Vietnam with my company, leading my squad. I felt that I had abandoned them there. They were still going out on sweeps, ambush patrols, and search and destroy missions, which sometime during my tour had been renamed reconnaissance in force, for public relations reasons. I had become one of the seasoned veterans and recognized leaders of the 2d Platoon. I could still feel the pull of the unit. A long time passed before I no longer felt that I belonged out there with them, on patrol.

I was twenty-two years old and had spent almost 5 percent of my life engaged in combat. This has affected me in two ways.

A few days after coming home, I overheard a conversation between two people I didn't know while walking on a downtown street in my hometown. One of them was upset over something similar to errors in her bank records, perhaps a balance that didn't agree with the tally in her checkbook. The women were using voice inflections and displaying emotions that we used in Vietnam while discussing life or death matters such as how best to approach a dug-in enemy position and sustain the fewest casualties. But these people were not discussing an act that could result in their death, but something that simply did not matter that much. I was shocked that they could be so caught up in something so trivial.

Only a short time before, in another land, I and the others with whom I served had made numerous, daily decisions that affected whether we or others would live or die. Certainly, life's minor complications cannot be a big deal in comparison. It took me a while to reach the conclusion that because I had known the most difficult of times, my perspective of life's routine challenges was different from the normal paradigm. This has had a positive influence on my life. When I think that my troubles are significant, I remember those that I faced in Southeast Asia, and current challenges become relatively insignificant, then solvable.

While in Vietnam, I developed an appreciation for what I term "the smaller things in life." One day, after returning from a two- or three-day patrol, during which we had little sleep and had done a lot of humping the boonies in the heat and humidity, I sat down inside our perimeter and completely collapsed. The sun was beating on me, and the temperature was more than a hundred degrees. The sweat had soaked my uniform, and the only refreshment I had was warm water from my canteen. I felt miserable. I remember thinking that if I survived this, I would be happy for the rest of my life with little more than a shade tree and something cold to drink. I think about that often. It has helped me to appreciate minute matters that I would otherwise have dismissed or ignored.

When I returned from overseas, I still had six months to serve in the army. After a month's leave, I was ordered to report to Fort Dix, New Jersey, where I served in B Company, 5th Battalion, 2d Training Brigade, a basic training unit. I helped put through a cycle of new recruits, then became one of the unit's platoon sergeants. Despite twenty-some reenlistment talks and offers of an additional stripe and a cash bonus of $6,000 if I stayed in, I became a civilian again on May 7, 1969, two years after my induction as a draftee.

The war continued for several more years. I often wondered what happened to the men I knew who had remained in my platoon when I left Vietnam. I was also curious about the people I had trained at Fort Dix, most of whom most likely served in Southeast Asia as I did.

American combat troops were withdrawn from Vietnam in the spring of 1973. Only then did I stop feeling that I still belonged in Vietnam. Saigon fell to the North Vietnamese Army on April 30, 1975, soon after Congress withdrew funds for the war effort, despite President Gerald Ford's promise to the South Vietnamese government to continue military aid. The war ended six years after I was separated from military service.

The Viet Cong, who had fought bravely for many years to liberate their country, were assimilated into the NVA. The process had begun after the 1968 Tet Offensive when the north "helped" short-handed Viet Cong units by providing them with officers and NCOs. By the time Saigon fell, the NVA had taken over the Viet Cong to the extent that during the parade in Saigon two weeks after the Communist victory, the remaining Viet Cong soldiers were not allowed to march under the Viet Cong flag. Rather, they were dispersed among the various NVA units, a symbol that Vietnam, for better or worse, was once again united as one country.

The domino theory—which stated that if South Vietnam fell to communism, other countries would too, which was the theory that led us to war in the early 1960s—turned out to be a false doctrine. No other country has since fallen to communism. It is irrelevant in the long run whether the war was right or wrong or whether Vietnam has a Communist government. Using history's perspective, the matter may have been better served if left in the hands of the Vietnamese people themselves. What is relevant is that people such as Jerry from Tay Ninh or Tran Ngoc Bich from Dau Tieng, and millions like them, can now finally live in peace.

Vietnam today is the poorest country on earth, with one of the world's largest armed forces. Yet, the Vietnamese have two things that indicate better times ahead, which only they could have acquired: the right to govern their own nation and the hope for a better country and brighter future. Toward that end, I wish them the very best.

Author's note

Because this tale has been told from the author's perspective, it centers on my experiences and activities. This is certainly not to imply that the only significant events that occurred during my tour in Vietnam involved my participation. On the contrary, the young men with whom I served performed many heroic feats for which they have received far less honor or glory than they deserve. I was definitely not the only member of the 2d Platoon who explored tunnels, walked point, went on ambush patrols or listening posts, or received wounds. Almost everyone did. Many other members of my platoon performed feats of bravery that, sadly, may never become known. Nor is my platoon unique. There were countless others like it and surely some better.

Of the 2.8 million men who served in Vietnam, only a fraction experienced combat. Many more, however, served in hazardous support units such as artillery or helicopter units, and as such were exposed to the hazards of combat. There are many wonderful stories and personal examples that demonstrate the courage, dedication, and selflessness of those who served our country in America's longest war. If only a portion of their deeds could be told in coffee shops, community halls, classrooms, chat rooms, literature, and movies or on front porches, street corners, and television, America would be a richer country. Let their voices always be heard.

2D PLATOON CASUALTIES: OCTOBER 1967 TO OCTOBER 1968

Name	Date of death	Age	Comments
Anderson Turner	11 Nov 67	32	14 years of service
Bernard Mattson	12 Jan 68	20	From Peoria, IL
Brian Cady	14 Jan 68	20	
David Keister	14 Feb 68	19	Died in the hootch
Earl Mack	14 Feb 68	21	Died in the hootch
Richard Vellance	14 Feb 68	20	Died in the hootch
Ralph Williams	14 Feb 68	27	Our lieutenant
Roger Wilson	14 Feb 68	21	Died in the hootch
Joseph Gallagher	19 Feb 68	20	
Sam Stewart	19 Feb 68	19	
Joseph Zale	19 Feb 68	21	Medic
Bruce Dent	25 Feb 68	19	
Patricio Maldonado	27 Feb 68	24	Squad leader
Kellum Grant	4 May 68	20	